THE DESTRUCTION OF JEWISH CEMETERIES IN POLAND

Krzysztof Bielawski

Other Titles in this Series
Engaging Cultural Ideologies:
Classical Composers and Musical Life in Poland 1918–1956
Cindy Bylander

The Ghost of Shakespeare: Collected Essays
Anna Frajlich
Edited by Ronald Meyer

Complicating the Female Subject: Gender, National Myths,
and Genre in Polish Women's Inter-War Drama
Joanna Kot

For more information on this series, please visit:
academicstudiespress.com/polishstudies

THE DESTRUCTION OF JEWISH CEMETERIES IN POLAND

Krzysztof Bielawski

Translated by
Richard Bialy

ACADEMIC STUDIES PRESS

BOSTON

2024

Library of Congress Cataloging-in-Publication Data

Names: Bielawski, Krzysztof, 1972 –author. | Bialy, Richard, translator.
Title: The destruction of Jewish cemeteries in Poland / Krzysztof Bielawski;
  translated by Richard Bialy.
Other titles: Zagłada cmentarzy żydowskich. English
Description: Brookline, MA, : Academic Studies Press, 2024. | Series:
  Polish studies | "Polish version published by "Więź" in 2020." |
  Includes bibliographical references and index.
Identifiers: LCCN 2024017661 (print) | LCCN 2024017662 (ebook) |
  ISBN 9798887195698 (hardback) | ISBN 9798887196107 (paperback) |
  ISBN 9798887195704 (adobe pdf) | ISBN 9798887195711 (epub)
Subjects: LCSH: Jewish cemeteries—Poland—History—20th century. |
  Jewish cemeteries—Poland—History—21st century. |
  Cemeteries—Desecration—Poland—History. | World War,
  1939–1945—Destruction and pillage—Poland.
Classification: LCC DS134.55 .B5413 2024 (print) | LCC DS134.55 (ebook) |
  DDC 943.8/004924—dc23/eng/20240418
LC record available at https://lccn.loc.gov/2024017661
LC ebook record available at https://lccn.loc.gov/2024017662

ISBN 9798887195698 (hardback)
ISBN 9798887196107 (paperback)
ISBN 9798887195704 (adobe pdf)
ISBN 9798887195711 (epub)

Book design by Tatiana Vernikov
Cover design by Ivan Grave
Author's photo: Tadeusz Wrzesiński, MTJ Studio

Published by Academic Studies Press
1577 Beacon Street
Brookline, MA 02446, USA
press@academicstudiespress.com
www.academicstudiespress.com

Distinguished Sponsors

**The U.S. Commission
for the Preservation of America's
Heritage Abroad**
www.heritageabroad.gov

J-nerations Foundation
Forum for the Preservation
of the Jewish Heritage in EU
www.j-nerations.com

Friends of Jewish Heritage in Poland
A public charity devoted to preserving
the physical sites of Jewish heritage in Poland.
www.JewishHeritagePoland.org

Helen Albert and David Albert
In memory of our beloved mother
Diana Albert (Doba Drezner) of Serock

The Nissenbaum Family Foundation
www.nissenbaum.pl

**Faculty of History,
University of Warsaw**
www.historia.uw.edu.pl

**Rafael and Dorin Blau,
the Beiteinu Chaj Foundation**
Rescuing the Rutika synagogue
in Dzierżoniów (Reichenbach)
www.synagogarutika.com

Awards for the Polish version:

Józef A. Gierowski and Chone Shmeruk Award for the best academic publication
    on history and culture of Jews in Poland
Majer Bałaban Award for the Best Master and PhD Dissertations
    on Jews and Israel
Mieczysław F. Rakowski Award for the best dissertation
    on the Polish People's Republic
The General Conservator of Monuments' Award for the best dissertations
    on heritage protection
Jan Józef Lipski Master Thesis Competition

Polish version published by "Więź" in 2020

Table of Contents

Foreword

This book is not an easy read. But it is an important read. And in many respects an essential one.

Honoring the dead is a basic tenet of Jewish practice. In Judaism, cemeteries are sacred spaces. They are cemeteries "forever," even if there are no longer any headstones in place. Bodies may not be moved or disturbed, except under certain specific conditions. And there are various religious rules regulating visits.

In Poland, as in other countries whose Jewish population was destroyed in the Shoah, Jewish cemeteries take on a special role. They bear witness as the most widespread physical remnants of the pre-Holocaust Jewish world. By definition commemorative sites, Jewish cemeteries can thus serve as memorials not just to the individuals buried there, but to the Holocaust itself.

There are an estimated 1,200 Jewish cemeteries on the territory of today's Poland. They range from huge urban expanses, such as in Warsaw and Łódź, to remote village graveyards. For many, however, only their site is known, as they have been built over, bulldozed, used as quarries, or otherwise eradicated. Few, if any, surviving cemeteries have escaped damage of one sort or another. Some have only a scattering of standing headstones, or less.

Krzysztof Bielawski rescues Poland's Jewish cemeteries from oblivion by itemizing their annihilation in often excruciating detail. He chronicles how the Nazis and their collaborators deliberately targeted Jewish built heritage, including cemeteries, along with the destruction of the Jewish people. But, tackling a subject once virtually taboo, he goes much further, documenting in graphic terms how that destruction and desecration continued after the Holocaust under Poland's communist rule and even has gone on in the past three and a half decades of democracy.

His aim, he writes, is "to present the process of Jewish cemetery destruction in Poland as a result of human actions and to identify the perpetrators." Using archival material, legal records, official documents, first-hand testimony, written recollection, and interviews, he does just that.

And he presents a chilling picture.

Uprooted matzevot were crushed for gravel, repurposed as millstones, and used as raw material to construct buildings, pave roads and courtyards, and line drains and waterways. Housing developments, hotels, shops, schools, factories, clinics, markets, bus stations, and more were built atop cleared areas where bodies still lie buried. Human bones emerged during building works; they were tossed on trash heaps or shattered and mixed with sand as construction material.

The book is arranged both chronologically and by several broad themes:

- The destruction of Jewish cemeteries in the territory of today's Poland in 1933–45, through Nazi policies, military operations, and actions by the local population
- The destruction of Jewish cemeteries after 1945, via both state legislation and policy and the participation of the local populace,
- State policy regarding Jewish cemeteries after 1989,
- The destruction of Jewish cemeteries as perceived by Jews and by non-Jewish Poles.

The descriptions snowball as the book progresses, an avalanche of meticulously compiled evidence documenting both official policy and private operations. Bielawski cites orders, names names.

Importantly, he brings the story up to the present. He describes not only some modern episodes of destruction, but just as relevantly—or even more so—he notes the many initiatives to protect and recognize Jewish cemeteries that have been undertaken since the political changes of 1989, via state and local policy and also by the efforts of individuals, NGOs, descendants groups, and local and international Jewish organizations.

Anyone who has dealt with Jewish built heritage in Poland has had to reckon with the devastation of the country's Jewish cemeteries. We have all made guesses, broad-brush assumptions as to how and when and just what took place—and by whom.

Thanks to Krzysztof Bielawski's unflinching investigation, now we know.

Ruth Ellen Gruber
Director, Jewish Heritage Europe

Acknowledgments

This work would not have reached readers without the help of many people. The original, Polish version of the book was published thanks to Paweł Kądziela and Zbigniew Nosowski of the Więź Association. The Polish edition was sponsored by the Association of the Jewish Historical Institute of Poland, the Nissenbaum Family Foundation, and the Foundation for the Preservation of Jewish Heritage in Poland.

I want to thank the people and organizations that made publishing the English version possible: Alessandra Anzani, Matthew Charlton, Alana Felton, Daniel Frese, Prof. Andrzej Karcz, Becca Kearns, Diana Kim, Kira Nemirovsky, and Sasha Shapiro of Academic Studies Press, as well as Prof. Joanna Michlic and Prof. Jan Zbigniew Grabowski. I also appreciate help from Richard Bialy, who translated the book.

I thank all the many sponsors for their generosity: The U.S. Commission for the Preservation of America's Heritage Abroad, the University of Warsaw, Meir Yehiel Bulka of J-nerations Foundation, Dr. Dan Oren of Friends of Jewish Heritage in Poland, the Nissenbaum Family Foundation, David Albert, Helen Albert, Temple Israel of Great Neck, N.Y., Jeffrey Miller, Hatte Blejer, Josh and Amy Degen, Edward Janes, Ellen Mains, Alan Metnick, Robert Silverstein, Myrna Teck, Paul Walsky, Rafael and Dorin Blau of the Beiteinu Chaj Foundation, Jeffrey Cymbler, Malka Shacham Doron, Nira Fried, Chaim Prajs, Marsha Raimi, Duvid and Naomi Singer, Iwona Surleta, the Michael H. Traison Fund for Poland, Avner Yonai, and Menashe Zugman. Meir Yehiel Bulka organized a fundraising campaign in Israel and Dr. Dan Oren organized fundraising in the USA.

I am especially indebted to Jan Jagielski (deceased in 2021) of the Emanuel Ringelblum Jewish Historical Institute, Prof. August Grabski of the University of Warsaw, Maciej Rymkiewicz of the National Heritage Institute, and Prof. Andrzej Trzciński of the Maria Curie-Skłodowska University's Department of Jewish Culture and History in Lublin.

I owe a great debt to many people who supported me, shared their knowledge, material and photos, including Dr. Jakub Chmielewski of the State Museum at Majdanek, Moshe Goldwasser, Ruth Ellen Gruber, Prof. Leszek Hońdo, Piotr Kowalik, Prof. Ruth Leiserowitz and Michael Leiserowitz of the Juden in Ostpreussen Association, Wojciech Łygaś of the Nissenbsaum Family Foundation, Katarzyna Markusz, Dr. Sławomir Pastuszka, Dr. Krzysztof Persak, Piotr Puchta, Prof. Göran Rosenberg, Prof. Dariusz Rozmus, Janusz Skrzypczak, Philip Steele, Dr. Paweł Sygowski, Dr. Tomasz Wiśniewski, and Prof. Marcin Wodziński.

I also wish to thank my wife, Grażyna Bielawska, who for years has patiently supported me and endured my commitment to this work.

Krzysztof Bielawski

Abbreviations

- AAN—Archiwum Akt Nowych (New Acts Archive)
- AIPN—Archiwum Instytutu Pamięci Narodowej (Archive of the Institute of National Remembrance)
- AP Katowice—Archiwum Państwowe w Katowicach (State Archives in Katowice)
- AP Kielce—Archiwum Państwowe w Kielcach (State Archives in Kielce)
- AP Łódź—Archiwum Państwowe w Łodzi (State Archives in Łódź)
- AP Lublin—Archiwum Państwowe w Lublinie (State Archives in Lublin)
- AP Otwock—Archiwum Państwowe w Warszawie, Oddział w Otwocku (State Archives in Warsaw, Otwock Branch)
- AP Przemyśl—Archiwum Państwowe w Przemyślu (State Archives in Przemyśl)
- AP Siedlce—Archiwum Państwowe w Siedlcach (State Archives in Siedlce)
- AŻIH—Archiwum Żydowskiego Instytutu Historycznego im. E. Ringelbluma (Archive of The Emanuel Ringelblum Jewish Historical Institute)
- FJCP—Friends of Jewish Cemeteries in Poland
- NID—Narodowy Instytut Dziedzictwa (Institute of the National Heritage)
- UMCS—Uniwersytet Marii Curie-Skłodowskiej w Lublinie (The Maria Curie-Skłodowska University in Lublin)
- ŻIH—Żydowski Instytut Historyczny im. E. Ringelbluma (The Emanuel Ringelblum Jewish Historical Institute)

Chapter 1

Introduction

From the time Jewish communities began settling in Poland, at least 1,200 Jewish cemeteries were established within what constitute the country's present borders. This number was quoted by the census prepared in the years 2017–2019 by the Institute of National Heritage and the POLIN Museum of the History of Polish Jews, based on information collected on the Virtual Shtetl website (www.sztetl.org.pl). The list of these cemeteries has been verified by the Provincial Conservators of Monuments. When compiling the list, the Halachic principle was complied with, according to which a cemetery is the resting place of the dead awaiting the coming of the Messiah and as such, is not subject to eradication, but always "exists," even if there are no gravestones on its surface. The list includes cemeteries of varied condition (including those without gravestones, now built upon or otherwise devastated), those still active and those officially closed for burial purposes, as well as a dozen or so medieval cemeteries, whose location is today no longer known. Also included are the cemeteries established in the ghettos of Augustów, Białystok, Kielce, Legionowo, and Jewish War Cemetery No. 293 in Zakliczyn, where soldiers who perished during World War I are buried.[1] Not included in the list are the graves of Shoah (Holocaust) victims not located in Jewish cemeteries.

Jewish cemeteries in Poland have never been fully documented. They had been of interest to certain researchers and scientists as early as the beginning of the 20th century, but the Shoah interrupted their investigations. In the years of the Polish People's Republic, research into Jewish heritage was limited. It was not until the 1990s that there was a growing interest in the subject of Jewish cemeteries, which resulted in numerous articles, studies, books, albums and websites. This research concerns various aspects, including the history

---

1   During World War I, the Austro-Hungarian War Graves Department created cemeteries for fallen soldiers of Jewish origin within the existing cemeteries of Jewish communities or in their immediate vicinity (Rymanów). The cemetery in Zakliczyn is the only cemetery from this period in Poland, established by the War Graves Department far from a Jewish cemetery.

of cemeteries and sepulchral art, philological analysis of inscriptions, palaeography, and customs relating to funerals and memory of the dead. Lists of preserved gravestones are also being gradually created. Despite this, our knowledge of Jewish cemeteries in Poland is still meagre and the vast majority still remain to be professionally documented. Meanwhile, many of these objects are gradually deteriorating, thus limiting the field of research.

One of the gaps in historiography is the destruction of cemeteries. This process began on a large scale during the Second World War and continues to this day. Many Jewish cemeteries are now devoid of gravestones or have just a residual number still standing, lacking their original perimeter walls, markings and clear borders, often built upon and practically indistinguishable.

In Poland it is common to attribute the destruction of cemeteries exclusively or mainly to the Germans during the Second World War. In fact, local populations and the post-war Polish state have also participated in this process. This makes the subject a difficult one, and often evaded. Never before has any extensive research been conducted on the destruction of Jewish cemeteries. True, information concerning this process can be found in numerous sources and studies on cemeteries, the Shoah, local history, in the official documentation of local council offices and various organizations, but until today the issue has not been addressed in a fully comprehensive manner.

Particularly noteworthy is the book by Kazimierz Urban Cmentarze żydowskie, synagogi i domy modlitwy w Polsce w latach 1944–1966. Wybór materiałów[2] published in 2006. Its author discusses the post-war fate of property belonging to former Jewish communities, devoting much attention to the destruction of cemeteries, and including in its pages several hundred source documents from the Archives of New Records and the Jewish Historical Institute.

Another fundamental work is the book by Małgorzata Bednarek Sytuacja prawna cmentarzy żydowskich w Polsce 1944–2019, which was published in 2020.[3] This publication contains an in-depth analysis of the legal situation of Jewish cemeteries and presents evidence concerning frequent violation of the law by the state and other "users" of cemeteries. It constitutes extremely valuable

---

2   Urban Kazimierz, Cmentarze żydowskie, synagogi i domy modlitwy w Polsce w latach 1944–1966. Wybór materiałów (Kraków: Zakład Wydawniczy Nomos, 2006).

3   Bednarek Małgorzata, Sytuacja prawna cmentarzy żydowskich w Polsce 1944–2019 (Kraków – Budapest – Syracuse: Austeria, 2020).

source material and crucial information for representatives of the authorities, employees of conservation services, activists of organizations working to protect Jewish cemeteries, and historians.

Yechiel Weizman's book *Unsettled Heritage: Living next to Poland's Material Jewish Traces after the Holocaust*, published in 2022 by Cornell University Press, provides a historical and anthropological overview of the history and current state of Jewish cemeteries, synagogues, and other remnants of Jewish heritage in Poland.[4]

This book is based on the author's Jewish History and Culture thesis paper entitled *The Destruction of Jewish Cemeteries within the Boundaries of Present-day Poland since 1933*, as defended in 2019 at Warsaw University's Historical Institute. The thesis was awarded in four competitions, organized by The Emanuel Ringelblum Jewish Historical Institute, the Open Republic – Association Against Anti-Semitism and Xenophobia, the Polityka weekly, and the General Conservator of Monuments. In 2020 on the basis of the above thesis a Polish-language book *Zagłada cmentarzy żydowskich*[5] (Annihilation of Jewish Cemeteries) was published. The publication was supported by the Association of the Jewish Historical Institute of Poland, the Nissenbaum Family Foundation, and the Foundation for the Preservation of Jewish Heritage in Poland. In 2021 the book won the Józef A. Gierowski and Chone Shmeruk Award for the best academic publication in the field of the history and culture of Jews in Poland.

This book aims to present the process of Jewish cemetery destruction in Poland as a result of human actions and to identify the perpetrators. Analysis of various texts, iconographic sources and studies was carried out to this end. Also important has been the experience of the author, who since 2005 has been interested in the fate of Jewish cemeteries—initially as an amateur researcher and creator of the website www.cmentarze-zydowskie.pl, and since 2009 to 2024 as Jewish heritage specialist at the POLIN Museum of the History of Polish Jews. This experience was acquired through visits to cemeteries, his own research, participation in conferences, and by consulting with other people dealing with this subject.

---

4   Yechiel Weizman, *Unsettled Heritage: Living next to Poland's Material Jewish Traces after the Holocaust* (Ithaca: Cornell University Press, 2022).

5   Krzysztof Bielawski, *Zagłada cmentarzy żydowskich* (Warszawa: Więź, 2020).

A serious problem facing this research is the dispersed nature of the available resources and the lack of comprehensive studies. Sometimes, as a result of ignorance, for the sake of historical policy, or due to local solidarity, distortions occur, such as blaming only the Third Reich for the destruction of cemeteries, disregarding the participation of the local population and state authorities. In many cases, the process of cemetery destruction as well as the perpetrators of such acts could only be described on the basis of fragmentary information from different localities, which however, in the broader view, made it possible to recognize common characteristics of this phenomenon. The acts of destruction quoted in the book are not an exhaustive litany of such events; they are only a part of the whole and serve to exemplify the process of cemetery destruction.

This study concerns cemeteries located within Poland's present borders, as well as the destruction committed since 1933 (that is, since Adolf Hitler took power) in the former German territories that became part of Poland after 1945, and the rest of the country beginning on September 1, 1939. Reference to the period 1933–1939 is necessary in order to understand the situation of cemeteries in the Opole region, Lower Silesia, and parts of Great Poland, Pomerania, Warmia and Masuria.

The book does not address the destruction of cemeteries caused by natural factors. A proper study of that issue would require specialist, interdisciplinary knowledge in such fields as physics, chemistry, biology and geology. Reference is made to that process, however, with its most important elements being briefly presented.

In the following chapters various types of destruction and desecration are discussed, with a division into the periods up to 1945 and later, specifying particular perpetrators of such acts (including the German state, civilian populations and the Polish state). These are supplemented by chapters presenting the reactions of both Jews and Poles to the destruction of cemeteries. The issue of cemetery protection is also raised.

The book examines the acts in chronological order, while in the case of listing place names alphabetical order is maintained, with an indication of dates. In the Polish language version, quotes are included with their original spelling preserved, while foreign-language quotes are translated into Polish. Due to the laws on protection of personal data, in justified cases certain witnesses remain anonymous.

Chapter 2

The Destruction
of Jewish Cemeteries

A cemetery is a plot of land specially intended for the burial of the dead, and in the case of Jewish cemeteries, also for the burial of damaged religious writings. The following constitute the component parts of a cemetery:

- Graves, understood as specific sites where the dead are buried. In Jewish cemeteries in Poland, these are almost exclusively burials in earth. Unlike Christians, Ashkenazi Jews did not and do not bury their dead in crypts, sarcophagi and urns. Cremations and urn fields are extremely rare, and concern only those who have undergone extensive acculturation.[1]

- Gravestones occurring in various forms: stelae (commonly called matzevahs), gravestones (pseudo-sarcophagi), ohels, inscription plaque enclosures, modified stelae, modest architectural and sculptural forms, architectural gravestones, and grave enclosures.[2]

- Forms of commemoration not directly related to any one burial place (symbolic gravestones, commemorative plaques, and monuments honouring victims of the Shoah).

- Buildings (pre-funeral buildings, administrative and utility buildings, the homes of caretakers and gravediggers, coach houses and garages).

- Roads and pathways.

- Enclosures, gateways and wicket gates.

- Additional infrastructure, including paved walkways, stairs, bridges, main water installations, benches, rubbish bins, lighting, drainage systems, and monitoring systems.

- Markings (information boards, signposts).

- Graveyard foliage.

---

1   In Poland pre-war urn graves are to be found in, among other places, the cemeteries in Starogard Gdański, Warsaw, and Wrocław.

2   Teresa Klimowicz, Paweł Sygowski, Monika Tarajko, and Andrzej Trzciński, *Cmentarze żydowskie. Podręcznik dobrych praktyk w ochronie dziedzictwa lokalnego* (Lublin: Stowarzyszenie Studnia Pamięci, 2018), 39–51.

- Spatial arrangements: division into sectors, a network of roads and paths, and the so-called Kohen pathways.[3]

The principle of the sanctity of gravesites is extremely important in Jewish tradition. The Talmud states: "It is forbidden to remove the dead or their bones from where they rest."[4] Contrary to the burial customs of various other denominations, where after a certain period of time it is permitted to dig up a grave, remove the existing remains, and place another body there, Jewish graves may not be tampered with and reused. Exhumation is only possible after obtaining the consent of a rabbi in certain instances: in the case of a decision by a public prosecutor's office, where a grave is threatened with destruction, where the remains are to be transferred to Israel, where a body is transferred to the grave requested by the deceased before his death, when a body is to be transferred from a cemetery of another religion to a Jewish cemetery, when the deceased has been buried by mistake next to a woman unrelated to him, when transferring a body mistakenly buried in a place chosen by another person, when moving a body mistakenly buried in a double grave next to the wrong person, or when transferring a body to a family grave. Jewish burial customs do not permit exhumation of the bodies of those who died for their faith (Hebrew: kidush ha-Shem—"for the sanctification of [the Lord's] Name") and were buried at the place of their execution (this mostly concerns victims of the Shoah).[5] In principle, any form of interference with the ground in which graves are located is forbidden. The remains of the deceased are to be left in peace to await the Messianic times. Rabbi Abraham Ginsberg, Director of the Committee for the Preservation of Jewish Cemeteries in Europe explained it thus:

> The combining of the soul and body after death constitutes a key aspect of our belief in the immortality of the soul. The soul suffers when the grave is violated or when disrespect is shown to what seem to be merely dry bones. The soul and spirit can only rest when the physical body in which they were located rests in a grave acquired in life or assigned after

---

3   Kohens (Hebrew: Kohanim) – descendants of Aharon from the tribe of Levi, in antiquity serving in the Temple of Jerusalem. Due to the specific requirements of maintaining their ritual purity (including a prohibition concerning contact with corpses), extraterritorial pathways are marked out in cemeteries, allowing them to enter a cemetery without having to approach the graves, which would expose them to impurity.

4   *The Jerusalem Talmud, Moed Katan* 2:4.

5   Aaron Felder, *Yesodei Smochos* (New York: Rabbi Aaron Felder, 1978) 49, 54–56.

death. [...] Jewish law states that the ground covering a grave belongs to the deceased and must not be interfered with in any way, as that would disturb the deceased.[6]

In Orthodox Judaism, a number of recommendations and prohibitions apply to cemeteries, including a ban on treading on graves, generating profit from gravestones and the grass growing in the cemetery, or planting flowers and trees on graves.[7]

The above described principles include a range of definitions of Jewish cemetery destruction. While in virtually every culture the destruction of graves and their consecrated soil (i.e. gravestones, buildings, and other elements of infrastructure) are considered to be acts of vandalism, in the case of Jewish cemeteries, additional acts likewise considered forms of destruction include any interference with the ground in the burial area, including archaeological research, the excavation or repositioning of gravestones, or the removal of the root systems of trees and shrubs.

As a rule, Jewish cemeteries are maintained by religious organizations, which is why other undesirable actions include placing the symbols of other faiths on them. For the religious and traditionalists, it is unacceptable to carry out burials of non-Jewish individuals in Jewish cemeteries[8] or to engage in any activities that are contrary to tradition, such as the grazing of livestock, eating and drinking in the cemetery, or generating profit from the cemetery.[9] It is worth noting, however, that the degree to which these rules are followed depends on the customs of the local Jewish community.

The destruction of Jewish cemeteries should be examined in relation to the above-described components of cemeteries and moral issues. In addition to the mechanically caused destruction by humans, it is also necessary to bear in mind

---

6   "Understanding of the value of Jewish cemeteries," Abraham Ginsberg, accessed June 30, 2020, https://sztetl.org.pl/en/tradycja-i-kultura-zydowska/religia/jak-rozumiec-wartosc-zydowskich-cmentarzy.

7   Felder, *Yesodei Smochos*, 49, 127–128.

8   One of the challenges of today's Jewish communities in Poland is the issue of burying the dead of so-called mixed marriages. Jews sometimes expect their non-Jewish spouses to be buried in a Jewish cemetery in a grave alongside their own. A few years ago, a separate section was created for such burials at the Jewish cemetery in Warsaw.

9   Salomon Ganzfried, *Code of Jewish law (Kitzur Schulchan Aruch). A compilation of Jewish laws and customs* (New York: Hebrew Publishing, 1927), 105.

the damage caused by the effects of water, atmospheric gases, air pollution, temperature changes, biological factors (heterotrophic and autotrophic microorganisms, nitrifying bacteria, algae, lichens), metal corrosion, overgrown cemetery vegetation, strong winds, lightning discharges, floods, fires, mining damage, processes affecting sloping ground (runoff, drainage and subsidence of soil), the presence of animals (for example, the digging of burrows in the burial area, the building of beaver dams causing a rise in water levels and the flooding of cemeteries, and leaving faeces that may react chemically with stone materials).

Also important are demographic changes, including the waves of migration at the turn of the 20th century and after Adolf Hitler came to power, and above all the changes caused by the Shoah. A good example from the period before 1933 is the case of the Jewish community in Cieszowa. As a result of migration to large urban and industrial centres, by 1905 not a single Jew lived in that village, and the keys to their cemetery were left in the care of a Catholic priest.[10] The greatest changes were of course caused by the Shoah, as a result of which nearly 90% of Polish Jews were murdered,[11] while most of the survivors gradually left the country,[12] and for reasons of safety, those who decided to remain very often chose not to return to their home towns, preferring to settle in large cities (including those in lands annexed in 1945 from the territory of the Third Reich). As a result, hundreds of cemeteries and millions of graves were deprived of guardians.

Another significant factor is the insufficient activity in terms of the day-to-day maintenance of gravestones and other cemetery infrastructure. This is

---

10 Jan Myrcik, *Pro Memoria. Cmentarz żydowski w Cieszowej* (Tarnowskie Góry: Dom Kultury im. W. Roździeńskiego, 2011), 18.

11 The exact number of victims is unknown. Historians estimate that of the approximately 3.35 million Jews living in Poland in 1939, no less than 2.7 million people met their death during the Second World War, and no more than approximately 425,000 survived, with victims representing 80% of the population and survivors 12.7%. See: Albert Stankowski and Piotr Weiser, "Demograficzne skutki Holokaustu," in *Następstwa Zagłady Żydów. Polska 1944–2010*, ed. Feliks Tych and Monika Adamczyk-Garbowska (Lublin – Warszawa: Wydawnictwo UMCS, Żydowski Instytut Historyczny im. E. Ringelbluma, 2011), 15.

12 The majority of survivors left Poland. 92,000 Jews emigrated between July 1946 (the Kielce pogrom took place on July 4) and February 1947. Later the emigration became much more difficult. After 1956 new waves of migration took place. From 1955 to 1959 more than 18,700 Jews from the Soviet Union came to Poland. On the other hand, in the 1950s many Jews emigrated (51,000 people to Israel only). In 1961 approx. 31,000–36,000 Jews lived in the country. After the antisemitic campaign (so called March '68) in 1967–1969, at least 13,000 Jews were forced to emigrate.

mainly a result of the demographic catastrophe that was the Shoah. Proper care of cemeteries far exceeds the capabilities of the Jewish organizations existing in Poland today. State institutions and non-Jewish social organizations are likewise unable to effectively take care of all cemeteries as objects of local cultural heritage.

It should be emphasized that destruction of cemeteries also took place in earlier times. Evidence of this can be found in one of the entries of the Statute of Kalisz dated August 16th 1264, in which Polish prince Bolesław the Pious imposed a severe punishment on anyone destroying Jewish cemeteries: "If a Christian should in any way ravage or invade a cemetery, we order that he be severely punished according to the custom and laws of our land and that all his property, by whatever name it may go, be transferred to our treasury."[13] This problem probably affected many Jewish communities, as confirmed by the widespread employment of cemetery caretakers (for example in Przemyśl in 1743 a cemetery guard was employed to ensure that the fences around the gravesites were not dismantled and the stone and wooden gravestones were not knocked down).[14] Similarly, not without good reason the entrance to the 18th-century cemetery in Wrocław featured a warning carved into the stone: "Whoever disturbs this place of peace, will be struck with an axe. The axe will cut off his hand if he desecrates any grave here."[15]

Some destruction of cemeteries took place as a result of anti-Jewish riots (including those in Przemyśl in 1571)[16] and military operations (such as those in 1655 in Sandomierz during the Swedish-Polish war, when "cemetery gravestones were chopped up and scattered").[17] There were also cases of cemeteries being destroyed as a result of decisions by rulers. At least several cemeteries in Silesia, including those in Legnica, Świdnica and Wrocław, were liquidated in

---

13 *Dzieje Żydów w Polsce. Wybór tekstów źródłowych XI–XVIII wiek*, ed. Paweł Fijałkowski (Warszawa: Żydowski Instytut Historyczny, 1993), 17.

14 Andrzej Trzciński and Marcin Wodziński, "XVI-wieczne macewy ze starego cmentarza żydowskiego w Przemyślu," in *Żydzi i judaizm we współczesnych badaniach polskich, t. II, Materiały z konferencji*, ed. Krzysztof Pilarczyk and Stefan Gąsiorowski (Kraków: Księgarnia Akademicka, 2000), 115–116.

15 Maciej Łagiewski, *Macewy mówią* (Wrocław: Zakład Narodowy im. Ossolińskich, 1991), 33.

16 Trzciński and Wodziński, "XVI-wieczne macewy ze starego cmentarza żydowskiego w Przemyślu," 116.

17 Majer Bałaban, *Historja i literatura żydowska ze szczególnem uwzględnieniem historji Żydów w Polsce*, vol. 3 (Lviv: Zakład Narodowy im. Ossolińskich, 1925), 270.

the fourteenth and fifteenth centuries, following the expulsion of Jews from those towns.[18] The oldest known Jewish cemetery in Warsaw was destroyed at the turn of the 16th century in connection with the expulsion of Jews and the subsequent privilege of "*de non tolerandis Judaeis*" granted by king Sigismund I the Elder.[19] In 1733, the nobility of the Liw region,[20] demanding that members of parliament make efforts to prevent Jews from leasing land and to impose crown duties, also demanded the liquidation of recently established Jewish cemeteries.[21]

In the past—certainly in the second half of the 19th century—graves were destroyed due to the superstitions of the Christian population, which consisted of digging up corpses from Jewish cemeteries and using them as a "cure" for humans and animals or as a means of supposedly preventing the poisoning of sheep.[22] The causes of destruction were however often much more mundane, such as the grazing of livestock. Such was the case in Chęciny where, after a hailstorm in 1912, Christians began to graze their cattle near the Jewish cemetery, resulting in damage to some gravestones and the perimeter wall. The local bishop was asked to intervene, and the case dragged on until at least 1933, when "due to numerous cases of the cemetery's desecration by unidentified perpetrators," the Jewish community decided to hire a caretaker.[23] In his book on Jewish cemeteries in Warsaw, Ignacy Schiper devoted much space to "suburban scoundrels," especially active at the end of the 19th century, prowling the cemetery on Gęsia Street:

> Systematically falling victim to their thievery were such items as iron gratings forming the fencing around gravestones, the more expensive

---

18 Marcin Wodziński, *Hebrajskie inskrypcje na Śląsku XIII–XVIII wieku* (Wrocław: Towarzystwo Przyjaciół Polonistyki Wrocławskiej, 1996), 44–46.

19 Ignacy Schiper, *Cmentarze żydowskie w Warszawie* (Warszawa: Maor, 1938), 2–3.

20 Liw is a village (former town) in east-central Poland.

21 *Żydzi polscy 1648–1772: źródła*, ed. Adam Kaźmierczyk (Kraków: Uniwersytet Jagielloński. Katedra Judaistyki, 2001), 109.

22 Alina Cała, *Wizerunek Żyda w polskiej kulturze ludowej* (Warszawa: Oficyna Naukowa, 2005), 192; Alina Cała, *Asymilacja Żydów w Królestwie Polskim 1864–1897* (Warszawa: Państwowy Instytut Wydawniczy, 1989), 180–181; Hanna Węgrzynek, "Praktyki medyczne we wczesnonowożytnej Polsce i ich wpływ na funkcjonowanie oskarżeń o mord rytualny," *Czasy Nowożytne*, no 25 (2012): 109–110.

23 Agnieszka Sabor, *Sztetl. Śladami żydowskich miasteczek. Działoszyce, Pińczów, Chmielnik, Szydłów, Chęciny. Przewodnik* (Kraków: Austeria, 2005), 145.

headstones, the metal parts of decorations on monuments, money boxes, etc. To load their loot, handcarts were often brought right into the cemetery itself. [. . .] Even sand, which was plentiful in the cemetery, proved a lure to the thieves [. . .] At that time, these dregs of society chose the Jewish cemetery as a place for night-time trysts with prostitutes.[24]

However, the scale of destruction was certainly not as great as it was after 1939.

It should be noted that the intensified antisemitism of the interwar period, with its escalation in the second half of the 1930s, did not lead to many acts of vandalism in Jewish cemeteries. The aggression of antisemites was manifested in, among other things, physical violence against Jewish people, the demolishment of their stalls, shops and other premises, separate seating for Jews in universities, and their expulsion from institutions and various organizations. It seems that destruction of cemeteries during pogroms and other similar activities was sporadic, one example being the smashing of gravestones during the anti-Jewish acts of peasants in Oświęcim in late 1918 and early 1919.[25]

At the same time, the oldest cemeteries, dating back several hundred years and not actively used, were often in poor condition at the beginning of the 20th century due to, among other things, stone erosion and lack of regular maintenance. Avraham Blushtein thus described the cemetery in Międzyrzec Podlaski, probably established in the 16th century: "For many years no one had been buried in the old cemetery, the matzevahs had become overgrown with tall, wild grasses, and even though the graves of ancestors were no longer visited by anyone, they were signs of antiquity."[26] In 1916, in the oldest cemetery of Sandomierz, historian Majer Bałaban found "all the gravestones [. . .] broken and destroyed."[27] In 1935, he described the 16th-century Remuh cemetery in Kraków in similar terms: "The cemetery itself leaves a depressing impression; the monuments are mostly destroyed, have become embedded in the ground,

24 Schiper, *Cmentarze żydowskie w Warszawie*, 189.

25 Konrad Zieliński, *Stosunki polsko-żydowskie na ziemiach Królestwa Polskiego w czasie pierwszej wojny światowej* (Lublin: Wydawnictwo UMCS, 2005), 431.

26 Avraham Blushtein, "Di Brisker Gas," in *Sefer Mezrich*, ed. Yitzchak Ronkin and Binem Heller (Tel Aviv: Ha-Merkaz ha-Mezritshai be-Israel ve-Irgune bene irenu be-tefutsot, 1978), 607; Jerzy Sobota and Andrzej Trzciński, *Cmentarze żydowskie w Międzyrzecu Podlaskim* (Lublin: Wydawnictwo UMCS, 2009), 62–63.

27 Majer Bałaban, *Zabytki historyczne Żydów w Polsce* (Warszawa: Instytut Nauk Judaistycznych, 1929), 112.

or lie flat at the base of others that are still standing [. . .] However, all the monuments have been irretrievably lost."[28] Ojzasz Mahler echoed those sentiments, writing: "Here and there, gloomy gravestones, overgrown with vegetation, protrude from the ground. Time has wiped away their inscriptions, sculptures and various ornaments. A large section of the cemetery is almost empty."[29] However, this does not change the fact that at the beginning of the Second World War, there were hundreds of cemeteries in Poland with thousands of gravestones, pre-funeral and other buildings, various forms of perimeter fencing and other elements of cemetery infrastructure. Also, the oldest cemeteries, closed for further burial purposes, were respected burial sites and—again quoting Awraham Blusztejn—"signs of antiquity,"[30] essential for maintaining Jewish traditions and identity.

---

28 Majer Bałaban, *Przewodnik po żydowskich zabytkach Krakowa* (Kraków: Stowarzyszenie Solidarność – B'nei Brith, 1935), 76.

29 Ojzasz Mahler, *Przewodnik po żydowskich zabytkach Krakowa* (Kraków: Ojzasz Mahler, 1935), 32.

30 Blushtein, "Di Brisker Gas," 607.

Chapter 3

Jewish Cemeteries in Poland before 1939

Jews established cemeteries in the territory that is now Poland from practically the very beginning of their settlement. Evidence of this can be found in, among other things, medieval matzevahs, the oldest of which marked the grave of David, son of Sar Shalom, who died in Wrocław on August 4th 1203.[1] The size of cemeteries varied, depending on the history and demographic development of a given community. The smallest plots measured about 0.05–0.07 hectares. Metropolitan cemeteries covered an area much larger (in Warsaw, about 33 hectares; in Łódź, 42 hectares). It was not uncommon for several cemeteries to be established over time in one and the same town. There arose as many as eight burial sites in the history of Kraków's Jews, and five in Warsaw. The creation of new cemeteries was due to the development of settlements, as well as the expulsion of Jews from a given town and their re-settlement,[2] the filling up of previously used necropolises, and the establishment of new burial sites outside built-up areas, initiated at the end of the 18th century—an action that concerned cemeteries of all denominations. The latter actions were due to increased awareness of the importance of sanitation. In Austria, the relevant orders were issued by Emperor Joseph II Habsburg on December 11th 1783 and August 23rd 1784. This imperial warrant also covered those areas of Poland partitioned by the Habsburg Monarchy and included an order for the closure in 1799 of the cemetery at the Remuh synagogue in Kazimierz (a district of Kraków since 1800) and the opening of a new cemetery on today's Miodowa Street.[3] In Prussia, a decree to establish cemeteries outside city limits was issued in 1773, and on May 24th 1814, a royal decree was issued ordering Jewish families living more than a mile from a cemetery to create their own burial sites.

---

1   Wodziński, *Hebrajskie inskrypcje na Śląsku XIII–XVIII wieku*, 167–170.

2   Such situations took place in among other places Lwówek, Świdnica, Warsaw and Wrocław.

3   Leszek Hońdo, *Nowy cmentarz żydowski w Krakowie* (Kraków: Księgarnia Akademicka, 2005), 14.

Since due to state policy, Jewish communities in Prussia were relatively small, this edict resulted in the creation of numerous minor cemeteries. In many cases these cemeteries conducted only 150-200 funerals over the next 120 years, that is until the outbreak of World War II.[4] On February 18th 1792, an Official Proclamation for Free Cities with Regard to Cemeteries was issued in the Polish-Lithuanian Commonwealth. This instructed magistrates to establish cemeteries outside their townships, emphasizing that the new provision applied "not only to Christian cemeteries, but also to those places where Jews of whatever faith are buried." In those areas of Poland partitioned by the Russian empire, the issue of arranging and locating cemeteries was regulated by the Tsar's decree of March 13th 1817 concerning burial of the dead, and the May 31 1846 order issued by the Administrative Council of the Kingdom of Poland recommending the establishment of cemeteries outside built-up areas.[5]

It should be noted that the 19th century saw a significant increase in the number and size of Jewish cemeteries. This was largely due to the introduction of the laws described in the previous paragraph and a dynamic increase in the number of individual Jewish communities, caused by industrialization, changes to the regulations affecting Jewish settlement, and migrations from regions affected by pogroms.

Table 1. Jewish population in selected towns in central Poland[6]

Year	1808	1827	1857	1897	1921
Błonie	20	4	88	1027	1262
Góra Kalwaria	60	500	1298	n/a	2961
Gostynin	131	425	645	1760	1831
Grodzisk Mazowiecki	317	636	786	n/a	2756
Mszczonów	485	1011	1693	2437	2188
Płock	1932	3412	5259	7480	7352

---

4   Wodziński, *Hebrajskie inskrypcje na Śląsku XIII–XVIII wieku*, 60.

5   Jacek Kolbuszewski, *Cmentarze* (Wrocław: Wydawnictwo Dolnośląskie, 1996), 182.

6   Bohdan Wasiutyński, *Ludność żydowska w Polsce w wiekach XIX i XX. Studjum* (Warszawa: Wydawnictwo Kasy im. Mianowskiego, Instytut Popierania Nauki, 1930), 20–25.

The way cemeteries were organized reflected the customs and wealth of local Jewish communities. In small, poor shtetls in Podlasie or Mazovia, cemeteries were sometimes surrounded only by an earth embankment, gravestones were limited to modest stelae made of stones found in the fields, wood or slabs of sandstone, and pre-funeral buildings were timber-built. In large towns, cemeteries were usually enclosed by walls, and imposing buildings were erected on them, where the ritual ablution of corpses was performed and a cemetery administrator held office. From the nineteenth century onwards, evidence of an urban population's material and moral diversity could be seen in its gravestone monuments, which began to take on ever more sophisticated forms, their designers being recognized sculptors. Over decades or even centuries of use, certain cemeteries became filled with thousands of graves. The number of those buried between 1806 and 1939 at the cemetery on Warsaw's Gęsia Street is estimated at between 120 and 150 thousand.[7]

The cemetery—next to the mikveh and the synagogue—is one of the most important objects in every Jewish community. It is an important component of the property of the religious community that in the past was called the kehilla, constituting a territorial unit of the Jewish population's self-government with legal status. Direct administration of a cemetery is entrusted to a Chevra Kadisha Brotherhood (Aramaic: Sacred Brotherhood). The functioning of cemeteries is regulated by the internal regulations of Jewish communities (including Chevra Kadisha statutes) and the overriding state legislation.

In the Second Polish Republic (from 1918 to the WWII), cemetery issues were governed by the following legal acts: the Act of March 17th 1932 on the burial of the dead and determining the cause of death, and the November 30th 1933 Ordinance of the Minister of Social Welfare on the burial of the dead and determining the cause of death.

Under the Act, the right to establish, maintain, and close cemeteries was granted to municipalities and state-recognized religious associations and other religious legal entities. It was permissible to use a closed cemetery for other purposes, but this was subject to a protection period of 50 years from the last burial and on condition of preserving its historic and artistic elements (with the possibility of their removal to another place). The state guaranteed itself the possibility of closing and expropriating religious cemeteries for reasons of public

---

7   Henryk Kroszczor and Henryk Zimler, *Cmentarz żydowski w Warszawie* (Warszawa: Państwowe Wydawnictwo Naukowe, 1983), 5.

interest, including the closure of cemeteries "under exceptional circumstances" and requisitioning them for other purposes within 50 years since the last funeral. The act allowed for the re-use of graves after 20 years since the last burial, except for those with historical or artistic value. It also allowed for the exhumation of a corpse at the justified request of the deceased person's family with the permission of the general administrative authority, at the request of a judicial authority, on the recommendation of an administrative authority in the event of suspicion that the death was due to a contagious disease unidentified during the deceased's life, and by order of an administrative authority in the event of an intention to use the cemetery for another purpose. The act also provides for criminal prosecution of anyone desecrating cemeteries.[8]

The November 30th 1933 Ordinance of the Minister of Social Welfare on the burial of deceased persons and determining the cause of death specified the manner of dealing with corpses, the rules governing the location of cemeteries, the building of perimeter fences and the management of pre-funeral houses. According to this ordinance, human remains were considered "the remains of a corpse that were excavated while digging a grave, and any human body parts detached from the whole, as well as ashes obtained by the incineration of human corpses." The ordinance also detailed the method of dealing with cemeteries in the context of protecting objects of historic substance.[9]

The above regulations did not take into account the rules of the Halacha religious law and Jewish tradition, in particular the impossibility of liquidating cemeteries. In the interwar period however, such cases were only sporadic. In 1938, in connection with the expansion of the aeroplane production plant in Mielec, the state authorities attempted to expropriate the local cemetery, and in the same year closed the cemetery in Falenica due to its location in a built-up area.[10]

---

8   Act dated March 17th 1932 on burying the dead and determining cause of death, Journal of Laws No. 35/1932, entry 359.

9   Regulation of the Minister of Social Welfare dated November 30th 1933 on burying the dead and determining cause of death, issued in consultation with the Minister of Internal Affairs and the Minister of Religious Denominations and Public Education, Journal of Laws 1934 issue No. 13, entry 103.

10 Archiwum Akt Nowych (hereinafter: AAN), Ministerstwo Opieki Społecznej w Warszawie, ref. no. 15/696, Zamknięcie cmentarza żydowskiego w Falenicy, ref. no. 15/704, Zamknięcie cmentarza żydowskiego w Mielcu.

Chapter 4

The Destruction of Jewish Cemeteries in the Territory of Current-Day Poland, 1933-1945

4.1. Cemeteries during the Third Reich

There are areas within Poland's present borders which before the Second World War constituted territory of the Third Reich. The local Jewish communities in those lands had suffered repression as early as the 1920s due to growing antisemitic sentiments. In 1923–1932, before Hitler came to power, Germany recorded 125 cases of Jewish cemeteries being devastated, four of these occurring in Silesia, namely in Löwenberg in Schlesien, Breslau, Kieferstädtel and Trebnitz.[1] According to Alina Cała, they were "most likely spontaneous" and negligible in number, committed by the Nazis.[2] (For comparison: in the years 2002–2012 some 89 various acts of destruction and desecration of Jewish cemeteries were reported in Poland.[3]) After 1933, such acts of destruction also took place, for instance during Kristallnacht (or the Night of Broken Glass, a pogrom against Jews carried out by SA paramilitary forces and civilians throughout Nazi Germany) on November 9–10th 1938. The literature on this subject claims that all (or almost all) Jewish cemeteries were desecrated on that night, although in reality the actions of the Nazi militants consisted primarily of physical aggression against individuals, depriving them of their freedom, and the plunder and

---

1   Wodziński, *Hebrajskie inskrypcje na Śląsku XIII–XVIII wieku*, 62.

2   Alina Cała, *Żyd – wróg odwieczny? Antysemityzm w Polsce i jego źródła* (Warszawa: Żydowski Instytut Historyczny im. E. Ringelbluma, 2012), 606.

3   A list of devastated Jewish cemeteries, compiled by Małgorzata Płoszaj, commissioned by POLIN Museum of the History of Polish Jews in 2012.

destruction of apartments, shops, establishments and synagogues.[4] Reinhard Heydrich's first report, drawn up shortly after Kristallnacht, contains information about the arrest of 174 people, the burning of 191 synagogues, the demolition of 76 synagogues, along with the destruction of 11 and demolition of 3 community houses and cemetery chapels.[5] In detailed reports from 70 cities of the so-called Breslau SS Oversection, destruction of cemeteries (or more precisely, pre-funeral buildings) appears only in the case of Hirschberg and Jägerndorf, a town now located in the Czech Republic.[6]

What is known is that during the events relating to Kristallnacht, cemeteries were devastated in among other places Dyhernfurth (where most of the gravestones were said to have been overturned),[7] Greifenhagen and Naugard (where gravestones were smashed),[8] Hirschberg im Riesengebirge (where the interior of the pre-funeral building was demolished and its windows were broken),[9] Kolberg,[10] Köslin,[11] Lauenburg in Pommern,[12] Stettin,[13] Swinemünde (the pre-funeral buildings were set on fire in these five cities, while Kolberg's pre-funeral building was eventually turned into a stable for a nearby military unit),[14] and Schweidnitz (where the gravestones were smashed by a group led by Horst

---

4   Wodziński, *Hebrajskie inskrypcje na Śląsku XIII–XVIII wieku*, 62.

5   Karol Jonca, *"Noc kryształowa" i casus Herschela Grynszpana"* (Wrocław: Wydawnictwo Uniwerystetu Wrocławskiego, 1998), 208.

6   Zygmunt Hoffman, "Noc Kryształowa na obszarze Wrocławskiego Nadodcinka SS," *Biuletyn Żydowskiego Instytutu Historycznego w Polsce*, no. 2/98 (1976): 75–96.

7   Bernhard Brilling, *Die jüdischen Gemeinden Mittelschlesiens. Entstehung und Geschichte* (Stuttgart: W. Kohlhammer, 1972), 68.

8   AAN, Ambasada RP w Berlinie, ref. no. 474/875, Raport 3/25 Konsula RP Wacława Brzezi-Russockiego dla Ambasady RP w Berlinie; Eryk Krasucki, *Historia kręci drejdlem. Z dziejów szczecińskich Żydów* (Łódź: Księży Młyn, 2018), 99.

9   Hoffman, "Noc Kryształowa na obszarze Wrocławskiego Nadodcinka SS," 87.

10 Hieronim Kroczyński, *Kronika Kołobrzegu* (Kołobrzeg: Wydawnictwo Le Petit Café, 2000), 314.

11 Jonca, *"Noc kryształowa" i casus Herschela Grynszpana*, 176.

12 Magdalena Abraham-Diefenbach, Jenny Gebel, and Michał Szulc, "Lębork," in *Śladami żydowskimi po Kaszubach. Przewodnik. Jüdische Spuren in der. Kaschubei. Ein Reisehandbuch*, ed. Mirosława Borzyszkowska-Szewczyk and Christian Pletzing (Gdańsk – Lübeck – München: Academia Baltica, Instytut Kaszubski w Gdańsku, 2010), 362.

13 AAN, Ambasada RP w Berlinie, ref. no. 474/875, Raport 3/25 Konsula RP Wacława Brzezi-Russockiego dla Ambasady RP w Berlinie.

14 Jonca, "'Noc kryształowa' i casus Herschela Grynszpana," 173.

Mann, a physical education teacher).[15] In Gleiwitz, some of the fittings of the pre-funeral building were burned (its caretaker preventing an attempt to set fire to the entire building), and its windows were also broken.[16]

In Lauenburg in Pommern, a month after the events of Kristallnacht, the businessman Walter Graff asked the city authorities to sell him the damaged pre-funeral building. In his application dated December 14th 1938, he wrote: "I kindly request you sell me this ruin. I would like to renovate the still standing part and use the rooms for the production of tobacco and snuff [. . .] The Jewish cemetery can remain where it is, it doesn't bother me. Jews could be given access to that area from the side road (Sophienweg). Besides, I would put up my own wall that would separate my yard from the cemetery [. . .] Heil Hitler! Walter Graff." The Fritz Rummel company in turn offered to demolish the pre-burial building free of charge in exchange for the opportunity to remove the resulting rubble.[17]

In the spring of 1939 the destruction of the cemetery in Schneidemühl began. The town's German administration forced the Jewish community to agree to the demolition of its pre-burial building. All graves less than 40 years old were exhumed and moved to another cemetery. A surrounding wall was knocked down and gravestones were removed along with all metal elements, including the gates and the ironwork surrounding graves. A municipal park was then established on the site of the cemetery.[18]

On July 4th 1939, the Nazi authorities established the Association of Jews in Germany (Reichsvereinigung der Juden in Deutschland)—a civil law association that the Jews remaining in Germany were compelled to join. The previously existing German communities and other Jewish organizations were made illegal and all their properties—including cemeteries—were taken over by the new Association.[19] The Security Police forced the Association of Jews in Germany to

---

15 "'Noc Kryształowa' i pogrom Żydów w Świdnicy," Horst Adler, accessed June 30, 2020, http://www.mojemiasto.swidnica.pl/?p=1047.

16 Bożena Kubit, *Max Fleischer i jego dzieło. Historia żydowskiego cmentarza i domu przedpogrzebowego w Gliwicach* (Gliwice: Muzeum w Gliwicach, 2018), 68–69.

17 Irena Elsner, *Żydzi w Lęborku i w powiecie lęborskim do 1945* (Amberg: Elsir, 2017), 192–193.

18 Peter Simonstain Cullman, *Historia gminy żydowskiej z Piły od roku 1641 do Holokaustu* (Piła: Stowarzyszenie Inicjatyw Społecznych Effata, 2017), 173–174.

19 Diemut Majer, *"Narodowo obcy" w Trzeciej Rzeszy. Przyczynek do narodowo-socjalistycznego ustawodawstwa i praktyki prawniczej w administracji i wymiarze sprawiedliwości ze szczególnym*

gradually put the cemeteries up for sale. Their advertisements, sent directly from the Association's Berlin headquarters and its local offices, included a description of the site for sale, its location, surface area and price. Among other buyers or interested parties were towns or municipal councils (Gogolin,[20] Glatz, Löwen, Lüben, Namslau, Sprottau, Schweidnitz, Winzig, Görlitz, and Trachenberg), Catholic parishes (Strehlen), stonemasons (Gross Wartenberg, Landeshut), entrepreneurs (Freiburg), private individuals (Jauer), and the hitherto caretakers of such sites (Grünberg in Schlesien). As a rule, the price demanded per square metre was low, anywhere from 10 pfennigs to 4 marks.[21] It is worth noting that the purchase agreements stipulated that the graves (that is, the plots in which the deceased rested) should be left undisturbed for 30 years (in a part of the country where a period of 40 years, as adopted in Prussia, normally applied) dating from the most recent burial, and guaranteed relatives of those buried there the right to visit the cemetery. However, gravestones were treated as movable property. Gravestones from the cemetery of the former Jewish community in Frankfurt an der Oder, which buried its dead in that part of the city constituting today's Słubice, were valued at 22 reichsmarks per ton.[22] The concluded agreements had to be additionally approved by the local administrative authorities and the Reich's Main Security Office.

On June 10th 1943, local units of the Association of Jews in Germany were dissolved and all its property was seized by the state secret police (Gestapo). Tax offices were entrusted with the responsibility of selling this property off. This process, however, was beset by a significant legal flaw—seizure of property did not mean acquisition of ownership. The former owner, that is, the Association of Jews in Germany, was denied participation in the activities that made it possible to dispose of the property, including the transfer of ownership. In such

---

uwzględnieniem ziem wcielonych do Rzeszy i Generalnego Gubernatorstwa (Warszawa: Wydawnictwo Prawnicze, 1989), 114.

20   Stefan Spychalski, "Dyskryminacja ludności żydowskiej na terenie b. rejencji opolskiej," *Biuletyn Żydowskiego Instytutu Historycznego w Polsce*, no 3/91 (1974): 53–57.

21   Franciszek Połomski, "Zawłaszczenie i sprzedaż cmentarzy żydowskich w latach II wojny światowej na Śląsku. Ze studiów nad prawem własności w III Rzeszy," *Studia nad faszyzmem i zbrodniami hitlerowskimi* 11, no. 815 (1987): 304–328.

22   Eckard Reiss, "Makom tov – der gute Ort – dobre miejsce. Cmentarz żydowski Frankfurt nad Odrą / Słubice (Makom tov – der gute Ort – a good place. The Frankfurt an der Oder / Słubice Jewish Cemetery," in *Makom tov – der gute Ort – dobre miejsce. Cmentarz żydowski Frankfurt nad Odrą / Słubice*, ed. Eckard Reiss and Magdalena Abraham-Diefenbach (Berlin: Vergangenheits Verlag, 2012), 43.

a situation, the German administrative authorities had only the right to manage the property. This gave rise to numerous doubts and fears among both those offering the cemeteries for sale and the buyers. As late as 1944, officials admitted that despite their sale, the gravestones were still the property of Jews ("Grabdenkmaler [. . .] noch den Juden gehören"). As a result, sale and purchase contracts had to contain a clause under which the purchaser exempted the German state from any claims by third parties.[23] Formal requirements, legal ambiguities, and protracted negotiations resulted in long drawn out proceedings. For example, the cemetery belonging to the aforementioned abolished Jewish community in Frankfurt an der Oder was not sold to the city until December 2nd 1944.[24] Until the end of the war, no buyer was found for the cemetery plot in Glogau, though its matzevahs (Jewish gravestones) were sold in 1943 to stonemasons.[25] The cemetery in Oppeln was purchased by its former gravedigger, a member of the NSDAP (the National Socialist German Workers Party) named Hoffman. After removing the gravestones from the children's section, he used the space thus recovered to establish a garden.[26]

Until the end of the war, German officials were unable to develop uniform rules for dealing with Jewish cemeteries in the Third Reich. On the one hand, local municipal offices demanded the liquidation of these cemeteries, while on the other, the authorities required compliance with the pre-war law on cemeteries, which for sanitary reasons forbade the disturbance of graves for 30–40 years after a body was buried, and also ensured a separate burial place for the last Jews living in a given town (funerals in "Aryan" cemeteries not being possible). Due to the lack of consistent regulations, along with a time-consuming procedure for the sale of plots, the final fate of cemeteries often remained in a state of suspension.

In 1942, the Reich's History of the New Germany Institute initiated a research project entitled *Securing the historical and anthropological material of Jewish cemeteries in Germany*. Part of the project involved exhuming skulls and

---

23 Andreas Wirsching, "Jüdische Friedhöfe in Deutschland 1933–1957," *Vierteljahrshefte für Zeitgeschichte* 50, no. 1 (2002): 27.

24 Reiss, "Makom tov – der gute Ort – dobre miejsce," 43.

25 Połomski, "Zawłaszczenie i sprzedaż cmentarzy żydowskich w latach II wojny światowej na Śląsku," 313.

26 Archiwum Żydowskiego Instytutu Historycznego im. E. Ringelbluma (hereinafter: AŻIH), Relacje. Zeznania ocalałych, ref. no. 301/2455, Anna Dziuba's testimony, 1.

other bones from cemeteries and recording the personal data of the deceased as found on their gravestones. The material obtained was to be used for research on the Nazi theory of race. It is not known, however, whether and from which cemeteries in eastern Germany such bones were collected. At the end of 1942, on the orders of the authorities, numerous cemeteries were stripped of all metal elements, such as gates, fences, and barriers, which were then melted down in foundries and used to produce weapons for the German armed forces.[27]

Regardless of official attempts to manage Jewish cemeteries, they were also devastated by the local population. In the winter of 1941, the residents of Löwen dismantled the cemetery's wooden fence and cut down its stand of trees, also stealing gravestones and a hearse. In September 1943, Lower Silesia's over-President of the Treasury, after visiting the cemetery in Sagan, remarked: "Destruction by local youths is still continuing."[28]

Despite a much longer-lasting risk of destruction that began in 1933, many cemeteries in Germany survived the war in fairly good condition. In her testimony written in 1946, Ida Gliksztejn,[29] conscious of the massive destruction of cemeteries in central and eastern Poland, noted: "It seems all the more strange that at the same time there were Jewish cemeteries in Germany that were not only totally undisturbed but even carefully maintained by caretakers who remained at their posts even after the last Jew had been deported from the town."[30]

Although the present study concerns localities within the borders of modern-day Poland, it is worth noting that, paradoxically, one of the best-preserved Jewish cemeteries in Europe is that in Berlin's Weissensee district.[31] Writing about cemeteries in the present-day Lubush Province, Andrzej Kirmiel, historian and director of the Alf Kowalski Regional Museum in Międzyrzecz,

---

27 Wirsching, "Jüdische Friedhöfe in Deutschland 1933–1957," 1–40.

28 Połomski, "Zawłaszczenie i sprzedaż cmentarzy żydowskich w latach II wojny światowej na Śląsku," 316, 327.

29 Ida Gliksztejn, Alta Iska Rapaport, *secundo voto* Weber, *tertio voto* Jarkoni (1906 Józefów nad Wisłą – 1997 Ramat ha-Sharon) – a teacher, in the years 1941–1942 a clerk in the Lublin Judenrat, from 1945 a secretary in the Bytom Jewish Committee, associate of the Central Jewish Historical Commission. In 1957, she emigrated to Israel, where she worked at the Yad Vashem Institute and the Union of Former Concentration Camp Prisoners.

30 AŻIH, Relacje. Zeznania ocalałych, ref. no. 301/3546, Ida Gliksztejn's testimony, 1.

31 In 1943, the Berlin city authorities eliminated the second Jewish cemetery on Grosse Hamburger Strasse and turned it into a park.

stated that they generally survived the Second World War without major damage, while their significant destruction took place only after 1945.[32]

Demographic changes (the emigration of Jews from Germany in the 1930s, the extermination of most of the remainder, and after 1945, the arrival in cities of people repatriated from the east, with the simultaneous expulsion of the indigenous population) make it considerably difficult to determine the fate of cemeteries in German territories that are now located in Poland. This has been compounded by a historical policy, according to which the destruction of cemeteries was often blamed entirely on Germans. The cemetery in Słupsk (German: Stolp) may serve as an example. In a note drawn up on March 20th 1989, Ewa Błaszczyk, the Słupsk Province's commissioner for Religious Affairs stated: "According to archival materials, the cemetery was liquidated before 1933, and the 86 people supposed to be buried there were interred during the First World War."[33] Contradicting this is the history of the funeral of Sima Staw, who died in June 1945 and was buried in that cemetery. A photograph of her grave, taken on or shortly after the funeral, was published by Göran Rosenberg in his book *A Brief Stop on the Road from Auschwitz*. At that time, the cemetery had been partially devastated (a horticultural farm was established on its oldest section in 1942), but the photo shows rows of gravestones still standing, with no sign of damage. When in 1985 family members tried to find Sima Staw's grave, they found the cemetery razed to the ground.[34] A similar picture emerges when we examine the history and state of preservation of Jewish cemeteries in many other places, such as Lower Silesia.

4.2. Destruction, Desecration, and Administration of Property in Areas Conquered by the Third Reich

For Jewish cemeteries in territory occupied by Germany in 1939, the fate awaiting them was much worse than that of cemeteries located in the Third Reich.

---

32 Andrzej Kirmiel, "*Żydowskie ślady na Ziemi Lubuskiej*," in *Makom tov – der gute Ort – dobre miejsce. Cmentarz żydowski Frankfurt nad Odrą / Słubice*, ed. Eckard Reiss and Magdalena Abraham-Diefenbach (Berlin: Vergangenheits Verlag, 2012), 223.

33 AAN, Urząd do Spraw Wyznań, ref. no. 132/314, Obiekty judaizmu woj. słupskiego, 115.

34 Göran Rosenberg, *Krótki przystanek w drodze z Auschwitz* (Wołowiec: Wydawnictwo Czarne, 2014), 199–200.

Cemeteries in the General Government were afforded practically no protection—the Germans destroyed them ruthlessly. In contrast to cemeteries in Germany, cemetery plots in the General Government were not subject to sale, but there are known cases of gravestones being sold.[35]

The situation was slightly different in the case of cemeteries in those Polish territories annexed by the Third Reich in 1939, including the Łódź, Pomerania, Poznań, and Śląsk Provinces, part of Mazovia, and the Kielce, Kraków, and Suwałki Provinces. The available sources suggest that in their case the German administration had no consistent rules of procedure. The property of these Jewish communities was not taken over by the Association of Jews in Germany, and for a long time the issue of trade in such property was not formalized—as late as January 1944, the Tax Office in Chrzanów was unsure whether it could offer Jewish cemeteries for sale.[36] The rule affording graves thirty years of protection was treated selectively. In Kleczew, where both Polish and Jewish slave labourers removed gravestones from the local cemetery on the orders of the Germans, human remains were also disinterred. The German guards ordered the body of one of the men recently buried there to be lifted and placed in an upright position, so that the deceased could "supervise" the slave labourers.[37] However, efforts were made to follow the rules at least in some of the cemeteries. In the ruling of July 1st 1941, the Oświęcim authorities emphasized:

> Closure of the cemetery does not automatically mean that when its current purpose is discontinued the area will be turned over to general street traffic. Following appropriate arrangements and after no less than 40 years [. . .], the cemetery may be razed to the ground, which action will also require police approval. We do however retain the right to issue such a permit before the expiry of the 40-year period, as long as this raises no particular objections on the part of the police or sanitation

---

35 Aleksander Bieberstein, *Zagłada Żydów w Krakowie* (Kraków–Wrocław: Wydawnictwo Literackie, 1985), 230.

36 AŻIH, Dokumenty niemieckie 1944–1939, ref. no. 59/233, Chrzanów. Starostwo Powiatowe, 26.

37 Anetta Głowacka-Penczyńska, Tomasz Kawski, and Witold Mędykowski, *The first to be destroyed. The Jewish community of Kleczew and the beginning of the final solution* (Boston: Academic Studies Press, 2015), 138.

services. If necessary, corpses that have not yet decomposed will be buried elsewhere in accordance with the regulations.[38]

As in the territory of the pre-war Third Reich, efforts were probably made to maintain some cemeteries as places for the separate burial of Jews who died or were killed under various circumstances, and only from 1942 onwards were regulations on a larger scale introduced regarding the status of cemetery plots. This can be seen in an official letter written on February 24th 1943 by the President of Upper Silesia:

> In view of the deportation of Jews, the use of existing Jewish cemeteries is totally out of the question. I agree to such cemeteries being closed. Such closures may be effected by political communes after obtaining the consent of the authorized custodial establishments. Closure of cemeteries requires authorization by the local government's president as the national police authority. Jewish cemeteries, once closed, can immediately be turned into planted walks. Any other use requires the approval of the local government's president as the police authority. I wish to emphasize that the sites of Jewish cemeteries and the gravestones located on them are managed by a custodial entity. Political municipalities should be afforded the right of first refusal on the sale of such sites.[39]

Similarly in Toruń, the procedure for closing that city's cemetery commenced in 1942 after the authorities had made sure that there were no Jews in the city.[40]

Deserving particular attention is the case of the cemeteries in the Free City of Gdańsk (German: Danzig). In the spring of 1939, the Synagogue Community's governing body, in view of the need to cover the emigration costs of its members, signed an agreement with the city authorities concerning the sale of its property, in which it was stipulated that the cemeteries would remain intact until 1948.[41]

---

38 Wojciech Gałosz, Marcin Karetta, Jacek Proszyk, and Artur Szyndler, *Cmentarz żydowski w Oświęcimiu. Historia, symbole, przyroda. The Jewish Cemetery in Oświęcim. History, Symbols, Nature* (Oświęcim: Centrum Żydowskie w Oświęcimiu, 2018), 14–15.

39 AŻIH, Dokumenty niemieckie 1939–1944, ref. no. 233/59, Chrzanów. Starostwo Powiatowe, 6.

40 Magdalena Niedzielska, *Cmentarz żydowski* (Toruń: Wydawnictwo Adam Marszałek, 2010), 36.

41 Grzegorz Berendt, "Żydzi," in *Encyklopedia Gdańska*, ed. Błażej Śliwiński (Gdańsk: Fundacja Gdańska, 2012), 1155–1156.

The first destruction of Jewish cemeteries on the territory of Poland's Second Republic occurred as a result of military operations in 1939. Graves, gravestones and other elements of cemetery infrastructure were destroyed during bombardments and battles in areas where cemeteries were located and due to their being designated defensive positions. This issue is discussed in more detail in the chapter *Destruction as a result of military operations*.

During the initial period of the war and occupation, Wehrmacht soldiers and those of other units were already devastating and desecrating Jewish cemeteries. Several such events were reported by Rabbi Szymon Huberband of the Oneg Shabat group, which was established by Emanuel Ringelblum and created the Warsaw Ghetto's Underground Archives. His descriptions of those acts were based on his own experiences and the accounts of witnesses who were herded into the Warsaw ghetto after 1940.

On the eve of the Sukkot on September 22nd 1939, in Piotrków Trybunalski—the town where Szymon Huberband was a rabbi—the Germans used the synagogue and the neighbouring house of religious studies to lock up Polish prisoners of war. The next day, they ordered sewage pits to be dug in the cemetery adjacent to the synagogue complex. Some of the matzevahs were uprooted and used to form a pavement leading from the synagogue to the latrine. A few days after the end of the Sukkot, this latrine was dismantled by Bundists led by Abraham Wajshof—a Bund activist and member of Piotrków Trybunalski's town council and Jewish community.[42] In retaliation, the Germans took 22 hostages, demanding that the Jewish community pay a contribution of 20,000 zlotys and deliver up eggs and butter. The community was also required to rebuild the latrines for the prisoners of war and they were duly set up just outside the burial ground, in the courtyard of the Jewish hospital.

In Radomsko, most likely also in the first months of the occupation, the Germans dug up the graves of the Rabinowicz dynasty's tzadiks in their search for valuables allegedly hidden in the cemetery. The cemeteries in Dobrzyń, Przasnysz, and Rypin were stripped of their matzevahs and ploughed up. A cemetery was also damaged in Suwałki.[43] According to Anna Bieniaszewska,

---

42   Szymon Huberband, *"Życie religijne podczas wojny,"* in *Archiwum Ringelbluma. Konspiracyjne Archiwum Getta Warszawy. Pisma rabina Szymona Huberbanda*, vol. 32, ed. Eleonora Bergman and Anna Ciałowicz (Warszawa: Żydowski Instytut Historyczny im. E. Ringelbluma, 2017), 125.

43   Szymon Huberband, "Zagłada bożnic, bejt ha-midraszy i cmentarzy," in *Archiwum Ringelbluma. Konspiracyjne Archiwum Getta Warszawy. Pisma rabina Szymona Huberbanda*, vol. 32,

in 1939 the cemetery in Golub "was blown up together with its pre-funeral building."[44]

In 1940, the grave of Tzadik Elimelech was dug up in Leżajsk. According to the account given by Józef Dec and Mieczysław Pudełkiewicz, two Leżajsk residents, Józef O. and Józef Ż., were ordered to do so by the Germans and worked under the supervision of the gendarmes Johann Keipr, Stanisław Werner, and Michał Nabrzeżny. The gravesite's wooden ohel was dismantled, and the bones and relics of holy vessels were disinterred. For several days, the bones lay under the nearby trees, while one of the local youths carried Elimelech's skull around on a stick, scaring children with it.[45]

It can be assumed that the destruction of cemeteries in the early years of the war and occupation was random, part of a series of repressions committed against Jews by soldiers of the victorious German army brought up on antisemitic ideology. The smashing of matzevahs and profanation of graves, along with other things such as physical violence, desecration of synagogues, the burning of religious books, the shearing of men's sidelocks and beards, and forcing them to clean the streets—was above all one of many actions aimed at humiliating the Jewish population. In time, this destruction began to be a more planned process connected to the Nazi "management" of cemetery property in the form of stone and other materials. For example, in 1942 the Governor of the Lublin District, in connection with plans to build and repair roads, demanded an inventory of cemeteries and an estimate of the number of gravestones.[46]

The Germans used Jewish forced labourers, prisoners of war of various nationalities and local populations to carry out the actual work of devastating cemeteries. For Jews, this was an additional, extremely painful form of repression. The Germans not only used their labour, but at the same time severely humiliated them, ordering them to dig up graves, destroy the gravestones of family and community members, and to use matzevahs for various construction works. Research conducted by Dr. Tomasz Wiśniewski has shown that work was

ed. Eleonora Bergman and Anna Ciałowicz (Warszawa: Żydowski Instytut Historyczny im. E. Ringelbluma, 2017), 217–218, 223, 246, 249, 253.

44 Anna Bieniaszewska, *Shalom znad Drwęcy. Żydzi Golubia i Dobrzynia* (Toruń: Wydawnictwo Adam Marszałek, 2016), 241.

45 "*Święta Kuczek już nie będzie. Żydzi w Leżajsku,*" Juliusz Ulas Urbański, accessed June 30, 2020, http://ulas2.republika.pl/ulas.htm.

46 Archiwum Państwowe w Lublinie (hereinafter: AP Lublin), Urząd Okręgu Lubelskiego, ref. no. 498/30, Schriftwechsel, Anfragen. Amtliche Anfragen, 149.

carried out by, among others, Polish peasants, forced to provide horse-drawn carts and transport the "spoils" (in some cases being rewarded with permission to take a number of gravestones).[47] In Bydgoszcz, teenagers from the German Bromberg Erziehungslager prison camp for juveniles removed matzevahs from the cemetery on the Dąbrowskiego Hill.[48] Gravestones from Lublin cemeteries were broken up by Jewish prisoners of war from the camp at No. 7 Lipowa Street and probably Poles from one of the forced Construction Service (German: Baudienst) camps.[49]

The Germans used Jewish gravestones on a massive scale to harden roads and pavements, as curbs and as building material. Gravestones from cemeteries in Poznań, including the Jewish graveyard on Głogowska Street and the Christian graveyard on Bukowska Street, were used on such construction sites as the motorway to Berlin, the Rusałka artificial lake, and new villas built in the city. The work was performed by prisoners from camps such as those in Żabikowo, Krzyżowniki and Junikowo. Gravestones were torn from the ground and cut up into smaller pieces. Forced labourers were ordered to dig up graves, open coffins and search through the human remains. According to the *Information Bulletin* of the Government Delegation for Poland, "the Germans carrying out the work got the Jews drunk and then forced them to rob the dead of all valuables, including the gold from their teeth."[50]

In 1940, the matzevahs from the Sochaczew cemetery were used to build military facilities, including those at the Bielice airport. During this work, the ohels of tzadik Awraham Bornsztajn and rabbi Eliezer ha-Kohen were damaged.[51] In Skierniewice, gravestones were used to strengthen a dam built on the river to create a bathing area.[52] In mid-1940, the Germans dug up the graves in the Drobin cemetery, gravestones were torn out, and a sports field was laid out

---

47 Consultation with Dr. Tomasz Wiśniewski on June 10, 2018.

48 Małgorzata Wąsacz, "Po żydowskim cmentarzu na Wzgórzu Dąbrowskiego nie ma już śladu," *Gazeta Pomorska*, June 7, 2006.

49 AŻIH, Relacje. Zeznania ocalałych, ref. no. 6669/301, Roman Chwedkowski's testimony, 6.

50 Anna Ziółkowska, *Obozy pracy przymusowej dla Żydów w Wielkopolsce w latach okupacji hitlerowskiej (1941–1943)* (Poznań: Wydawnictwo Poznańskie, 2005), 47–50.

51 Hercke Tylman, Hirshel Gothelf, and Shlomo Jakubowicz, "Tsvangs-arbet," in *Pinkas Sokhatshev*, ed. Avraham Shmuel Shtein, Gabriel Weissman (Jerusalem: Irgun Yotsei Sokhatshov be-Israel: 1962), 393.

52 Edward Włodarczyk, *Z dziejów Żydów skierniewickich* (Skierniewice: Wojewódzka Biblioteka Publiczna w Skierniewicach, 1993), 154.

Figure 4.1. In Mogielnica the Germans used tombstones to pave the forecourt of a gendarme post. This young Pole is showing bones from the destroyed graves. September 1942. Author unknown, Janusz Skrzypczak's collection.

on the site. As Rabbi Szymon Huberband reported, as a result of this destruction "the bones and skeletons of the dead were strewn all over the streets of the town." Only some time later did the Germans allow the bones to be collected and reinterred.[53] In Bydgoszcz, work on the demolition of the cemetery began in February 1940 and lasted until March. The Germans ordered the matzevahs to be broken down into smaller, cobble-sized pieces, which were used to harden the paths leading to the city's water tower.[54] In Rajgród too, the Germans ordered Jews to smash gravestones and use them to harden the roads.[55] Some of the stones were used as rubble filling for the foundations of a house erected next to the water mill on the Wojda estate.[56] In some places—including Biłgoraj, Łosice, Mogielnica, Sobienie-Jeziory, Wieruszów, and Wyszków—matzevahs

---

53 Huberband, "Zagłada bożnic, bejt ha-midraszy i cmentarzy," 224.

54 Wąsacz, "Po żydowskim cmentarzu na Wzgórzu Dąbrowskiego nie ma już śladu."

55 AŻIH, Relacje. Zeznania ocalałych, ref. no. 301/2600, Lejb Lewentin's testimony 02.07.19471.

56 Janusz Sobolewski, "Zabytki powiatu grajewskiego," *Rajgrodzkie Echa*, no. 7/306 (2016): 26.

were used to pave the forecourts of German gendarme posts. In Proszowice Germans used tombstones to strenghten banks of the Szreniawa river.[57]

Gravestones from the Mława cemetery were used by the Germans to erect monumental pillars at the entrance to the Truppenübungsplatz Mielau military training ground, commonly known as "New Berlin," established in 1940.[58] Matzevahs from Jordanów and Nowy Targ were used in the construction of the Security Police and Security Service Officer Training School in Rabka, including the wide stairs leading to the roll-call square. On the orders of the school's commander, Wilhelm Rosenbaum, the Jewish forced labourers placed these stones with the epitaphs face up, and those made of black marble were arranged in the shape of the eagle featured in the coat of arms of the Third Reich. Zdzisław Olszewski, who witnessed the construction and use of those stairs, in 1997 wrote: "The Hebrew inscriptions carved on the paving stones of 'Rosenbaum's Staircase' were viewed with appreciation and laughter by various dignitaries of the SS, SA and SD, invited by Rosenbaum to enjoy these sacrilegious, Nazi freak shows."[59] In Izbica, gravestones were used to tile the walls of the local jail. In the opinion of a local journalist, the Gestapo commander Kurt Engels "wanted them [the Jews] to understand that their last living act was the erection of their own tomb."[60] Matzevahs from Końskie were also treated as building materials, used in the construction of a fattening pen for pigs and an observation tower at the manor house in Modliszewice, then occupied by the district administrator Eduard Fitting.

In Chodzież, matzevahs were used to pave the roads and paths leading to the sanatorium. The work was carried out by Jewish prisoners from the camp established in mid-1941. The situation was similar in Oborniki, where Jews and British prisoners of war were forced to work. According to Anna Ziółkowska,

---

57 POLIN Museum of the History of Polish Jews (hereinafter: POLIN), Oral History Collection, ref. no. 549, Piotr Kopeć's testimony.

58 *Materiały źródłowe do historii Żydów Mławy i powiatu mławskiego w XVIII–XX wieku*, ed. Leszek Arent, Piotr Grochowski, and Przemysław Miecznik (Mława: Towarzystwo Przyjaciół Ziemi Mławskiej, 2016), 196.

59 Grzegorz Moskal, Michał Rapta and Wojciech Tupta, *Mroczne sekrety willi "Tereska": 1939–1945* (Wadowice: Grafikon, 2009), 126–128.

60 Robert Kuwałek and Weronika Litwin, *Izbica. Opowieść o miejscu* (Warszawa: Fundacja Ochrony Dziedzictwa Żydowskiego, [no date]), 11; "Niemcy użyli Żydom," Adam Jaworski, accessed June 30, 2020,https://web.archive.org/web/20160309084125/http://www.roztocze.net/newsroom.php/21919_Niemcy_ul%C5%BCyli_%C5%BBydom_.html.

director of the Museum of Martyrdom in Żabikowo, destruction of Jewish cemeteries in that area around Poznan the Germans called Warthegau was a common practice, especially after May 30th 1940.[61]

Jewish gravestones were also used to pave roads in the Treblinka and Majdanek camps. In the first of these, matzevahs, probably from the cemetery in Kosów Lacki, 8 kilometres away, were used to lay the so-called Black Road between the death camp and the labour camp. Usually, when hardening roads, matzevahs were laid flat or—after being smashed up—as paving. A different technology was used in Majdanek: smashed gravestones were placed upright between the curbs and a layer of gravel was spread over them. In 2015, the State Museum at Majdanek exhibited the remains of one of the original roads from the camp's economic section. Broken matzevahs were also used to form the plinth beneath a statue of a turtle, which, according to its creator, prisoner Albin Maria Boniecki, symbolized the slogan "Work slowly." About this case Jerzy Kwiatkowski wrote:

> Our field contains a considerable amount of limestone from our own quarries, and besides this, gravestones from the Jewish cemetery in Lublin. These have been brought in by civilian farm carts and are already broken up, to be destroyed immediately. They are mostly sandstone, but there are also examples of grey marble and expensive black Swedish granite. They feature weathered Hebrew inscriptions, covered with moss, although some are still fresh with shiny gold lettering. Working this field is a commando of about 30 Steinklopfers (stone breakers), prisoners with weak legs, who in a sitting position break up cemetery monuments into rubble to be spread on the entrance road and paths. I am taking pieces of these gravestones in order to make this plinth and thus symbolically protect at least some of them from total desecration. May they bear up this symbol of the resistance movement and form a 'component part' of the same.[62]

Similarly, in Kazimierz Dolny,

> The Jews themselves, under Nazi supervision, tore out the old stone matzevahs from the Jewish cemetery and, for their even greater humiliation, paved the paths leading to the Gestapo headquarters established in

---

61 Ziółkowska, *Obozy pracy przymusowej dla Żydów w Wielkopolsce w latach okupacji*, 52–53.

62 Jerzy Kwiatkowski, *485 dni na Majdanku* (Lublin: Wydawnictwo Lubelskie, 2018), 135.

the Reformed Franciscan monastery, and the courtyard of the town hall, and used them to lay paths leading to the privies in those of the town's properties that had been requisitioned as housing for officers.[63]

These works in Kazimierz Dolny were recorded by an unknown amateur film-maker. The 45-second colour film is currently in the private collection of Tomasz Wiśniewski. It shows a group of Jews digging in the sloping cemetery under the supervision of German guards, young hotheads from the Todt organization, two women with bouquets of flowers flirting with them, labourers driving piles into the ground and forming the slope of the hill into stepped terraces and the already levelled lower section of the necropolis with a wooden latrine. Testimony concerning the horror experienced by the forced labourers in Kazimierz Dolny was given in Edith Klein's account recorded in 1989:

> The Germans used to take Jewish boys and girls to work. [...] The was a Jewish cemetery next to the public school I went to [...]. This was a cemetery for very religious rabbis [...]. When the Germans took over the school, they wanted to make a soccer field on the cemetery. We girls had to ... [she stops at this point and begins to cry]. It was a quite old cemetery. Everything was lying out in the open, chests, bones, garbage ... We found a head, just a skull. They put it on a stick and put it in front of the school for everybody to see it, making fun of it and taking pictures.[64]

The cemetery in Brzeziny likewise became a source of building materials. Here too, local Jews were forced to work tearing out matzevahs and using them on local construction sites. Jan Bryksa recalled the scene:

> All our men, young and old [were forced] to build a dyke on the pond or went straight to the Jewish cemetery to rip out the matzevahs. Later, they placed them on the southern side of the wall, in rows several dozen metres long. The Germans did various things with those matzevahs. They laid a bridge over the park's pond, used as a fire fighting reservoir at the junction of Staszica and Mickiewicza Streets, opposite the post office. They lined the entire reservoir with Jewish gravestones—the bottom, the sides [...]. The Germans also used them to pave the road in Dąbrówka near Brzeziny [...]. In January 1945, they were still using

---

63 Andrzej Sas-Jaworski, *Dzieje Żydów kazimierskich* (Warszawa: Subdan Agencja, 1997), 62.

64 USC Shoah Foundation, Visual History Archive, ref. no. 54163, Edith Klein's testimony.

them to build barricades [. . .]. And target practice was carried out on them, mainly by Volksdeutsch, gendarmes and the Volkssturm. They set the gravestones up as targets and shot at them with rifles, sometimes even throwing grenades.[65]

In Osięciny, the Germans ordered the Jews to level the hill on which their cemetery was located. The sand thus obtained was then transported to Osięciny's town centre and used for road works and to fill the muddy town square. After the sand had been scattered on the square, the Germans forced the Jews to dance there.[66]

Figure 4.2. Tombstones used to pave a street in Radom. Date and author unknown, collection of the Jacek Malczewski Museum in Radom.

In Rybnik, Jewish forced labourers along with the town's non-Jewish residents were put to work destroying the cemetery. According to Joanna

---

65 "Brzeziny żyją na macewach," Michał Gołąbek, accessed June 30, 2020, http://www.e-kalejdoskop.pl/wiadomosci-a230/brzeziny-zyja-na-macewach-r669/pdf.

66 Jan Cybertowicz, Jarosław Kotuniak, *Z dziejów Osięcin i okolic* (Osięciny–Włocławek: Lega, 2006), 220–221.

Gabowicz's account, in March 1940 Gestapo officers gathered up a group of Jews, who were escorted to the cemetery and forced to remove the gravestones, load them onto horse-drawn carts, demolish the cemetery's pre-funeral building and level the terrain.[67] In 2004, Mirella Michnik, a pupil at Secondary School No. 2 in Rybnik, wrote in detail about the destruction of the cemetery in an essay prepared for a history competition set by the Shalom Foundation. She based her description on the account given by Jan Kołowrot, a resident of Rybnik:

> Some of the graves had already been exhumed. Coffins were removed from other open graves. Those made of lead-zinc and soldered were heated and taken apart, while those of copper and brass were dismantled. Skeletons were taken out of their coffins. Some of them were still covered by scraps of clothing. The prisoners broke these skeletons up with shovels, split skulls, smashed jaws, and removed any dental bridges. They were looking for gold bracelets, signet and other rings, earrings, and gold teeth. They wore gloves for this work. 'We were guarded by a Gestapo officer in a black uniform. He stood next to a large bucket of chlorinated lime. The bucket was intended for valuables found on the corpses. [...] Prisoners were not allowed to talk to each other. The exhumation work consisted in the prisoners first digging up any valuable or useful items around the gravestones. At first, the older graves went untouched. Apparently they had orders to concentrate on opening those graves with the most expensive headstones.'[68]

The cemetery was transformed into a park. The soil mixed with bones was transported by horse-drawn carts and lorries to several different places, used among other things to fill in the pond near the church. At the priest's request a dozen or so altar boys participated in this work. One of them was Franciszek Musiolik:

> I was an altar boy in that church from January 1940 to the end of '43. At that time, the Germans were liquidating the Jewish cemetery and this earth, mixed with corpses and bones, had to be removed somewhere. And here in this valley was a pond. Except that there was no spring supplying water to this pond. [...] The Germans said they would fill in this pond. [...] The Germans brought along these dead men's bones, coffin

---

67 AŻIH, Relacje. Zeznania ocalałych, ref. no. 301/2652, Joanna Gabowicz's testimony, 1.

68 Shalom Foundation, Collection of works from the "History and Culture of Polish Jews" competition, ref. no. 262/V/2004, Mirella Michnik, Śladami Żydów *rybnickich*, Rybnik 2004.

boards and so on. It was stored. . . by the cartful. They dumped their loads and a whole heap was left. [...] The German parish priest Klimza[69] asked us, there were nearly 20 of us altar boys, to take care that the terrain was levelled. So I worked there maybe 80 or 100 hours. At that time, my brother was Oberministrant, senior altar boy. He took notes on who worked how many hours, because the priest had promised to pay for the work. [...] The fact is one felt, seeing those bones and skulls, well for me, a 12-year-old boy, it was literally nauseating. But we didn't want to refuse the parish priest. We did "what had to be done."[70]

In an interview with Adrian Karpeta from the Regional Weekly *Nowiny*, Franciszek Musiolik added: "The priest said that there were human remains in this earth and that we were to treat them with respect. Whenever we came across a skull we tried to cover it over as soon as possible. We didn't recognize any of the other bones."[71]

In Radom, the Germans probably only began the destruction of the cemetery as late as the spring of 1943, after exterminating most of the Jewish inhabitants. They left groups of labourers in the city. One of these, quartered in a labour camp on Szkolna Street and consisting of about 100 people, was directed to remove gravestones. The stone obtained in this way was sold, used for paving streets and in construction works, including the building of a hangar at the airport.[72]

Some acts of destruction may be considered as serving primarily the desecration of graves and the humiliation of the Jews. According to the notes of Rabbi Szymon Huberband, in an indeterminate period—but certainly before May 10th 1942—in Ciechanów, the Germans intended to use the ohel of rebbe Awraham Landau as a privy.[73] In the *Yisker-bukh fun der Tshekhanover yidisher*

---

69   Franciszek Klimza (1892–1975) was a Pole, who in 1939–1944 was a substitute vicar in Rybnik.

70   "Opowieść o likwidacji cmentarza żydowskiego w Rybniku," Franciszek Musiolik, accessed June 30, 2020, https://www.youtube.com/watch?v=UP866a8uXpI.

71   "Rybnickie Pokłosie," Adrian Karpeta, accessed June 30, 2020, http://nowiny.rybnik.pl/artykul,29477,rybnickie-8222-poklosie-8221-wstrzasajaca-relacja-swiadka-likwidacji-cmentarza-zydowskiego.html.

72   Sebastian Piątkowski, *Radom w latach wojny i okupacji niemieckiej (1939–1945)* (Lublin–Warszawa: Instytut Pamięci Narodowej, 2018), 451.

73   Szymon Huberband, "Dziennik 9–19.05.1942," in *Archiwum Ringelbluma. Konspiracyjne Archiwum Getta Warszawy. Pisma rabina Szymona Huberbanda*, vol. 32, ed. Eleonora

kehile, however, Binyamin Appel states that after removing the tzadik's bones, the ohel was used as a tool shed and in the end completely demolished.[74]

Among the most drastic examples of cemetery destruction and related martyrdom of the Jewish population was the establishment of the forced labour camp in Plaszow in the autumn of 1942, transformed into a concentration camp on January 10th 1944. This camp was located on the site of two adjacent cemeteries, the first being the cemetery of the former community in Podgórze,[75] founded in 1888 at No. 25 Jerozolimska Street and the second being the cemetery of the Jewish Religious Community in Kraków, operating since 1932, located at No. 3 Abrahama Street and No. 14 Jerozolimska Street. After the ghetto was closed and burial of the dead in the cemeteries on Miodowa Street and Jerozolimska Street was forbidden, the latter cemetery became the only official burial place for Kraków's Jews.[76] The Germans used Jewish forced labourers for construction work, including a group of engineers, one of these being Jakub Stendig, head of the Jewish community's construction department. Gravestones were torn out of the ground and used for construction work and for hardening the camp's roads, alleyways and the backyards of houses inhabited by the SS. The camp's buildings were located directly over graves and during construction work, the unearthing of bones and decayed human remains were a regular occurrence. Within the grounds of the cemeteries at No. 3 Abrahama Street and No. 14 Jerozolimska Street, the barracks of the men's camp were erected and the roll-call yard was marked out. In the south-west section, two reservoirs for fire-fighting purposes were dug, as required by the company insuring the camp's infrastructure. The building of the Chevra Kadisha holy brotherhood was commandeered as a billet for the SS, as well as a prison and torture chamber for the camp's inmates. Its basement was converted into 20 punishment bunkers for those forced to spend their sentences standing up, five general cells and one cell for those sentenced to suffer in total darkness. The Germans converted the pre-funeral building into a stable and a pigsty. In the

---

Bergman and Anna Ciałowicz (Warszawa: Żydowski Instytut Historyczny im. E. Ringelbluma, 2017), 58.

74   Binyamin Appel, "In the Years of the German Extermination of the Jews," in *Yisker-bukh fun der Tshekhanover yidisher kehile*, ed. A. Wolf Yassini (New York: JewishGen, 2013), 253.

75   On July 14, 1936, the Ministry of Religious Denominations and Public Education issued a decision to merge the Jewish communities of Podgórze and Kraków into one Jewish Religious Community in Kraków.

76   Bieberstein, *Zagłada Żydów w Krakowie*, 228.

cemetery at No. 25 Jerozolimska Street, a zone was established for new arrivals to the camp who automatically underwent quarantine. This included two barracks. The cemetery's monumental pre-funeral building was transformed into a bathhouse and delousing station.[77]

Prisoner Matys Brunnegraber recalled the work on constructing the camp as follows:

> We demolished the cemetery wall, which took a long time, as it was very thick. We had to break up the gravestones with pickaxes, the graves themselves were levelled and piles were driven into soil to provide foundation support for the barracks. These piles were driven into graves to a depth of one metre. [...] A Bager[78] dug up the soil, unearthing the bones of skeletons. Whenever a skull was encountered, the Bagermeister ordered the Jews to remove any gold teeth and bridges and took them away.[79]

Jakub Stendig's account includes a gruesome description of the work he had to carry out:

> We're digging holes for these piles, and at a depth of 80 centimetres the chalky white belly of a perhaps one-year-old corpse appears. The Rotten-fuehrer [...] grabs a pickaxe and stabs it from above right in the belly, to make way for the pile to be driven [...] and then... as if in protest, like a geyser the contents of the belly burst up and fill the whole area with an incredibly powerful stench. Another pile fared better, because it fell straight into the arms of a corpse.[80]

Involved in the construction of the camp's fence was Shalom Leser, who during Amon Göth's trial in 1946 testified: "There were still fresh, swollen corpses in the holes we were digging for the posts. On one occasion my pickaxe struck a leg with a shoe still on it. [...] There were graves all around and many corpses covered with earth to a depth of just 30 centimetres.[81]

---

77 Ryszard Kotarba, *Niemiecki obóz w Płaszowie 1942–1945* (Warszawa–Kraków: Instytut Pamięci Narodowej, 2009), 48.

78 Mechanical excavator.

79 AŻIH, Relacje. Zeznania ocalałych, ref. no. 301/3546, Matys Brunnegraber's testimony, no date, 3–4.

80 AŻIH, Archiwa Wojewódzkich Komisji Historycznych, ref. no. 303/XX/558, Kraków, WŻKH, Jakub Stendig, Stary podgórski cmentarz, 17.

81 *Proces ludobójcy Amona Goetha przed Najwyższym Trybunałem Narodowym*, ed. Nachman Blumental (Warszawa – Kraków – Łódź: Centralna Żydowska Komisja Historyczna w Polsce, 1947), 218.

While the camp was in operation, the Germans decided to build a new bathhouse. The building was located in the former cemetery of the Podgórze commune, and while digging the foundations, "in almost every square metre of the excavation the labourers encountered corpses, which were dug up in one place and then thrown into pit dug in another area. In this way, the new delousing plant was built on corpses."[82]

In June 1944, during the construction of a railway line, the Germans blew up the pre-funeral building. They left its west wing standing, as it housed a water-pumping facility needed for the functioning of the camp.

Figure 4.3. The pre-funeral house at the cemetery in Podgórze being blown up, 1944. Author unknown. Collection of the Institute of National Remembrance.

In the summer of 1944, in view of the approaching eastern front, traces of the crimes committed in the Plaszow camp were erased. According to various sources, between August and October, the Germans began burning the corpses of those people who had been buried in a mass grave next to the pre-funeral

---

82 Archiwum Instytutu Pamięci Narodowej (hereinafter: AIPN), Oddziałowa Komisja Ścigania Zbrodni Hitlerowskich przeciwko Narodowi Polskiemu, ref. no. Ds. 38/67, Protokół oględzin terenu obozu koncentracyjnego w Płaszowie przeprowadzonych przez sędziego St. Żmudę, 35.

building. The bodies were unearthed and cremated on pyres. The work was carried out by Jewish prisoners from the so-called Ausgrabenkommando, under the supervision of German Kapos.[83]

A forced labour camp—called Judenfriedhof or Lager II Buchenwald—was established in the cemetery in Oświęcim. From November 1941, prisoners from Poland, Belgium, France and Ukraine, who worked for IG Farben, were housed in barracks in the northern section of this cemetery. On the orders of the Germans, hundreds of gravestones were used as foundations for what is today Dąbrowskiego Street, among other things.[84]

The cases cited above show that cemetery plots also became the subject of secondary development. In 1940, the Germans laid out a football playing field at the cemetery in Kleczew,[85] and a park in that of Piła.[86] On June 25th 1942, the Ghetto Overseers in Łódź headed by Hans Biebow informed the Jewish Elders of the intention to remove the gravestones from the Wesoła Street cemetery so that it could be used as a lumber yard for the adjacent Timber Products Establishment.[87] In Krakow, the Germans built barracks at the Miodowa Street cemetery.[88] A warehouse was erected at the extreme end of the cemetery in Mielec, adjacent to the railway line, and soil and clay was removed from the rest of the site.[89] In 1942, a garden centre was established at the Ostrów Wielkopolski cemetery on J. Słowacki Street and one of its underground tombs was used as a cold store for seedlings and flowers. The second cemetery in Ostrów was levelled and transformed into a town square.[90] The Germans organized the cultivation of vegetables on the site of the cemetery in Zamość. Ruth Bauernschmidt, who was deported from Dortmund to Zamość, wrote in a letter to her parents on June 16th 1942: "We have been set to work gardening and have had to clean up

83 Kotarba, *Niemiecki obóz w Płaszowie 1942–1945*, 151.

84 Gałosz, Karetta, Proszyk, and Szyndler, *Cmentarz żydowski w Oświęcimiu*, 14–15.

85 USC Shoah Foundation, Visual History Archive, ref. no. 24854, Bert Gembicki's testimony.

86 Simonstain Cullman, *Historia gminy żydowskiej z Piły od roku 1641 do Holokaustu*, 173–174.

87 Archiwum Państwowe w Łodzi (hereinafter: AP Łódź), Przełożony Starszeństwa Żydów w Getcie Łódzkim, ref. no. 1081, Kronika getta łódzkiego, 379.

88 AŻIH, Relacje. Zeznania ocalałych, ref. no. 301/248, Moses Goldberg's testimony, 1.

89 Urban, *Cmentarze żydowskie, synagogi i domy modlitwy w Polsce w latach 1944–1966*, 255.

90 Maciej Zenon Maśliński, "Ostrowskie lapidaria – cmentarze żydowskie," in *Ostrowskie Studia. Studia Iudaica Ostroviensia*, vol. II, ed. Jarosław Biernaczyk (Ostrów Wielkopolski: Gmina Miasto Ostrów Wielikopolski, 2009), 291–292.

and manage the old cemetery, where vegetables and other edible seedlings are now planted."[91]

In the spring of 1941, in Przeworsk, a town from which the Germans had expelled almost all the Jews in the first months of the war, the Town Council leased the Jewish cemetery to Helena R. "for the purpose of herding cattle for an annual fee of 10 zlotys."[92] In 1942, grass was harvested from the Jewish cemetery in Warsaw for the production of mattresses, and beet, cabbage, tomato and potato plantations were established there, run by the German company Ost-deutsche Bautischlerei-Werkstätte and the Toporol Society for the Promotion of Agriculture.[93] Although these crops were grown on land not yet occupied by graves, and Toporol was a Jewish organization of pre-war origin, from the point of view of the more religious, deriving material benefits from a cemetery could be considered profanation. With regard to the greenery of cemeteries, the *Kitzur Shulchan Aruch* codex clearly states: "One should not [. . .] harvest any vegetation that grows there. One is, however, permitted to pick fruit from trees that, although planted in a cemetery, do not grow directly above graves."[94] In the eyes of Halacha (Jewish law), supplying the ghetto population with vegetables can be considered the suspension of everyday rules for a higher purpose, the saving of lives (pikuach nefesh in Hebrew).

The Germans also demolished and razed cemetery buildings. One such destroyed facility was the building in Warsaw's cemetery at Gęsia Street. Despite the plundering of graves and various other thefts, this cemetery survived the years 1939-1943 in relatively good condition. On May 15th 1943, German soldiers blew up and burned down the synagogue and the pre-funeral building at the entrance to the cemetery. Jürgen Stroop (SS commander and Chief of Police in occupied Poland) planned for the Great Synagogue on Tłomackie Street to be blown up on that same day, but its destruction was postponed until

---

91 Ralf Piorr and Peter Witte, *Ohne Rückkehr: Die Deportation der Juden aus dem Regierungsbezirk Arnsberg nach Zamosc im April 1942* (Essen: Klartext Verlag, 2012), 192.

92 Archiwum Państwowe w Przemyślu (hereinafter: AP Przemyśl), Akta miasta Przeworska, ref. no. 137/1399, Dochody budżetowe, 64.

93 Joseph Kermish, *To live with honor and die with honor!. . .* (Jerusalem: Yad Vashem, 1986), 536; Janina Bauman, *Zima o poranku* (Kraków: Znak, 1989), 77; Anna Grasberg-Górna, "Dziennik (25.08.–4.09.1942)," in *Archiwum Ringelbluma. Konspiracyjne Archiwum Getta Warszawy. Dzienniki z getta warszawskiego*, vol. 23, ed. Katarzyna Person, Michał Trębacz, Zofia Trębacz (Warszawa: Żydowski Instytut Historyczny im. E. Ringelbluma, 2015), 393.

94 Ganzfried, *Code of Jewish law*, 105; Felder, *Yesodei Smochos*, 49.

May 16th. Both operations—blowing up the cemetery buildings and the Great Synagogue—were intended as the symbolic culmination of the "great action," namely the murder of Warsaw's Jews and suppression of the Ghetto Uprising.[95]

Cemeteries were often destroyed as a result of executions carried out in them. These involved the firing of weapons accompanied by ricochets that damaged gravestones, perimeters and buildings. Traces of shots fired are visible on the inner side of the brick wall of the cemetery in Siedlce, where in August 1942 the Germans shot local Jews.[96] According to Dariusz Rozmus, the pockmarks on the gravestones in Pilica could have arisen as a result of just such an execution.[97] In Góra Kalwaria, the Germans threw the victims of executions into the cemetery well, used for ritual ablution. After the war, activists of the local Jewish Committee—deeming this water no longer potable—were forced to fill in the well and dig a new one.[98]

The digging of mass graves also contributed to considerable destruction, including the excavation of earlier burials. In 1942, a dozen or so Jews in Nowy Targ were forced to remove gravestones and in their place dig a pit intended as a mass grave.[99] In all likelihood such a situation also arose in Warsaw, where mass graves were dug for tens of thousands of people in one of the oldest sections of the Jewish cemetery. According to a report by the head of Intelligence for the 12th District of the National Armed Forces Czesław Zawadzki, whose alias was "Gozdawski," 100 metre long pits were dug at the cemetery in Kosów Lacki, in which were buried the bodies of those who died or were killed while being transported to the Nazi death camp in Treblinka.[100]

Some mass graves used in cemeteries were later opened at the order of the Germans in order to remove any traces of their crimes. Zofia Skoczek from

---

95 Jürgen Stroop, *Żydowska dzielnica mieszkaniowa w Warszawie już nie istnieje!* (Warszawa: Instytut Pamięci Narodowej, 2009), 101–102.

96 Edward Kopówka, *Żydzi w Siedlcach 1945–1850* (Siedlce: Stowarzyszenie Tutaj Teraz, 2009), 364.

97 Dariusz Rozmus, "Zagadnienie ochrony prawnej zabytków ze starego cmentarza żydowskiego w Pilicy." *Roczniki Administracji i Prawa* 2015, no. XV (2), 93.

98 An unrecorded interview with Feliks Karpman, conducted by Krzysztof Bielawski on April 18, 2010.

99 Karolina Panz, *"Zagłada żydowskich mieszkańców Nowego Targu w perspektywie mikrohistorycznej – głosy, obrazy, przybliżenia i oddalenia"* (PhD diss., University of Warsaw, 2018), 257, 409.

100 Artur Ziontek, *Żydzi Kosowa Lackiego* (Kosów Lacki: Miejsko-Gminny Ośrodek Kultury w Kosowie Lackim, 2016), 100.

Szczebrzeszyn testified: "About 500 people—men, women and children—were executed en masse at the Jewish cemetery. [. . .] After the first of these actions, the Germans dug up the mass graves and began to take the rotting bodies away by vehicle in the direction of Zamość."[101] Similar events took place in Siedlce, where "in 1943 the Nazis brought a transport of Jews [. . .]. These Jews were tasked with digging up mass graves and burning the corpses."[102] In the summer of 1944, the exhumed remains of murdered Jews and Soviet prisoners of war were burned on a huge pyre at the Jewish cemetery in Sandomierz, and the ashes were buried in pits measuring approximately 3 x 20 metres.[103] Also in 1944, the bodies of Shoah victims removed from cemeteries were also burned in Jadów, Sieniawa and Węgrów.[104]

Destruction of cemeteries also involved the destruction of gravestones of considerable historical and artistic value. Matzevahs from the 700-year-old cemetery in Kalisz were smashed to form cobblestones with which streets were later paved. They were also used to build an embankment along the Prosna River.[105] Among others not spared this destruction were renaissance gravestones from cemeteries dating back to the 16th century in Kraków and Przemyśl. These not only marked burial sites, but also constituted a valuable source for research into the history and culture of local Jewish communities.

Destruction of the gravestones of respected rabbis and tzadiks was particularly traumatic for the more religious. Also destroyed were cemetery records such as burial registers and the chronicles of the Chevra Kadisha brotherhoods. In Krakow, the Germans burned all items of a liturgical nature and books found in the cemetery.[106]

Both then and today, Jewish cemeteries are maintained by religious organizations, and one of their fundamental principles forbids the burial of non-Jews.

---

101 AŻIH, Relacje. Zeznania ocalałych, ref. no. 301/5503, Zofia Skoczek's testimony, 2.

102 AŻIH, Relacje. Zeznania ocalałych, ref. no. 301/5862, Jontel Goldman's testimony, 1.

103 Piotr Sławiński, "Dzieje i przestrzenna organizacja cmentarzy," in *Cmentarze żydowskie w Sandomierzu*, ed. Sławiński (Sandomierz: Armoryka, 2011), 85–86.

104 Marian Karczewski, *Czy można zapomnieć?* (Warszawa: PAX, 1969), 121; Jerzy Czechowicz, *Zarys historii Żydów w Jarosławiu i okolicy* (Rzeszów: Wydawnictwo Edytorial, 2015), 158; AŻIH, Relacje. Zeznania ocalałych, ref. no. 301/ 6043, Władysław Okulus's testimony, 5–6.

105 AŻIH, Relacje. Zeznania ocalałych, ref. no. 301/567, Gedala Goldman's testimony, undated, 5.

106 AŻIH, Relacje. Zeznania ocalałych, ref. no. 301/1216, Bolesław Szyjut's testimony, 23.11.1945, 1.

In this context, burying non-Jews in them should be considered actions that contravene Halacha. Such situations arose in the years 1939-1940, when the Germans shot and buried several hundred Poles—mainly representatives of the intelligentsia—at the Jewish cemeteries in Aleksandrów Łódzki, Lublin,[107] Kalisz, Konin, Kościan, Rypin, Skarszewy, Sieradz, Szubin, Śmigiel, Świecie, and Żnin.[108] Victims of executions, including a Roma and Sinti group and members of the Polish resistance, were buried in the Jewish cemetery in Łódź.[109] At the turn of September 1944, the cemetery on Warsaw's św. Wincentego Street became the place of execution for residents of the capital (for example, an unnamed priest was shot on August 24th 1944), who were shot and buried in previously dug pits.[110] After the war, a significant number of these victims were exhumed and their bodies transferred to parish and communal cemeteries.

What should also be considered the desecration of Jewish cemeteries was the placing of symbols of other denominations on their premises. In 1942, the Germans intended to set up a crematorium at the cemetery on Kraków's Miodowa Street. Its design included a large cross to be hung above a catafalque. However, the plan to build this crematorium was never fulfilled.[111]

4.3. Destruction as a Result of Military Operations

Probably the first Jewish cemetery to suffer damage during World War II was the cemetery in Krzepice—a town some 5 kilometres from the then Polish-German border. According to materials collected by local historian Romuald Cieśla, at around 5:00–6:00 a.m. on September 1st 1939, several tanks of the

---

107 During the exhumation in 1947 it was found that there were latrines located on the mass graves in the cemetery on Kalinowszczyzna Street. See: *Biuletyn Żydowskiej Agencji Prasowej*, May 6, 1947.

108 Maria Wardzyńska, *Był rok 1939. Operacja niemieckiej policji bezpieczeństwa w Polsce. Intelligenzaktion* (Warszawa: Instytut Pamięci Narodowej, 2009), 153, 166, 175, 207, 207, 210–211.

109 Joanna Podolska, *Spacerownik. Łódź żydowska* (Łódź: Agora, 2009), 219.

110 AIPN, Główna Komisja Badania Zbrodni Hitlerowskich w Polsce, ref. no. GK 182/83, Protokoły przesłuchania świadków w sprawie zbrodni hitlerowskich dokonanych w czasie Powstania Warszawskiego, 1–27.

111 Leszek Hońdo, *Dom przedpogrzebowy przy żydowskim nowym cmentarzu w Krakowie* (Kraków: Universitas, 2011), 88.

German 4th Armoured Division entered the cemetery, knocking down its perimeter wall.[112]

Due to their walls and gravestones providing protection against missiles, and sometimes also in view of their elevation, some cemeteries became strategic points during hostilities. During the September 1939 campaign, at least several cemeteries—including those in Bolszewo, Warsaw, and Seroczyn—became defence points established for the Polish Army.[113] In Zakroczym, the construction of fortifications led to conflict between Jewish community representatives and the army. A delegation led by a rabbi, demanding an end to the excavation of the graves, was repelled by soldiers throwing stones. Following negotiations, the unit's commander modified the plan "so that not so many dead would have to be disturbed."[114] In 1939, the wall of the cemetery in Warsaw's Bródno district was damaged "as a result of hostilities."[115]

The cemetery in Filipów was in the immediate path of the German fortifications that were erected in the years 1940–1941 and again in 1944 along the border with the Soviet Union. During the occupation, German soldiers tested their rifles by firing at the cemetery wall in Pruszków and destroyed it. According to regional historian Marian Skwara, damage to some gravestones was probably caused by their bullets.[116] In Żabno too, Wehrmacht soldiers smashed part of the cemetery's wall during exercises using anti-tank guns.[117] In Brzeziny, members of the Volkssturm and gendarmes used matzevahs for target practice, and in

---

112 Romuald Cieśla, *Blask dawnych Krzepic* (Krzepice: UMiG w Krzepicach, 2007), 57.

113 Yoav A. Sapir, "Bolszewo," in *Śladami żydowskimi po Kaszubach. Przewodnik. Jüdische Spuren in der. Kaschubei. Ein Reisehandbuch*, ed. Mirosława Borzyszkowska-Szewczyk and Christian Pletzing (Gdańsk – Lübeck – München: Academia Baltica, Instytut Kaszubski w Gdańsku, 2010), 110; NN, "Wspomnienia z pierwszych miesięcy okupacji w Warszawie (09.1939–01.1940 r.)," in *Archiwum Ringelbluma. Konspiracyjne Archiwum Getta Warszawy. Getto warszawskie*, part 1, vol. 33, ed. Tadeusz Epsztein, Katarzyna Person (Warszawa: Żydowski Instytut Historyczny im. E. Ringelbluma, 2016), 4–6.

114 AŻIH, Archiwum Ringelbluma, ref. no. ARG I 1085 (Ring. I/943), NN, Zakroczym, 1.

115 "Wydział Statystyczny," in *Archiwum Ringelbluma. Rada Żydowska w Warszawie*, Vol. 12, ed. Szymon Morawski, Beata Jankowiak-Konik (Warszawa: Żydowski Instytut Historyczny im. E. Ringelbluma, 2014), 470.

116 Marian Skwara, *Pruszkowscy Żydzi. Sześć dekad zamkniętych Zagładą* (Pruszków: Powiatowa i Miejska Biblioteka Publiczna im. H. Sienkiewicza w Pruszkowie, 2007), 244.

117 Paweł Domański, *Izraelici w Żabnie* (Żabno: Mała Poligrafia Redemptorystów w Tuchowie, 2003), 67.

1945 used them again to build barricades.[118] The cemetery in Konin was transformed into a training ground for German soldiers.[119]

In 1939–1945, three cemeteries in Wrocław (then called Breslau) were damaged. Willy Cohn wrote about one such event in his diary: "February 24th 1940. Breslau, Saturday. A strange event occurred at our cemetery in Cosel.[120] One of the planes flew too low and collided with the dome of the chapel, which caught fire and burned down. The plane crashed and the entire crew was killed."[121] The cemetery's administration building was handed over to the Wehrmacht to be used as a warehouse.[122] Another Jewish cemetery, located on today's Gwarna Street, opposite the railway station, became of interest to railway officials, who intended to requisition the site and build an air-raid shelter for about 3,000 passengers. Ultimately, due to the complications concerning purchase of the cemetery from the Jewish Association in Germany, Wrocław's city authorities agreed to build a smaller shelter.[123] It is not known whether this construction work was ever completed. During archaeological digs conducted in 2013 and 2017, a reinforced concrete beam measuring 2x7x16 metres was unearthed, but it has not been possible to establish whether or not this was an element of the bunker's structure.[124]

During the war, the cemetery on today's Ślężna Street in Wrocław also suffered damage. In 1945, German and Soviet units clashed on its grounds. Evidence of this can be seen in the bullet marks still visible on some of the gravestones and tombs.[125] Colonel Mikhail Machov took part in that battle: "Our

---

118 "Brzeziny żyją na macewach," Michał Gołąbek, accessed June 30, 2020, http://www.e- kalejdoskop.pl/wiadomosci-a230/brzeziny-zyja-na-macewach-r669/pdf.

119 Letter from the Provincial Conservator of Monuments in Konin to Damian Kruczkowski, November 5, 2005 (case number Ko.WN.5183.1637.1.2015). The letter in Krzysztof Bielawski's possession.

120 The cemetery was established in 1902 on today's Lotnicza Street.

121 Willy Cohn, Żadnego prawa – nigdzie. Dziennik z Breslau 1933–1941 (Wrocław: Via Nova, 2010), 324.

122 Tamara Włodarczyk and Jerzy Kichler, Przewodnik po żydowskim Wrocławiu (Wrocław: Ad Rem, 2016), 145.

123 Wodziński, Hebrajskie inskrypcje na Śląsku XIII–XVIII wieku, 55–56.

124 Jerzy Kichler, "Agonia cmentarza, czyli rzecz o wrocławskim kirkucie," Midrasz, no. 4 (198), 34.

125 Maciej Łagiewski, Stary cmentarz żydowski we Wrocławiu (Wrocław: Muzeum Architektury, 2006), 7.

battalions had already occupied part of the cemetery between Sztabowa, Śleż-na and Komandorska streets. [. . .] On February 26th, the Germans launched a strong counterattack from Śleżna Street. We found ourselves surrounded. The companies fighting in the cemetery retreated in the face of overwhelming enemy forces."[126]

On February 15th 1944, two bombs fell on the cemetery in Słubice during an RAF air raid on Frankfurt on the other side of the Oder River. As a result of these explosions, a number of graves were destroyed, and a wall of the pre-funeral building collapsed.[127]

In 1944, the Sarnaki cemetery was used as an observation post for an SS unit participating in V2 rocket testing. In a trench dug on the site, soldiers took cover at the signal of an incoming missile.[128]

According to the findings of Prof. Jan Paweł Woronczak, the smashing of some matzevahs and the creation of a crater in the corner of the Kromołów cemetery could have been the result of an explosion of ammunition and pyrotechnic materials stored in box plate tombstones. The author did not say whether this ammunition was stored by German soldiers or members of the Polish resistance movement.[129]

Due to its strategic location, the cemetery in Nowogród, located on the high banks of the Narew River, right next to a bridge, was transformed into a defensive redoubt in the years 1944-1945. One of Nowogród's residents said of it:

> It was here that the front line was held up from October to January, and the Soviet troops were lined up here, and on the other side of the Narew there is an island, [indistinct], there they made a bridgehead and sent punishment battalions there [. . .]. Here [in the cemetery] there were gun emplacement trenches, some quite large and even bigger, in fact they were proper dugouts. And there the soldiers slept, spent the night and so on. [. . .] Here, like this house on the left, was a German tank, four others were burnt out [indistinct]. That's where their. . . trenches were, down

---

126 Michał Żywień, "Cmentarz żolnierski w Krzykach," in *Kalendarz wroclawski* (Wrocław: Towarzystwo Miłośników Wrocławia, 1967), 126.

127 Reiss, "Makom tov – der gute Ort – dobre miejsce," 42–43.

128 Alfons Filar, "Przesyłka z Sarnak," *Perspektywy*, June 23, 1973, 39.

129 Jan Paweł Woronczak, "*Cmentarz żydowski w Kromołowie jako tekst kultury*" (University of Wrocław, 1999), 8–9.

there, and the trenches were lined with boards, that's where soldiers were [buried].[130]

The depressions in the cemetery's grounds left by the gun trenches are still visible today.

In the spring of 1944, the 16th-century cemetery in Lublin, located on a hill to the east of the city centre, was partially destroyed. The Germans ordered trenches to be dug there, and on May 11th 1944, during an air raid on Lublin, Soviet planes dropped several bombs on the cemetery. David Tevel Mendelsohn's matzevah, pierced by a missile bears witness to that event.[131] According to Mieczysław Zych, a Lublin resident born in 1926, in the spring of 1944, the Todt organization labourers dug seven tunnels in the cemetery hill (six of which were completed, the seventh being not fully dug out) for the storing of ammunition. Each of them probably reached about halfway into the hill, was about 2 metres wide and about 2.5 metres high. According to Mieczysław Zych, the depressions in the terrain of the cemetery that still exist today were caused by the collapse of those tunnels.[132]

A deep excavation that passed through the cemetery at Olkusz probably served as an anti-tank trench.[133] Similar trenches were built in 1944 at the Kłodawa cemetery, where the Germans set up light artillery positions,[134] and in the eastern part of the Betsche cemetery, during creation of the Tirschtiegel Fortified Region. The latter works were performed by Soviet prisoners of war.[135] In Skorogoszcz, the Germans built a defensive bunker on the Jewish cemetery,[136]

---

130 Interview with an unnamed resident of Nowogród, recorded by Krzysztof Bielawski on July 11, 2010. The recording in Krzysztof Bielawski's possession.

131 Andrzej Trzciński, *Świadkiem jest ta stela. Stary cmentarz żydowski w Lublinie* (Lublin: Wydawnictwo Uniwersytetu Marii Curie-Skłodowskiej, 2017), 64–65, 688.

132 Archiwum Państwowego Muzeum na Majdanku, Spuścizna Roberta Kuwałka, ref. no. XXIV–30/1/9, 120–121.

133 Dariusz Rozmus, *Cmentarze żydowskie ziemi olkuskiej* (Kraków: Oficyna Cracovia, 1999), 27.

134 Barbara Gańczyk, Bartłomiej Grzanka, Adam Maliński, *Kłodawskie cmentarze* (Kłodawa: Ireneusz Niewiarowski, 2015), 89.

135 Maciej Borkowski, Andrzej Kirmiel, Tamara Włodarczyk, *Śladami Żydów. Dolny Śląsk, Opolszczyzna, Ziemia Lubuska* (Warszawa: Muzeum Historii Żydów Polskich POLIN, 2008), 79.

136 "Skorogoszcz," Krzysztof Bielawski, accessed June 30, 2020, http://cmentarze-zydowskie.pl/skorogoszcz.htm

and in Wałcz and Szczecin, they built shelters for the civilian population.[137] The two concrete air-raid shelters and a fire protection water tank were built at the cemetery in Oświęcim, which was additionally damaged during an Allied air raid on the town and the resulting bomb craters are still visible in its grounds.[138]

During the Warsaw Uprising, significant destruction of graves and gravestones took place at the Jewish cemetery on Warsaw's Okopowa Street, where from the 6th to 11th of August 1944 fierce battles were fought between the units of the Home Army and units of the German 9th Army. A record of those skirmishes was provided by Witold Sikorski, known as "Boruta" from the "Rudy" company of the Home Army's "Zośka" battalion:

> Andrzej and I are lying between three large tombs [. . .]. Every dozen or so seconds a whistling mortar projectile flies by [. . .]. I felt one of these monuments collapse onto my head. A tremendous force crushes me to the ground [. . .]. On the spot where the light machine gun was being fired there is only the gun left. Next to it are several fresh shell craters." Skirmishes in the Warsaw cemetery were also recalled by Wojciech Szymanowski, alias "Synon" of the Home Army's "Maciek" company: "I took some of our lads and made my way to the Jewish cemetery [. . .]. Our position is located in the centre of the facility, with the right and left wings extending over a hundred metres [. . .]. Around 4 a.m. I am wakened by movement in our tomb [. . .]. The Huns are pressing their attack harder and harder. The four of us repel their assault and throw grenades. The German fire power is getting stronger and more accurate, bullets are whizzing closer and closer. Hidden behind gravestones, we fire back with series after series from our sten guns. The headstone I'm hiding behind is already pockmarked by bullets.[139]

The cemetery also served as a reception site for airdrops from RAF planes. It is very likely that those heavy containers damaged numerous matzevahs.

---

137 Brigitte Kropp, "Auf den Spuren der judischen Gemeinde von Deutsch Krone," in *Heimatstadt-Heimatkreis Deutsch Krone*, ed. Hans-Geord Schmeling (Bad Essen: Verein Deutsch Krone Heimathaus e.V.: 1996), 277–280; AIPN, Ministerstwo Spraw Wewnętrznych w Warszawie, ref. no. IPN BU 1585/7150, Mniejszość żydowska – cmentarze wyznania mojżeszowego w Polsce, 15.

138 Gałosz, Karetta, Proszyk, Szyndler, *Cmentarz żydowski w Oświęcimiu*, 14.

139 *Pamiętniki żołnierzy baonu "Zośka": Powstanie Warszawskie*, ed. Tadeusz Sumiński (Warszawa: Nasza Księgarnia, 1959), 114, 153.

Figure 4.4. A German gun placed in what is likely the Kolno cemetery, 1944 (?).
Author unknown, Tomasz Wiśniewski's collection.

In 1945, the front line passed through the cemetery in Pszczyna. The effects of this are bullet holes on the gravestones and a later repaired hole in the wall of the pre-funeral building caused by a shell.[140] A dozen or so matzevahs in Miejsce also have holes in them. According to Halina Łabęcka, researching cemeteries in the Opole region, this happened during the Soviet army's attack in 1945. In that same year, a Red Army unit was stationed at the cemetery in Słubice prior to the Berlin Operation.[141]

The Jewish cemetery in Jedwabne was transformed into a battlefield at least twice. The first time was in June 1941, when, according to testimony given in 2002 by one of the witnesses for the investigation into the murder of the Jewish population: "there was a bit of shooting, because some Russkis had taken up defence positions on Jewish graves." The second skirmish took place on January 23rd 1945, during the Red Army offensive. As early as between June and

---

140 Correspondence with Sławomir Pastuszka on February 17, 2018. The letter in Krzysztof Bielawski's possession.

141 Reiss, "Makom tov – der gute Ort – dobre miejsce," 42–43.

September 1944, the Germans dug trenches in the shape of a broken line in the eastern part of the cemetery. They set up anti-aircraft guns on the field just north of the cemetery. Traces of those trenches, now in the form of shallow depressions, are still visible in the cemetery today.[142]

4.4. Participation by Local Populations in the Destruction of Cemeteries, 1939–1945

Jewish cemeteries were not devastated solely by the German occupiers or on their orders. Some residents of varied nationality, including Poles and Germans, also voluntarily participated actively in this process. During the war, those cemeteries that since the beginning of the 19th century had been established outside built-up areas were usually located some distance from the ghettos, and were thus most often unattended and easily plundered. Virtually anything of any value fell prey to local inhabitants. Gravestones were torn out and removed, walls and buildings, such as pre-funeral buildings, administrative facilities and the ohels of rabbis and tzadiks were demolished, and trees were cut down. The materials thus obtained were used for construction works, hardening courtyards, as grinding wheels or as gravestones in cemeteries of other denominations. Wood from matzevahs, fences, buildings or felled trees was used as fuel and building material. All and any metal elements were also desirable items plundered. Graves were dug up in search of valuables—mainly gold dental crowns.

It should again be emphasized that thefts from these cemeteries and their destruction was not a new phenomenon and did not occur only during the war, but following its outbreak, this practice intensified dramatically. An unnamed woman, appearing in the Ringelblum Archive under the pseudonym or diminutive name of Nacia, described the "action" of felling trees that took place in January 1940 in Głowno's 18th-century cemetery:

> At dawn, a mob of poverty-stricken goyim entered the cemetery and began to chop down trees. The sound of chopping wood could be heard for two days, it took just two days to strip the cemetery of all its dignity and majesty. The priest's protestations to stop hacking and disturbing the peace of the dead were to no avail. Neither did the disapprobation of

---

142 "Postępowanie o umorzeniu śledztwa," Radosław Jacek Ignatiew, accessed June 30, 2020, http://ipn.gov.pl/ftp/pdf/jedwabne_postanowienie.pdf.

richer Poles help any. They kept chopping . . . And not satisfied with just the tree trunks, they started digging up the roots. They began digging, and knocking down monuments.[143]

According to regional historian Tomasz Romanowicz, probably in the spring of 1941, after the deportation of Jews from Głowno to Łowicz, the cemetery was destroyed by the Germans, who ordered drainage ditches to be lined with its gravestones.[144]

A rather vague mention of another attempt to search for "diamonds" at the Warsaw Bródno cemetery appeared in Adam Czerniaków's Journal entry for January 4th 1940.[145] In the report of the Jewish Council's chairman for the period May 8-14 1940, concern about "the increasing number of cases of monuments in cemeteries being damaged" and the related need to erect new walls and repair existing ones was mentioned, and the report for the period from May 29th to June 11th mentioned the need to set up guard posts at the cemetery on Okopowa Street in order to discourage "social lowlifes from congregating" and reduce thefts from the cemetery.[146] In June of the same year, Adam Czerniaków twice noted destruction of cemeteries, first in Wola: "The authorities dealt with a rabble in the cemetery (Babice),"[147] and then in Bródno: "Zbytkower's[148] grave badly damaged. Youths are entering the cemetery and smashing gravestones with hammers."[149]

It is not known whether it was the German administration or individuals who were responsible for the damage to the cemetery on Okopowa Street, described on March 29th 1940 by Emanuel Ringelblum: "All the trees have been cut down. And there were some really beautiful poplars, chestnuts and other

---

143 AŻIH, Archiwum Ringelbluma, ref. no. ARG I 743 (Ring. I/438), N. N. (Nacia), Wspomnienia z pobytu w Głownie, 13.

144 Tomasz Romanowicz, *Dzieje społeczności żydowskiej w Głownie* (Głowno: Poligrafia, 2014), 90.

145 Adam Czerniaków, *Adama Czerniakowa dziennik getta warszawskiego*, ed. Marian Fuks (Warszawa: Państwowe Wydawnictwo Naukowe, 1983), 74–75.

146 "Wydział Statystyczny," 474, 510.

147 Czerniaków, *Adama Czerniakowa dziennik getta warszawskiego*, 119.

148 Szmul Zbytkower (1756 – 1801) was a merchant, banker, purveyor and agent of the last Polish king Stanisław August Poniatowski.

149 Czerniaków, *Adama Czerniakowa dziennik getta warszawskiego*, 126.

trees. All the pews have been stolen, as well as some slabs of marble. One can now see the whole cemetery at a glance, but it looks like a bald head."[150]

In a letter dated July 11th 1940 to the Polish Police's 2nd Precinct, the Jewish Council in Lublin wrote:

> Recently, the historic Jewish cemetery at No. 10 Sienna Street has been robbed by criminals who cut down trees, destroy monuments and cause other damage. This is witnessed by the caretaker, who is unable to prevent it on his own. Branches have been lopped off in the past, such vandalism being sporadic, but now, due to a sense of impunity, it has become systematic, and no longer branches, but whole trees are cut down, as happened on July 8th this year, when four linden trees were chopped down in one go.[151]

The incidents described by Adam Czerniaków concern the period before the establishment of the Warsaw ghetto. It can be assumed that the process of damaging cemeteries intensified after the Jewish population had been forced into the ghettos, and especially following their extermination in 1942. This hypothesis is confirmed by some source materials. In the village of Jeleniewo, from which Jews were deported to Suwałki at the end of 1939, and then to ghettos in the Lublin region, "Poles took the gravestones and stole everything during the German occupation."[152] In Zgierz, the cemetery was damaged at the very beginning of the occupation, and these acts of destruction increased after the deportation of the Jews[153] on December 26th or 27th 1939:

> The cemetery was also desecrated, with the Polish population playing a significant role in this. One Saturday morning, Poles breached the high wooden cemetery fence and began to steal gravestones. One of the Jews, together with the gravedigger Berl Helman, ran to the magistrate demanding his intervention. They were told that the police would respond, but nothing was done. A few hours after the incident, two policemen came along, but there was no longer any trace of the fence. A little later,

---

150 Emanuel Ringelblum, *Kronika getta warszawskiego wrzesień 1939–styczeń 1943* (Warszawa: Czytelnik, 1988), 114.

151 AP Lublin, Rada Żydowska w Lublinie, ref. no. 891/177, Wydział Stanu Cywilnego. Cmentarz, 51.

152 "Interview with two Jeleniewo residents," Herman Storick, accessed June 30, 2020, http://cmentarze-zydowskie.pl/jeleniewo_wywiad.htm.

153 In 1941, there were 83 Jewish forced laborers and members of their families in the town.

after the expulsion of the Jews, all the gravestones were removed and the ohels over the rabbis' graves were demolished. The streets were paved with these gravestones and some ancient pine trees were uprooted and later used as construction timber. Finally, the Germans ploughed the cemetery over.[154]

In his book *Wielkie Oczy. Studia z dziejów wieloetnicznego galicyjskiego miasteczka* (The history of the multi-ethnic Galician town Wielkie Oczy) Krzysztof Dawid Majus wrote: "Shortly after the deportation of all the Jews from Wielkie Oczy (June 10th 1942), the cemetery was devastated by the remaining residents and people resettled here from Trościaniec. The steles were broken up (the larger ones with the help of horses) and taken away for construction purposes."[155] The situation was no different in Sławatycze, where during the war almost all the matzevahs were stolen, "such actions being condoned by the gendarmes."[156] In Sandomierz, a month after the deportation of Jews that began on October 29th 1942, "demolition of Jewish houses began. [. . .] The Jewish cemetery was demolished. The surrounding wall was pulled down and the gravestones were used to pave streets or else the peasants took them to the countryside and used them for construction purposes."[157] According to Jakub Stendig, as soon as the ghetto in Kraków had been liquidated and its last inhabitants had been deported to the camp in Plaszow (March 13-14th 1943), "idle onlookers" began to plunder graves and destroy the gravestones in the cemeteries on Szeroka Street and Miodowa Street.[158]

An eyewitness to the destruction was Guta Szynowłoga-Trokenheim, who in 1942, together with her daughter, found shelter in the gatehouse of the Jewish

---

154 Danuta Dombrowski and Abraham Wein, "Zgerzsher Yidn unter der daytschisher groyl-ok- upatzye," in *Sefer Zgerzsh: tsum ondenk fun a Yidisher kehile in Poyln*, ed. Dawid Stokfisz (Tel Aviv: Irgun yotsei Zgerzsh be-Israel, 1975), 546–547.

155 Krzysztof Dawid Majus, *Wielkie Oczy. Studia z dziejów wieloetnicznego galicyjskiego miasteczka* (Przemyśl: Południowo-Wschodni Instytut Naukowy, 2013), 336–337.

156 Krzysztof Gruszkowski, *Nad starym Bugiem w Sławatyczach* (Biała Podlaska: ARTE, 2012), 104.

157 AŻIH, Relacje. Zeznania ocalałych, ref. no. 301/17, Henryk Scharff's testimony, 2.

158 Jakub Stendig, "Dewastacja cmentarzy, bóżnic i zabytków żydowskich Krakowa podczas okupacji hitlerowskiej," in *W 3-cią rocznicę Zagłady ghetta w Krakowie*, ed. Michał Borwicz, Nella Rost, and Józef Wulf (Kraków: Centralny Komitet Żydów Polskich, 1946), 187–188.

cemetery in Chęciny, inhabited by the Christian caretaker Karol Kiciński. In her book *Życie w grobowcu* (Life in a tomb) she wrote:

> People also come to get stone to repair pavements, they break up the gravestones and take whatever they need. I shudder at the very thought of such desecration. Why don't they do this in other cemeteries? [...]. Grandpa [Karol Kiciński] brought wood from the cemetery and found it very difficult to chop. It's wood from a gravestone, he said, looking at me [...]. In past centuries, people usually made grave markers of wood. Much later they started using stone. This cemetery has been in operation for over four hundred years. There were many wooden grave markers here, but the peasants took a lot of them away for firewood. Who could have stopped them? He kept chopping with all his might.[159]

The events described by Guta Szynowłoga-Trokenheim took place at the end of 1942, after the extermination of the Jews from Chęciny.

In his account of the destruction of the cemetery in Jędrzejów, Menachem Horowicz recalled:

> One day I noticed that peasants were tearing up the matzevahs and using them to pave a road on sand, to make it easier to walk on. There was a particularly large number of these matzevahs in places where [...] cows were herded to graze. [...] Peasants dismantled the cemetery's walls and stole the bricks they needed for new construction. The peasants additionally demolished headstones and stole anything from the cemetery that might be valuable in any way.[160]

In an interview conducted in 2014, Stanisława Konieczna from the village of Suchowola near Chmielnik mentioned 17 farmers by name, who "under the cover of night" transported matzevahs to their farmyards. According to her account, in which she quoted information obtained from her brother, this was believed to have occurred in 1942, and the excuse for this was apparently in order to "save at least some matzevahs from the Germans."[161]

---

159 Guta Szynowłoga-Trokenheim, *Życie w grobowcu* (Warszawa: Ypsylon, 2002), 100, 112.

160 Yad Vashem Archive, YV Relations Department, ref. No. O.3/1316, Menachem Horowicz's testimony.

161 *"Nasi sąsiedzi –Żydzi." Z dziejów relacji polsko-żydowskich na Kielecczyźnie w XX wieku*, ed. Agnieszka Dziarmaga, Dorota Koczwańska-Kalita, and Edyta Majcher-Ociesa (Kielce: Instytut Pamięci Narodowej, 2017), 223.

A glaring example of destruction committed by the local population is the case of the Jewish community cemetery in Parysów. Established at probably the end of the 18th or the beginning of the 19th century, the cemetery is located about 3 kilometres southeast of Parysów, in the forest south of the village of Starowola. According to conversations with residents, the Germans removed selected gravestones from the cemetery during the Second World War. The remaining destruction was the work of some peasants, stealing bricks from the cemetery's perimeter wall and almost all the gravestones. In 2009, the author of this book was informed about a cowshed built of matzevahs in Starowola, and duly visited the site. It turned out that the building was made of brick pillars taken from the demolished cemetery wall, while between these were arranged gravestones fashioned from glacial erratic granite boulders held together by mortar. These had not been plastered over, which meant that the gravestone inscriptions were still visible. During a stay in Starowola lasting several hours, it was possible to establish that the village had three such cowsheds made of matzevahs. Single gravestone fragments were also found in other buildings: in a nearby bridge, as the foundations of a barn, and as a step in front of a wooden privy. Within the grounds of the cemetery itself were found numerous depressions and a spot where gravel had been excavated, leaving human bones

Figure 4.5. Matzevahs in the wall of a barn in Starowola near Parysów, 2020.
Photo: Krzysztof Bielawski.

exposed. At that time, the cemetery had only one gravestone, which lay in a dug up grave.

The process of the Starowola cemetery's destruction was described by Jerzy P., a resident of the village:

> There were pillars of red brick and sliding logs of oak. And there was this fence. There were pine and spruce trees... They ripped it all up [...]. It was a large cemetery, over a hectare. The Germans took those whetstones away[162] [...]. In the very middle, among the graves was a small building. Rabbis were buried there. Right in the middle of the cemetery, I could even show you where today. They smashed it up, destroyed it...
> —The Germans?
> —No. After the Germans had killed the Jews, they ordered the village elder to plough up the Jewish cemetery with a horse, and then spruce trees were planted. And now there's a forest. And there it stands, hard to say whose it is. People took those stones and bricks and built barns. Still during the occupation, in nineteen forty-three. People built three barns using materials from that cemetery. We used to call it the "kerkut" and that's what we still refer to it as. Everyone says "kerkut." And the Germans took the stones away to Garwolin. The Germans took them all. And then, after the war, the village elder ploughed the kerkut up and afforested it.[163]

It is worth noting that despite the 64 years that had passed since the end of the war (this account was recorded in 2009), Jerzy P. remembered that the cemetery was destroyed in 1943. It is very likely the ceasure was the final extermination of the inhabitants of the Parysów ghetto, which took place on September 27th 1942. The certainty that nobody was left to protest the destruction of the cemetery may have encouraged local peasants to take the matzevahs away and demolish the wall. The barns made of stolen gravestones could not have been built before the spring of the following year, when the weather allowed construction work to begin.

The year 1943 also features in documents from an investigation conducted by the Polish Militia in 1965 concerning a path laid with matzevahs on a farm in

---

162 The person interviewed called the sandstone tombstones, from which the peasants made grinding wheels "stones." The issue is discussed in the chapter *Participation of the local population in the destruction of cemeteries after 1945.*

163 Interview with Jerzy P. recorded by Krzysztof Bielawski on September 20, 2009. The transcription in Krzysztof Bielawski's possession.

the village of Karolina near Mińsk Mazowiecki. These officers determined that in 1943 the owners of the property bought the gravestones from "immigrants working at the time for the Germans."[164] It was probably also in 1943 (in 1941 according to other sources) that the mayor of Jaśliska, Wincenty N. together with Julian G. bought matzevahs from the Germans and used them to build a dam and raise the water level at the mill.[165]

Participation by some of the Polish population in the destruction of cemeteries was a practically nationwide phenomenon. An account similar to that concerning Starowola was submitted by the previously mentioned resident of Nowogród:

> They destroyed it during the war. After 1939, it must be admitted, people began demolishing it. They took this material to use as foundations, hauling it away in carts for foundations, and after 1939 they took it away in wheelbarrows. They were made of sandstone, quite large, they cut them in half, and they dug them up here.[166]

Destruction of cemeteries often involved the plundering of graves. This happened at, among others, the Jewish cemetery in Warsaw. These "cemetery hyenas" included officers of the Jewish Police Service (in German: Jüdischer Ordnungsdienst). In September 1941, Emanuel Ringelblum wrote about them: "At night they dig up graves, pull any gold teeth from the corpses and rip their shrouds off. Recently, there was a disciplinary investigation into Jewish policemen who had engaged in this desecration. In a word, the very dregs of society."[167] The desecration of corpses was well remembered by Włodzimierz Derecki, alias "Kazik," member of the assault battalion of the People's Army,[168] who in August 1944 fought in the Wola cemeteries complex:

---

164 AIPN, Ministerstwo Spraw Wewnętrznych w Warszawie, ref. no. IPN BU 00231/205/6, Materiały dotyczące Leftwich-Lewkowitza Josepha i Morejno Wawa, 269.

165 "Epilog działań Nieformalnej Grupy Kamieniarzy Magurycz. Rok 2006," http://www.magurycz.org/spr2006.pdf, accessed June 30, 2020; Andrzej Potocki, Żydzi w Podkarpackiem (Rzeszów: Libra, 2004), 71.

166 Interview with an unnamed resident of Nowogród, recorded by Krzysztof Bielawski on July 11, 2010. The recording in Krzysztof Bielawski's possession.

167 Ringelblum, Kronika getta warszawskiego wrzesień 1939–styczeń 1943, 322.

168 People's Army (Polish: Armia Ludowa) was an underground organization during World War II, set up by the communist Polish Workers' Party.

> We jumped over a wall and entered the Jewish cemetery [...]. The pits there had been dug by so-called dentists, that is to say people who dug up graves and pulled any gold teeth. [...] The Jews who lay there usually had their heads exposed, with their teeth pulled out.[169]

The large number of cases of gold crowns being torn from skulls can be seen by the fact that after the war, at least in Warsaw and its outskirts, the word "dentist," used as a term to describe criminals involved in this practice, entered the colloquial vocabulary.[170]

In Warsaw, excavation of bodies possibly also took place in connection with the trade in places for individual graves, which were an expensive "alternative" to the burials in mass graves common at that time. Franz Mawick, the driver of a Swiss Red Cross mission, who visited the Warsaw ghetto in 1942, wrote about this:

> When the relatives of a Jew are able to pay a large sum, say 700 zlotys, they acquire the right to bury him in a single grave. The corpse is indeed buried separately, but space is limited, and the Germans are unwilling to lose such a good business, so another deceased person is soon buried in the same place. This later leads to quarrels in the cemetery, as over time several families claim the same grave.[171]

In the spring of 1943, a group of Klimontów residents dug up the mass grave of 68 people who had been murdered on November 30th 1942 and buried at the local Jewish cemetery. According to the account of the cemetery's prewar caretaker, as quoted by Lejb Zylberberg, "they dug up the corpses, looked for any dollars on them and pulled their gold teeth." In Klimontów, peasants also broke and open the cemetery's safe, in which Rabbi Simche Gelernter had hidden the Torah before being deported. They cut the parchment from the scroll and used it as lining for shoes.[172] The already quoted Jan Bryksa also described

---

169 Włodzimierz Derecki, accessed June 30, 2020, https://www.1944.pl/archiwum-historii-mowionej/wlodzimierz-derecki,837.html.

170 USC Shoah Foundation, Visual History Archive, ref. no. 16713, Maria Brzezińska's testimony.

171 Franz Blätter, *Warszawa 1942. Zapiski szofera szwajcarskiej misji lekarskiej* (Warszawa: Wydawnictwo Naukowe PWN, 1982), 71.

172 Joanna Tokarska-Bakir, *Okrzyki pogromowe, Szkice z antropologii historycznej Polski lat 1939–1946* (Wołowiec: Wydawnictwo Czarne, 2012), 88, 331.

the destruction of the genizah—a storeroom in which damaged liturgical books await burial—in the Brzeziny cemetery:

> On the western side of the hill, opposite the present Waryńskiego Street, the slope featured a semi-vaulted cellar. Parchments with Hebrew inscriptions were stored there. This cellar—as I remember—was always open; it had no lock. [...] As far as I can recall, it had always been there. After 1945 it was there, during the occupation it was there too; then parchments were selected from it, the inscriptions were scraped off and they were used for practical purposes [...]. This material was an excellent substitute for shoe leather. It's a different type of leather, but was basically great material. Of course, soles were wooden. It was sewn or stapled onto the sole, making shoes warm and waterproof. In addition, some people had foot wrappings or added straw, and thus had comfortable [footwear] for the whole winter.[173]

Some of the residents in Nowogród "went and looked for Jewish skulls and gold teeth."[174]

The Jewish cemetery in Bochnia was destroyed not only by the Germans, but also by "youths from outlying villages and urban scum." Oswald Szałowski, a Bochnia resident, described the cemetery as follows after visiting it in June 1944: "I went to see the cemetery where the local scum had been busy—looking for treasure, valuables and money buried by Jews. The gravestones are destroyed; slabs of marble and brass or bronze fittings have been torn out."[175]

In Krakow, the Maśnicki stonemasons advised the Germans on the sale of gravestones from the cemetery on Miodowa Street, helping them to evaluate the material.[176] After the war, the stonemason Moses Goldberg testified: "In this way, a whole slew of Krakow stonemasons thus acquired an unknown number of valuable Jewish gravestones, mostly from the cemetery. Some of these gravestones are still in their hands. As far as I know, these companies are either hiding

---

173 POLIN, Oral History Collection, ref. no. 589, Jan Bryksa's testimony.

174 Interview with an unnamed resident of Nowogród, recorded by Krzysztof Bielawski on July 11, 2010. The recording in Krzysztof Bielawski's possession.

175 Iwona Zawidzka, *Przewodnik po cmentarzu żydowskim w Bochni* (Bochnia: Muzeum im. prof. S. Fischera w Bochni, 2018), 18.

176 Bieberstein, *Zagłada Żydów w Krakowie*, 231.

them or transforming them into other gravestones."[177] In Aleksander Bieberstein's opinion, the execution of the cemetery's caretaker Pinkus Ladner, shot
in the autumn of 1943 was dictated by the desire to remove this witness to the
trade in matzevahs and illegal transactions related to this practice.[178]

Cemeteries were also destroyed by the German civilian population. In the
autumn of 1939, the perimeter fence and pre-funeral building in Dąbie were
dismantled by German farmers from the villages of Sobótka and Tarnówka,
including Cado and Schmidt, who used the material for construction work on
their farms. Some of the gravestones were also taken away at that time. In 1940,
these activities in Dąbie were conducted in an organized manner, under the aegis
of the local authorities. Gravestones were smashed and used to pave courtyards
on properties inhabited by officials, to build a road, and as fill for the foundations
of houses in a district intended for German settlers from the Black Sea. These
works were overseen by an engineer named Ulman, aided by a foreman Johann
Majewski (Jan Maciejewski). The administration official was the Volksdeutsch
Stefan Ropelski.[179] In Pobiedziska, settlers stole bricks from the cemetery
wall.[180] German colonists used gravestones from Sandomierz for construction
works on farms in Mokoszyn, Chwałki and Sucharzów.[181] This also happened in
Ryczywół.[182] In Koźmin Wielkopolski, members of the Hitlerjugend damaged
some of the matzevahs, knocking them over and smashing the ornamentation.[183]

---

177 AŻIH, Relacje. Zeznania ocalałych, ref. no. 301/248, Moses Goldberg's testimony, 1.

178 Bieberstein, *Zagłada Żydów w Krakowie*, 230. In Herman Ladner's testimony, this reason
for the murder is not mentioned. H. Ladner testified that his seven-year-old daughter Mala
and his father Pinkus Ladner were brought to Plaszow from the Gestapo headquarters
as "convicted[?] for hiding from the authorities," and the execution took place on
February 14, 1944. See: AIPN, Oddziałowa Komisja Ścigania Zbrodni Hitlerowskich
przeciwko Narodowi Polskiemu, ref. no. Ds. 38/67, Odpis protokołu przesłuchania świadka
Herman Ladner, 653.

179 Żydowski Instytut Historyczny im. E. Ringelbluma (hereinafter: ŻIH), Monuments
Documentation Department, the Dąbie Files, no reference number, Report by Zdzisław
Lorek of the District Museum in Konin dated 1991, typescript, no pagination.

180 Stanisław Zasada, "Macewy z jeziora," *Rzeczpospolita*, September 6, 2002.

181 ŻIH, Monuments Documentation Department, the Sandomierz files, J. Zub, Information
concerning the former Jewish cemetery on Sucha Street in Sandomierz, typescript, no pagination.

182 Adam Penkalla, *Żydowskie ślady w województwie kieleckim i radomskim* (Radom: Tramp,
1992), 152.

183 Maciej Ratajczyk, "Cmentarz żydowski w Koźminie Wielkopolskim," *Kwartalnik Historii
Żydów*, no. 3/259 (2016): 743.

The Först Stuckmantel company took away many of the most valuable gravestones from the cemetery on Kraków's Miodowa Street. According to master stonemason Moses Goldberg, "that company stole several wagon loads of gravestones and took them to Germany."[184] Matzevahs were being hauled away almost up to the last, before the arrival of the Red Army. The Germans formed five groups of forced labourers to tear up and smash gravestones. Among them was undermaster stonemason Bolesław Szyjut, who testified that stone monuments were loaded onto lorries and transported to the Steinschliff factory in the Sudetes.[185]

Worth mentioning are two known cases of destruction of graves and gravestones, which were caused by the will to save people from the Shoah. In the summer of 1942, during the extermination of Jews in the Warsaw ghetto, Mosze Aroniak and Ajzyk Posner arranged a hiding place in the Jewish cemetery on Okopowa Street.[186] Its construction in the cemetery's filled up 41st section, in a row of graves dating from 1879, almost certainly meant the necessity of exhuming the bodies of people buried there. To build the walls of this bunker, Aroniak and Posner used bricks from the cemetery wall or the mausoleum of Jewish fighters for Poland's freedom, and used gravestones to fashion its roof.[187] Matzevahs were also used to prepare a hideout for Guta Szynowłoga, her daughter Lilli and cousin Izaak Grynbaum at the cemetery in Chęciny.[188]

---

184 AŻIH, Relacje. Zeznania ocalałych, ref. no. 301/248, Moses Goldberg's testimony, 1.

185 AŻIH, Relacje. Zeznania ocalałych, ref. no. 301/1216, Bolesław Szyjut's testimony, 1.

186 The hideout was used by among others Mosze Aroniak, Dawid Płoński, Ajzyk and Guta Posner, Lea Stolbach and her son Abram. This shelter was discovered by the Germans on September 6, 1942, at which time some of the people in hiding lost their lives.

187 David Plonski (Yurek), [no title], in *We remember. Testimonies of twenty-four members of Kibbutz Megiddo who survived the Holocaust*, ed. Denise Nevo, Mira Berger (New York: Shengold Publishers, 1994), 133–134; an unrecorded telephone conversation between the author and Avraham Carmi (born Abram Stolbach) on April 28, 2019.

188 Szynowłoga-Trokenheim, *Życie w grobowcu*, 66–67.

Chapter 5

The Destruction
of Cemeteries after 1945

5.1. The Role of the Polish State as Legislator

The post-war Polish state—that is, the government and its state enterprises—was the second main factor after the local population responsible for the further destruction of Jewish cemeteries. This resulted from the introduction and application of regulations that restricted the development of Jewish organizations and deprived them of the right to ownership of the properties belonging to pre-war Jewish communities. Such regulations governed the functioning of cemeteries without respecting the principles stemming from religion and tradition. It was also the result of direct, active participation in the destruction of cemeteries, as well as a failure to provide them with sufficient protection.

On February 6th 1945, the Ministry of Public Administration issued *Circular No. 3 concerning the temporary regulation of religious affairs with regard to the Jewish population*, which stated that the State did not envisage the restoration of Jewish communities, and that until an Act regarding abandoned property came into force, all movable and immovable property of the pre-war communities was to temporarily remain under the management of the State Treasury. At the same time, the Ministry permitted the creation of Jewish Religious Associations (which in 1946 adopted the name Jewish Religious Congregations). These associations were to make it possible for members to freely practice their religion. For this goal to be achieved, the Circular required local elders to hand over their synagogues and cemeteries for use by the associations, and in the case of the latter, the Circular stated: "The issue of Israeli cemeteries will be settled by means of a separate regulation. Until then, they should remain under the management of the Jewish Religious Associations. However, the charging of any fees for grave sites in the cemetery will not be permitted."

The intention of the Circular's authors was to disrupt the legal continuity between pre-war and post-war Judaic organizations, convert the right to ownership of property into the right only to use it and consequently, transfer the property of Jewish communities to the State. This was an expression of the policy adopted by the new authorities, which aimed to restrict the role of religious organizations in the life of the country and bring about the nationalization of their property (in addition to Jewish organizations, many Christian churches and other religious associations also lost a considerable number of buildings) and at the same time—in view of Poland's general war damage—to avoid the need to return such property.[1]

As pointed out by Małgorzata Bednarek, in a real sense pre-war Jewish communities ceased to exist due to the murder of most of their members, but not in the legal sense, since they were not officially abolished by the Polish State, and the decisions issued by the Third Reich during the war were declared invalid. For this reason, the method used to disrupt the continuity between the communities and the Jewish Religious Associations and Jewish Religious Congregations amounted to a violation of the law.[2]

At the same time, the State aimed to regulate the legal status of real estate by issuing on March 2nd 1945 a *Decree on unoccupied and abandoned property*, on May 6th 1945 the *Act on unoccupied and abandoned property* and finally, on March 8th 1946, a *Decree on unoccupied property and formerly German-owned property*. The State Treasury took possession of movable and immovable property that due to the war was no longer in the possession of the owner or his legal successors. This decree provided the State Treasury and local government associations the possibility of obtaining ownership and title to unoccupied properties by a statute of limitations (so-called positive prescription, the acquisition of the right to immovable property due to its continuous and long-term use) after a period of 10 years had expired.

As a consequence of the Circular and Decree being signed, Jewish cemeteries formally became abandoned property. Jewish Religious Congregations could only be their users, not their owners, and in addition, could only use them in those places where their headquarters were located. They were also deprived of the right to ownership of the immovable property of pre-war Jewish

---

1   August Grabski and Albert Stankowski, *"Życie religijne społeczności żydowskiej,"* in *Następstwa Zagłady Żydów. Polska 1944–2010*, edited by Feliks Tych and MonikaAdamczyk-Garbowska (Lublin–Warszawa: Wydawnictwo UMCS, Żydowski Instytut Historyczny im. E. Ringelbluma, 2011), 216–217.

2   Bednarek, *Sytuacja prawna cmentarzy żydowskich w Polsce 1944–2019*, 217.

communities, which could be sold or rented, and the profits from the sale or rental of various buildings could be set aside to cover the costs of making cemeteries secure. This was the experience of, among others, the Jewish Religious Association in Dębica, which in 1946 asked local officials in vain for permission to sell three buildings of the pre-war Jewish community and allocate the funds thus raised to pay for the cemetery being tended and fenced off. Rzeszów's Regional Office of Trustees issued a negative decision, indicating that handing over the facilities for use by the Jewish Religious Association was not the same as granting the Association right of ownership.[3]

Not without significance was the subordination to the state of all activities by Jewish organizations in Poland, which from 1950 were limited to the Religious Association of the Judaic Faith in the Republic of Poland and the secular Socio-Cultural Society of Jews in Poland. Both organizations were under strict state control. The statute of the Religious Association of the Judaic Faith in the Republic of Poland, approved in 1966, stipulated that "the forms and scope of the Association's religious, charitable and economic activities must be approved by the state supervisory authority."[4]

On May 29th 1948, the Minister of Public Administration signed Circular No. 44, regulating the return of Jewish gravestones that had been used by the Germans during the war for paving roads, squares and other construction works. This was prompted by protests made by local Jewish organizations that were having difficulty overcoming the resistance of city officials. Under this Circular, local communities were required to return gravestones with inscriptions to Jewish organizations at their own expense. In the case of demands by Jewish organizations, gravestones without visible inscriptions could be returned at the applicant's expense.[5]

On September 13th 1956, the Ministry of Municipal Economics issued Circular No. 30, which sanctioned management of gravestones from abandoned cemeteries: "A gravestone without an owner [. . .] may be used for the

---

3   AAN, Ministerstwo Administracji Publicznej, ref. no. 794, Żydowskie Kongregacje Wyznaniowe i Naczelna Rada Religijna Żydów, 102–107.

4   Grabski and Stankowski, *"Życie religijne społeczności żydowskiej,"* 230.

5   AAN, Ministerstwo Administracji Publicznej, Ref. no. 1098, Wyznaniowe cmentarze żydowskie, 138.

construction of war cemeteries, mausoleums in municipal cemeteries and the execution of planned works related to cemeteries or gravesites."[6]

With regard to regulations concerning the functioning of the cemeteries themselves, until 1959 legal acts from the interwar period were applied, namely the *Act dated March 17th 1932 on burial of the dead and determining the cause of death*, and the *November 30th 1933 Ordinance of the Minister of Social Welfare on burial of the dead and determining the cause of death*. It was not until January 31st 1959 that the *Law on Cemeteries and Burial of the Dead* was passed, adapting the provisions of 1932 to the reality of the Polish People's Republic. The right to close cemeteries was granted the Minister of Municipal Economics in consultation with the Minister of Health, as and when requested by the competent presidium of a town's council, a housing estate or community, as agreed upon with the presidium of the provincial council. Closure of cemeteries of whatever faith additionally required the approval of the Office for Religious Affairs. Where a cemetery plot was intended to be used for a different purpose, the period of its protection was reduced from 50 to 40 years from the last burial taking place, with again the possibility of reducing this period "in cases of exceptional necessity with regard to public interest, state defence or for the implementation of national economic plans." Decisions in this respect had to be approved by the Minister of Municipal Economics in consultation with the Ministers of Health, Culture and Art and the Office for Religious Affairs. In the event of seizure of a cemetery plot for another purpose, the exhumation of bodies could be carried out at the expense of the person purchasing the land or its new user, based on the decision of the municipal economic authority, acting in consultation with the county sanitary inspector.[7]

Another important document was *Circular No. 11 issued by the Minister of Municipal Economics on August 3rd 1964 on the legal status of disused cemeteries constituting state property, managed and operated by Ministry of Municipal Economics authorities, as well as the financing, tending and maintenance of such cemeteries.* This Circular included a reminder that the obligation to maintain cemeteries owned by the state and not handed over for use by religious associations lay with the presidiums of town councils, estates, and communities. That obligation

---

6   AAN, Ministerstwo Gospodarki Komunalnej, ref. no. 9/20, Cmentarnictwo – korespondencja dotycząca zamknięcia cmentarzy żydowskich i ewangelickich, 6.

7   Ustawa z dnia 31 stycznia 1959 roku o cmentarzach i chowaniu zmarłych, Dziennik Ustaw Nr 11/1959, poz. 60, 61, 62.

ceased when a cemetery was requisitioned for another purpose and handed over to another purchaser or user. The obligation to manage religious cemeteries and cemeteries owned by the State but used by religious associations lay with the latter. The Circular specified that cemeteries owned by the State include disused cemeteries of various faiths and disused Jewish cemeteries constituting abandoned property that had become the property of the State by positive prescription (the acquisition of the right to immovable property due to its continuous and long-term use) and should be closed. The Circular called on local economic and housing management departments to sort out the legal status of cemeteries—both active and inactive—through court proceedings to declare acquisition of their ownership by the State by right of positive prescription and to close inactive cemeteries by no later than 1965. Financial aspects were an important issue. The circular stated that financing from the central budget of the Ministry of Municipal Economics to cover the costs of cleaning up closed cemeteries would cease on December 31st 1964. From the following year onwards, funds for cleaning up closed cemeteries were to be provided by the presidiums of national councils. At the same time, it was recommended that active cemeteries should be tended in such a way that they would not require any funds being spent on cleaning efforts after their closure.[8]

From 1972, as a result of an amendment to the law on cemeteries, their closure became simpler. Such decisions were made by the presidiums of provincial councils at the request of the presidiums of town councils, estates, or communities in which the cemeteries were located, after consulting the provincial sanitary inspector. Provincial authorities were authorized to decide on the use of cemetery grounds for other purposes once 40 years since the last burial had expired (in the case of cemeteries entered in the national register of monuments, the consent of the Minister of Culture and Art was required). Decisions to use cemeteries for other purposes before 40 years since the last funeral had expired depended on approval by the Ministry of Local Economics and Environmental Protection.[9]

---

8   Okólnik nr 11 Ministra Gospodarki Komunalnej z dnia 3 sierpnia 1964 roku w sprawie stanu prawnego nieczynnych cmentarzy, stanowiących własność Państwa, pozostających w zarządzie i użytkowaniu organów resortu gospodarki komunalnej oraz finansowania, porządkowania i konserwacji tych cmentarzy, Dziennik Urzędowy Ministerstwa Gospodarki Komunalnej nr 11/1964, poz. 56.

9   Ustawa z dnia 6 lipca 1972 roku o zmianie ustawy o cmentarzach i chowaniu zmarłych, Dziennik Ustaw nr 27/1972, poz. 193, 194.

As a result of the introduction of the above-mentioned legal acts, the fate of Jewish cemeteries was for all practical purposes dependent on the decisions of state authorities. Apart from several dozen cemeteries whose users were religious congregations,[10] as many as 94% of cemeteries went as "abandoned property" to non-Jewish users, who were required to maintain them. It was not difficult to predict that in many cases this situation would result in attempts to liquidate them. The Cemeteries Act of 1959 further shortened the period after which cemetery grounds could be used for other purposes from 50 to 40 years since the last burial. The Circular of 1964 clearly stipulated that as abandoned property, Jewish cemeteries became the property of the State due to the statute of limitations, and at the same time called on municipal and housing departments to initiate court proceedings in order to declare the State's acquisition of such property, while prohibiting the financing of clean-up operations in closed cemeteries from the central budget.[11]

The amendment to the law on cemeteries was a tool in the communist state's war waged against the Roman Catholic Church. At the same time, the overall policy of the authorities towards churches and religious associations should be borne in mind, as it aimed at eliminating them from the public arena. One of the elements of secularization was the gradual closure of religious cemeteries and the establishment of communal cemeteries.

On December 4th 1971, the Minister of Municipal Economics signed another Circular concerning cemeteries. This document essentially upheld the earlier findings. A significant alteration was the recommendation that in cases of designating closed cemeteries for other purposes, the rules governing their use should be followed in a manner ensuring respect for human remains. The ministry advised against requisitioning cemeteries to be used as "markets, garbage dump landfills, entertainment facilities (for example so-called fairgrounds)," at

---

10 On January 1, 1947, there were 80 Jewish Religious Congregations in Poland, which—according to the list prepared by the Organizing Committee of the Jewish Religious Community—made use of 68 active cemeteries. In reality, however, the number of cemeteries was imprecise. 11 congregations failed to submit any data, and the table also lists some cemeteries that did not exist. In total, the congregations were at that time the official users of only about 6% of Jewish cemeteries in Poland, half of which were located in former German territories. See: Grabski and Stankowski, *"Życie religijne społeczności żydowskiej,"* 220.

11 Urban, *Cmentarze żydowskie, synagogi i domy modlitwy w Polsce w latach 1944–1966,* 43–45.

Figure 5.1. The Jewish cemetery in Warsaw's Bródno district, 1947.
Author unknown, collection of the National Digital Archives.

the same time suggesting the creation of parks, green areas, housing estate foliage and forests in these areas.[12]

5.2. Practical Actions by the State Related to the Destruction of Cemeteries

From the very first months after the Eastern Front passed through Poland, state administration units undertook various actions leading to the destruction of Jewish cemeteries. In June 1945, on the orders of the town authorities in Kraśnik, a group of German residents, probably as part of their punitive hard labour,

---

12   Archiwum Państwowe w Warszawie, Oddział w Otwocku (hereinafter: AP Otwock), Urząd Miasta i Gminy Karczew, ref. no. 193/50, Likwidacja cmentarza żydowskiego w Karczewie, 1–5.

started levelling the oldest of the town's three Jewish cemeteries, preparing the plot to be used as a marketplace. This work was halted following intervention by the Central Jewish Committee.[13] The district manager apparently had no desire to depart from this plan and in August proposed setting up a staging post for farm carts there and in return proposed to the Jewish Committee that he would organize for the second cemetery to be fenced off and help in the exhumation of victims buried in various parts of the town. Also in 1945, a military unit in Nowy Targ used matzevahs to pave an airfield.[14] That same year, a transport base was established on the cemetery in Brodnica.[15] On the orders of the local administration in Słubice, the German inhabitants of Kunowice took a decorative fence from the cemetery, which was then used to fence off a mass grave for Soviet soldiers who had perished on February 3rd 1945, which was "decorated" with a display example of a Soviet ISU-122 self-propelled gun (years later replaced with a T-34 tank).[16]

Military units were stationed on at least three cemeteries. The Red Army established garrisons on cemeteries in Kraków's Podgórze district (using the infrastructure of the former German Plaszow labour camp) and in Zamość, where in the autumn of 1945, soldiers dug up graves during the construction of dugouts (officials visiting the cemetery in January 1946 found it full of "garbage, dirt, faeces, rubble and other debris" that poisoned the air).[17] The cemetery on Szubińska Street in Bydgoszcz was in turn occupied by the Polish Army.[18]

In the first post-war years, some of the cemeteries located in annexed former German territory fell victim to the so-called action of repolonizing Reclaimed Territories which involved removing German inscriptions from buildings, streets and even everyday objects. On September 28th 1945, the Municipal Council of Bielsko demanded the local Jewish Committee efface inscriptions in German from matzevahs, arguing that "the Polish population [. . .] is now

---

13   AŻIH, Centralny Komitet Żydów w Polsce, ref. no. 303/X/16, Wydział Budowlany, 4.

14   AAN, Urząd do Spraw Wyznań, ref. no. 45/476, Sprawa nagrobków cmentarnych, woj. krakowskie, 1–15.

15   AAN , Urząd do Spraw Wyznań, ref. no. 75/32, Związek Religijny Wyznania Mojżeszowego, 81.

16   Reiss, "Makom tov – der gute Ort – dobre miejsce," 48.

17   "Lokalizacja dawnych zamojskich cmentarzy w oparciu o archiwalne opracowania kartograficzne z XVIII-XX wieku," Jakub Żygawski, accessed June 30, 2020, http://zamosc.ap.gov.pl/images/AZ2015/007-034.pdf.

18   AAN, Ministerstwo Administracji Publicznej, ref. no. 199, vol. I, 107–109, 182–183.

striving for complete repolonization of Bielsko and reacts strongly to anything that is German."[19] This action was endorsed by the Provincial Office, claiming: "Bielsko [. . .] has always been German, and its German background has been thanks to real Germans, Polish renegades and, to a large extent, Jews who owned factories and property there."[20] Some of the inscriptions were removed by Jewish stonemason Szymon Wulkan. Presumably, the local Jews decided to protect the remaining monuments by turning them over so that their inscriptions faced the ground.[21] On April 26th 1948, the Ministry for Reclaimed Territories issued secret Circular No. 18 concerning "intensified repolonization of Reclaimed Territories," stating: "the action of removing German inscriptions should include: churches, chapels, cemeteries, roadside crosses, etc., and objects of religious worship, unless a given object is of outstanding historical value."[22] The paucity of Ministry for Reclaimed Territories documentation preserved in the Archives of New Records is insufficient to enable a broader investigation of this process in that area concerning Jewish cemeteries. What is known is that in their case the application of these recommendations caused controversy. The local officials in Chojnów were faced with a dilemma and asked the district manager how to proceed in the case of gravestones with epitaphs in both German and Hebrew. Following correspondence with the Provincial Governor, the district manager revoked the order to remove gravestone inscriptions.[23] The Supreme Religious Council of Polish Jews also protested with regard to this issue.[24] On the basis of the preserved gravestones and archival iconographic material, it can be concluded that the "repolonization" action also affected the cemeteries in Czechowice-Dziedzice, Racibórz and Żory, where

---

19 AAN, Ministerstwo Administracji Publicznej, ref. no. 199, vol. I, 22–28.

20 Archiwum Państwowe Katowice (hereinafter: AP Katowice), Urząd Wojewódzki Śląski w Katowicach, ref. no. 185/366, Sprawy świątyń, domów modlitwy, cmentarzy i urządzeń rytualnych, 5.

21 Jacek Proszyk, *Cmentarz żydowski w Bielsku-Białej* (Bielsko-Biała: Urząd Miejski w Bielsku-Białej, 2002), 86.

22 AAN, Ministerstwo Ziem Odzyskanych, Ref. no. 196/496, Repolonizacja Ziem Odzyskanych, 33.

23 Anna Jankowska-Nagórka, *"Deteutonizacja" Dolnego Śląska w latach 1945–1949 jako przykład polityki władz Polski Ludowej wymierzonej przeciwko niemczyźnie"* (PhD diss., Pedagogical University in Kraków, 2017), 72–73.

24 Dariusz Walerjański, "Zatarty ślad – historia cmentarzy żydowskich w Gliwicach," in *Żydzi gliwiccy*, ed. Bożena Kubit, Aleksandra Turek (Gliwice: Muzeum w Gliwicach, 2006), 162.

a significant number of German inscriptions were chiselled away or obliterated with mortar.[25]

The authorities of various localities treated as part of their assets those matzevahs that had been used during the war to pave roads and squares. In 1946, the District Jewish Committee in Rzeszów revealed that gravestones had been used by the town council to shore up the banks of the Wisłok River and that the town's authorities had sold about 3,500 other matzevahs.[26] That same year, the Biecz town council refused to hand over to the Jewish Committee free of charge gravestones that had been used to lay pavements, only allowing them to be taken back on condition that a new pavement was laid, with the Jewish Committee financing the materials and labour. Likewise the Gorlice authorities had no intention of returning matzevahs that the Germans had used to build stairs. In a letter to the provincial authorities the town's mayor claimed that "meeting the demands of the Jewish Committee would amount to the destruction of a major urban investment and would deprive the Market Square and the church of an important communication connection with one of the town's main streets." The case was taken to the central authorities and in 1948 the Ministry of Public Administration decided to prepare the previously mentioned Circular No. 44, ordering municipalities to return gravestones at their own expense.[27] However, in various towns, gravestones remained as a paving material for streets and squares. Such was the case for example in Baligród (in 1960 or 1961 the matzevahs lying on Baligród's market square were immortalized in the film *Ogniomistrz Kaleń*), Poddębice, Rymanów, and Tyczyna. In time, some of them were covered over with asphalt. In Kalisz, one can still see to this day in some streets (including Kazimierzowska Street) Hebrew letters on paving stones made of matzevahs.

In 1946, the Pińczów town council erected six residential barracks for the homeless in the local cemetery.[28] On March 21st 1946, the Poznań city council passed a resolution to requisition several religious cemeteries—including

---

25 Jan Delowicz, *Gmina wyznania mojżeszowego w Żorach 1511–1940* (Żory: Towarzystwo Miłośników Miasta Żory, 2018), 95.

26 AŻIH, Centralny Komitet Żydów w Polsce, ref. no. 303/XVI/176, Wydział Prawny, 1.

27 AAN, Ministerstwo Administracji Publicznej, ref. no. 1098, Wyznaniowe cmentarze żydowskie, 138.

28 Archiwum Państwowe Kielce (hereinafter: AP Kielce), Urząd Wojewódzki Kielecki II, Ref. no. 305/1519, Sprawy żydowskich związków religijnych, synagog i cmentarzy, 29.

a Jewish one with an area of 49,086 m²—for the expansion of the Poznań International Fair.[29]

Probably before 1947, the headquarters of a construction cooperative was established in the oldest cemetery in Siedlce.[30] In 1947, a dispute broke out in Mielec, where during the war the Germans had built a warehouse whose base dimensions were 27×104.5 metres, with one corner of the structure encroaching on the Jewish cemetery. After the war, this barrack was handed over to the County Agricultural and Commercial Cooperative. On July 4th 1947, the Presidium of the Municipal Council in Mielec decided to take over a 36 metre wide section of the cemetery plot adjacent to the warehouse. A protest by Leib S. Feuer of the Jewish Religious Congregation in Mielec was dismissed by the Ministry of Public Administration, which cited the "special economic value" of the warehouse, as it served as a depot for materials to be used in the reconstruction of a village and eventually for a delivery of 3 thousand tons of grain from the Soviet Union.[31] That same year, the Zamość town council began establishing a playground on the plot of its 16th-century Jewish cemetery and demolished its fence.[32]

In Puławy "just after the war" (according to a letter of the Presidium of the County Council), a concrete production plant belonging to the Municipal Communal Cooperative Company was located on the cemetery, using sand dug from the cemetery for its production process.[33]

In 1947 or 1948, the "Farmers Self-Help" Communal Cooperative in Grodzisk Mazowiecki took over the Jewish cemetery as its new user, gradually constructing buildings on the site.[34] Buildings were also erected on other cemeteries, including those in Maków Mazowiecki (a grain warehouse, in 1951), in Janów Lubelski (a base for the Regional Water and Sewerage Works, in

---

29 Janusz Ziółkowski, "Międzynarodowe Targi Poznańskie w przeszłości i obecnie," *Przegląd Zachodni*, no. 5–6 (1955): 206–207.

30 Mordechaj Canin, *Przez ruiny i zgliszcza. Podróż po stu zgładzonych gminach żydowskich w Polsce* (Nisza: Warszawa, 2018), 191.

31 AAN, Ministerstwo Administracji Publicznej, ref. no. 1098, Wyznaniowe cmentarze żydowskie, 155–160.

32 AŻIH, Komitet Żydowski i Wojewódzki Komitet Żydowski w Lublinie, ref. no. 37/355, Wojewódzki Komitet Żydowski w Lublinie, 5.

33 Archiwum Państwowe w Lublinie, Prezydium Powiatowej Rady Narodowej i Urząd Powiatowy w Puławach, ref. no. 746/39, Wydział Gospodarki Komunalnej i Mieszkaniowej, 66.

34 Eleonora Bergman, *Cmentarz żydowski w Grodzisku Mazowieckim. Studium historyczno-konserwatorskie*, (Warszawa: Stołeczna Pracownia Dokumentacji Dóbr Kultury, 1990), 27.

around 1953), in Jasło (a veterinary clinic, in around 1955), in Kazimierz Dolny (a school, in the 1950s), in Kruszwica (a sugar refinery, in around 1955), in Lipno (a veterinary clinic, in 1955), in Lubaczów (a firing range for the weapons section of the T. Kościuszko Secondary School, in the 1950s), in Łódź (a housing estate and a street, between 1949 and 1955), in Nowy Wiśnicz (an asphalt production plant, in 1959), in Opoczno (a bus terminal, in around 1958), in Sandomierz (a boarding school, between 1956 and 1960), in Szydłowiec (a Cooperative Department Store, and a furniture store, in 1959), and in Włocławek (a school, in around 1955).

In 1949, the Jewish Committee of Lublin Compatriots in Poland reported that the city authorities planned converting the 16th-century cemetery in Lublin into a park.[35] A year later, Kraków's city authorities intended to convert the 16th-century Remuh Cemetery into a green and gather up its gravestones to be placed around the grave of Rabbi Moshe Isserless Remuh.[36] Members of the Central Committee of the Polish United Workers' Party had a similar idea, calling for a park to be established on the site of the Jewish cemetery in Warsaw's Bródno district. The area was afforested and thousands of gravestones were moved to one side.

In 1953, the Office for Religious Affairs approved a request from the Presidium of the Grodzisk Mazowiecki town council, agreeing to the fence around the local Jewish cemetery being demolished and the material used for construction purposes by the Communications Equipment Factory.[37] That same year, the Presidium of the County Council in Wyrzysk applied for "the allocation of cemetery fences for road construction purposes."[38] Similarly, in Tarnów, part of the cemetery wall made of concrete slabs was dismantled and used for fencing around the nearby depot of the Kraków Engineering Works.[39]

At the same time, the property of former Jewish communities was being expropriated. As early as 1948, the Siedlce town council applied to expropriate,

---

35 AŻIH, Urząd do Spraw Wyznań, ref. no. 5b/31, Związek Religijny Wyznania Mojżeszowego w Polsce. Cmentarze żydowskie, 11.

36 AAN, Urząd do Spraw Wyznań, sygn. 5b/31, Związek Religijny Wyznania Mojżeszowego w Polsce. Cmentarze żydowskie, k. 11.

37 AAN, Urząd do Spraw Wyznań, sygn. 14/469, Rozbiórka ogrodzenia cmentarza Grodzisk, 1.

38 AAN, Urząd do Spraw Wyznań, sygn. 14/462, Nakło – przekazanie ogrodzenia cmentarnego, 2.

39 AAN, Urząd do Spraw Wyznań, sygn. 132/318, Obiekty judaizmu woj. tarnowskiego, 187.

among other things, an old people's home, an orphans' home, and a cemetery.[40] This process intensified in the 1950s, when a ten-year positive prescription clause began to be applied.

In the 1950s, the cemetery on Sosnowa Street in Białystok was covered with earth from excavations at nearby construction sites and the town's Central Park was then established on it. These earthworks were initially of an ad hoc nature, and later approved by the town's architect Michał Bałasz. In the 2015 documentary film *Central Park* directed by Tomasz Wiśniewski, Michał Bałasz explained the motives behind his decision:

> As a child, I was brought up to believe that a cemetery is some sort of sacred place and may not be desecrated. [. . .] But there was nothing here, no fences, no tidiness or order, only garbage cans, drunks sitting on matzevahs and swigging alcohol [. . .]. Not only that, but stonemasons began to actively steal the matzevahs from the place [. . .]. What was to be done? Put things in order and not desecrate. That was about all we could do. It certainly protected the place. I couldn't do anything more. Because I could have just left it like that, and it would have been devastated, destroyed, the stone would have been torn up. And this way [. . .] they can always be unearthed after a few years.[41]

In the years 1949-1954, the Łódź city authorities took charge of the oldest Jewish cemetery on Wesoła Street, established in 1811. Zachodnia Street was constructed to pass through its grounds, while the Construction Directorate of Workers' Housing Estates erected apartment blocks on the remaining part.[42] Plans were made to convert the second cemetery in Łódź, located on Bracka Street, into a park, but ultimately the destructive intervention of the town planners was limited to taking over part of the cemetery in order to extend Zagajnikowa Street.[43]

In 1954, a plan was made to pass an arterial road through the cemetery complex in Warsaw. This new street, including tram tracks, was to be an extension

---

40 AŻIH, Centralny Komitet Żydów w Polsce, ref. no. 303/XVI/178, Wydział Prawny, 21.

41 "Park Centralny," Tomasz Wiśniewski, accessed June 30, 2020, https://www.youtube.com/watch?v=NCC6n1N-8DU.

42 AAN, Urząd do Spraw Wyznań, ref. no. 22/417, Zamknięcie cmentarza w Łodzi, 11.01.1955, 9.

43 Ewa Wiatr, "Historia cmentarza," in *Monumenta et Memoria. Cmentarz żydowski w Łodzi*, ed. Leszek Hońdo (Łódź: Wydawnictwo Hamal Andrzej Machejek, 2016), 29–31.

of Gęsia Street,[44] passing through the Jewish and Evangelical-Augsburg cemeteries. In the case of the Jewish cemetery, the "cutting off of the area" (as it was
referred to in a Warsaw Architecture and Construction Board document) was
to apply to a strip 40 metres wide.[45] Ultimately, these plans were never implemented.

The destruction of cemeteries intensified in the 1960s. The process was
connected with an action aimed at bringing some order to cemeteries, and with
the adoption of the Act on Cemeteries in 1959, and the issuing on August 3rd
1964 of a circular concerning abandoned cemeteries. Perhaps also significant
was a tightening of the government's stance towards churches and religious associations, as well as the gradual rise to power of politicians from the so-called
Moczar team.[46]

At the end of the 1950s, officials at the Ministry of Municipal Economics
attempted to solve the issue of "abandoned cemeteries of foreigners," which
generated maintenance costs, disfigured the landscape, and kept police forces
busy in connection with theft and other criminal acts. In the years 1954-1956
the Ministry of Municipal Economics maintained a register of cemeteries. It
was found that, apart from active communal and religious cemeteries, there
were 5,941 abandoned cemeteries in the country covering a total area of approximately 3,520 hectares, including 584 abandoned cemeteries covering an
area of 392 hectares owned by religious associations (in the case of Jewish organizations, this involved only their use of the cemeteries) and 326 abandoned
cemeteries covering an area of about 166 hectares and marked for liquidation. The remaining 5,031 cemeteries covering a total area of approximately
3,000 hectares required further care and maintenance pursuant to statutory
provisions. In January 1958, the Ministry declared that

> the lack of proper care of cemeteries by the presidiums of the National
> Councils and the chronic lack of financial resources for their preserva-
> tion made these cemeteries, left to their own fate for 12 years, the sub-
> ject of various complaints due to their destruction and their dreadful

---

44 After 1955, Anielewicza Street.

45 AAN, Urząd do Spraw Wyznań, ref. no. 24/549, Sprawa trasy ul. Komunikacyjnej przez
    cmentarz żydowski, 4.

46 Mieczysław Moczar, real name Mikołaj Demko (1913 – 1986)—Polish politician, minister
    of internal affairs, leader of the so-called partisans fraction that played a key role in the antise-
    mitic campaign of 1967–1968.

condition only worsens with each passing year. Involvement of surveillance services in guarding cemeteries has often resulted in these employees being beaten up by various types of hooligans. Assistance from the
Civil Militia has been insufficient, and all offenses and crimes concerning desecration of corpses and the places of rest of the deceased have
rarely been the subject of court hearings, but have often caused indignation and bitterness among local citizens.

In order to prevent further destruction, the Ministry of Municipal Economics issued guidelines on dealing with abandoned cemeteries, and asked the Ministry
of Internal Affairs to increase supervision of cemeteries (as a result, about 200
perpetrators of destruction and theft were detained) and applied to the Ministry
of Finance for 60 million zlotys to cover the costs of bringing some order to the
same. These works were to be carried out "to a minimum extent" and included the repair of fences, removal of "gravestone rubble," protection of smashed
graves, collecting up scattered human remains, and basic care of cemetery
foliage.[47]

In 1958, in view of numerous protests by foreigners, mainly citizens of the
German Federal Republic, the authorities began a program of tidying up cemeteries which, due to the enormity of the task and increasing destruction, did not
bring forth dramatic results. On January 13th 1960, Zbigniew Januszko, deputy
chairman of the Planning Committee of the Council of Ministers, called on the
Ministry of Municipal Economics to deal with abandoned cemeteries, demanding that their liquidation be accelerated and that cleanup works be limited to
only those most necessary. In response, the Ministry of Municipal Economics
stated that "the cleaning up of inactive cemeteries would pertain to the entire
country and was aimed at closing those cemeteries (i.e. halting further burying
of the dead) and liquidating those cemeteries where the statutory 40-year period
of grave preservation since the last funeral had expired." The plans of the Ministry of Municipal Economics listed 5,941 cemeteries to be closed. That number
included 387 Jewish cemeteries, 48 of which were selected for liquidation.[48] It is
worth adding that at that time—thanks to a census carried out by the Office for

---

47   AAN, Ministerstwo Gospodarki Komunalnej, ref. no. 9/18, Cmentarnictwo – porządkowanie
     zdewastowanych, nieczynnych cmentarzy, 1–9.
48   AAN, Ministerstwo Gospodarki Komunalnej, ref. no. 9/20 Cmentarnictwo – porządkowanie
     zdewastowanych, nieczynnych cmentarzy, 8–20.

Religious Affairs in 1952—the central authorities knew about the existence of only 524 Jewish cemeteries.[49]

Resolutions on the closure of cemeteries were adopted by the presidium of the national council of the town, housing estate or community in which a given cemetery was located. Following agreement with the presidium of the Provincial Council, such resolutions were finally approved by the Ministry of Municipal Economics. These decisions concerned both individual cemeteries and whole groups. A "record-breaking" decision was made by the ministry on February 17th 1961, under which as many as 747 cemeteries of various denominations in the Szczecin Province (including 14 Jewish ones) were closed.[50] Often the resolutions concerned both the closure of a cemetery and also its use for other purposes. A search through the documentation of the Ministry of Municipal Economics, the Ministry of Local Economics and Environmental Protection, the Ministry of Administration, Local Economy and Environmental Protection, and the Office for Religious Affairs, as well as publications concerning regional historiography, revealed a decision to close 462 Jewish cemeteries.

Clearly the closure procedure was not carried out in the case of some cemeteries. This may have involved sites that were of no interest to the authorities in their urban planning or reorganization plans, or because such sites did not register as cemeteries in the minds of local officials due to all their gravestones and other above-ground traces having been previously removed.

On August 3rd 1964, the Ministry of Municipal Economics issued the previously mentioned Circular No. 11, which suspended central budget financing of cleanup operations in closed cemeteries. The local presidiums of national councils faced a choice: to finance the cleaning up of cemeteries from their own funds or else liquidate them. The decisions were easy to predict.

In the opinion of historian Piotr Pęziński, the tightening of the government's cemetery policy was related to the gradual inclusion of the "Moczar" faction in the apparatus of power.[51] It should be noted that as a result of numerous protests by Jewish communities in 1965, a circular was prepared at the Ministry of Municipal Economics aimed at limiting the liquidation of Jewish cemeteries,

49   Urban, *Cmentarze żydowskie, synagogi i domy modlitwy w Polsce w latach 1944–1966*, 325.

50   AAN, Ministerstwo Gospodarki Komunalnej, ref. no. 9/53, Decyzje o zamknięciu cmentarzy i przeznaczeniu ich na inny cel w województwie szczecińskim, 28.

51   Piotr Pęziński, *Na rozdrożu. Młodzież żydowska w PRL 1956–1968* (Warszawa: Żydowski Instytut Historyczny im Emanuela Ringelbluma, 2014), 224–227.

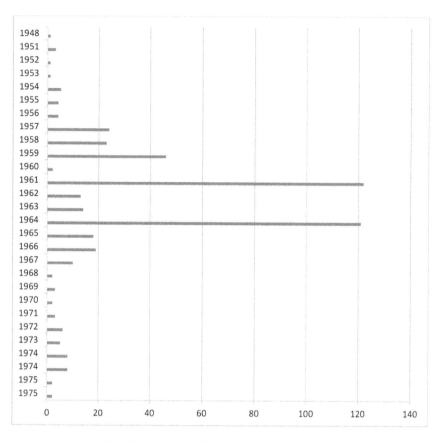

Resolutions on the Closure of Cemeteries By Year

In 1948, 1 Jewish cemetery was closed; in 1951—3; in 1952—1; in 1953—1; in 1954—5; in 1955—4; in 1956—4; in 1957—24; in 1958—23; in 1959—46; in 1960—2; in 1961—122; in 1962—13; in 1963—14; in 1964—121; in 1965—18; in 1966—19; in 1967—10; in 1968—2; in 1969—3; in 1970—2; in 1971—3; in 1972—6; in 1973—5; in 1974—8; and in 1975—2.

but the document was never announced or put into force. The attitude towards Jewish cemeteries of the Social and Administrative Department of the Ministry of Internal Affairs and the Administrative Department of the Polish United Workers' Party's Central Committee can best be seen in a secret note dated January 25th 1966, which is strongly critical of the Socio-Cultural Society of Jews in Poland:

> There are Jewish cemeteries in the country where no dead have been buried for several decades. These cemeteries are by nature historic

monuments and, in accordance with applicable regulations, should be liquidated within a specified period of time. The argument for organizing tidying up operations for such cemeteries and accepting further foreign funds, apart from those from the American Jewish Joint Distribution Committee[52] for their upkeep is unfounded.[53]

In the official position quoted above, one can see the insensitivity of officials to religious feelings and their ignorance of the rules resulting from Halacha. At that time, the head of the Administrative Department of the Polish United Workers' Party's Central Committee, overseeing religious matters, was General Kazimierz Witaszewski, known for his antisemitic views. The soon-to-be-launched antisemitic campaign to force the emigration of around 13,000 Jews, intimidate those who remained in the country and, consequently, restrict the activities of the Socio-Cultural Society of Jews in Poland and the Religious Association of the Judaic Faith in the Republic of Poland, created an even more convenient atmosphere for the destruction of Jewish cemeteries.

Pursuant to the Act of 1959, the use of a closed cemetery for another purpose could not take place until 40 years after the last person had been buried there. When establishing the date of the last funeral, they relied on death certificates, oral records of residents and dates engraved on gravestones, although it was certainly difficult for officials to check the latter—for example, employees of the Presidium of the National Council in Złotoryja admitted that they could not read dates written in the Hebrew alphabet.[54] For many cemeteries that were used at least until Operation Reinhardt in the years 1942–1943, and then often used to bury shot prisoners from the so-called residual ghettos or people caught hiding, the regulation meant having to wait until the mid 1980s before they could be liquidated. In this situation, the possibility of an earlier liquidation of a cemetery was frequently taken advantage of by citing "exceptional needs for reasons of public interest, defence of the State or for the implementation of national economic plans." The reasons given for the premature liquidation of

---

52 American Jewish Joint Distribution Committee (Joint) – Jewish charity organization, created in 1914.

53 AIPN, Ministerstwo Spraw Wewnętrznych w Warszawie, ref. no. IPN BU 1585/3607, Ludność żydowska w Polsce – sytuacja, 9.

54 AAN, Ministerstwo Gospodarki Terenowej i Ochrony Środowiska, ref. no. 1/30, Decyzje o zamknięciu cmentarzy i przeznaczeniu ich na inny cel w województwie wrocławskim, 2.

cemeteries were, among other things, due to the expansion of housing estates and workplaces, the need to clean up urban spaces and the establishment of green areas. Often, however, the reasons cited were bizarre, such as: the creation of a recreational and leisure route (Wągrowiec, in 1968),[55] the discovery of significant gravel resources in the cemetery (Międzyrzecz, in 1969),[56] and improvement of the "aesthetic condition of the town and for the good of cemetery matters" (Kłodzko, in 1971).[57] In 1966, the cemetery in Sulechów apparently had a negative impact on "the well-being of local residents," and the close vicinity of a football pitch, combined with the plans to build an international highway, meant that "the presence of the above cemetery in this area is absolutely inadvisable."[58] The only arguments cited for requisitioning the cemetery in Trzebnica for agricultural purposes were the very poor condition of the facility and the intention to include it in a "system of high and medium high vegetation to protect the town from westerly winds."[59]

In 1962, the Presidium of Warsaw's Wola District Council intended to close down a section of the cemetery on Okopowa Street, which "due to the sanitary regulations in force" was to apparently create "great difficulties" in the construction of new housing estates and a school. Citing a "shortage of public greenery," the Presidium applied for 24 hectares of the cemetery that covered a total area of 33 hectares to be converted to green areas. In the application dated March 24th 1962 it was stated: "The area currently being used [. . .] is circa 9.0 hectares, which fully meets the needs of the Jewish population, as this area constitutes 10% of the free burial space, as well as old graves that can be re-used. Apart from that, the Jewish population can use the communal cemetery."[60]

---

55 AAN, Ministerstwo Gospodarki Komunalnej, ref. no. 9/46, Decyzje o zamknięciu cmentarzy i przeznaczeniu ich na inny cel w województwie poznańskim, 18.

56 AAN, Ministerstwo Gospodarki Komunalnej, ref. no. 9/64, Decyzje o zamknięciu cmentarzy i przeznaczeniu ich na inny cel w województwie zielonogórskim, 78.

57 Ignacy Einhorn, Tomasz Jamróg, and Tamara Włodarczyk, *Dzieje społeczności żydowskiej w Kłodzku w XIX–XX w.* (Warszawa: Fundacja Ochrony Dziedzictwa Żydowskiego, 2006), 81.

58 AAN, Ministerstwo Gospodarki Komunalnej, ref. no. 9/64, Decyzje o zamknięciu cmentarzy i przeznaczeniu ich na inny cel w województwie zielonogórskim, 60.

59 AAN, Ministerstwo Gospodarki Terenowej i Ochrony Środowiska, ref. no. 1/31, Decyzje o zamknięciu cmentarzy i przeznaczeniu ich na inny cel w województwie wrocławskim, 231.

60 AAN, Ministerstwo Gospodarki Komunalnej, ref. no. 9/23, Cmentarnictwo – korespondencja dotycząca zamknięcia cmentarzy żydowskich i ewangelickich, 62–71.

In 1964, the cemetery in Kielce constituted "a serious obstacle in the district's urban planning."[61] The Presidium of the Municipal Council in Iwaniska motioned for the liquidation of the cemetery, which "in its current state is exposed to desecration, as it serves as pasture land for cattle and sheep, and besides that, is also a spreader of various types of weeds and pests." The same argument was used in Raków.[62] Two years later, the National Council in Krośniewice demanded the closure of the local Jewish cemetery because its location, among fields belonging to state-owned farms, on an "oval shaped" plot of land, made it difficult for tractor drivers to plough.[63]

Stanisław Podraszko, head of the Municipal and Housing Economics Department of the Presidium of the Provincial Council in Gdańsk, proved to be most inventive, writing in the resolution calling for the closure of 14 cemeteries (including a Jewish one): "Liquidation of abandoned cemeteries will have a positive effect with an improvement of public safety in the city (will contribute to facilitating the work of the Civil Militia)."[64]

In 1974, the Council Office in Wiżajny brought about the premature closure of the local cemetery and the establishment of a sports ground on it, arguing that such an investment was initiated by the Germans during the war, that 400 children attend the primary school, that a People's Sports Team is active in the village, and that the opening of a recreation and leisure facility will be a way of celebrating the 30th anniversary of the People's Republic of Poland.[65]

By decisions of local authorities, numerous cemeteries were fully or partially obliterated by the construction of new buildings.

---

61   AP Kielce, Provincial Office in Kielce, Ref. no. 1080/1067, Kielce – cmentarz żydowski na Pakoszu, 103.

62   AAN, Ministerstwo Gospodarki Komunalnej, ref. no. 9/29, Decyzje o zamknięciu cmentarzy i przeznaczeniu ich na inny cel w województwie gdańskim, 66–69.

63   AAN, Ministerstwo Gospodarki Komunalnej, ref. no. 9/38, Decyzje o zamknięciu cmentarzy i przeznaczeniu ich na inny cel w województwie łódzkim, 139.

64   AAN, Ministerstwo Gospodarki Komunalnej, ref. no. 9/29, Decyzje o zamknięciu cmentarzy i przeznaczeniu ich na inny cel w województwie gdańskim, 66–69.

65   AAN, Urząd do Spraw Wyznań, ref. no. 131/516, Cmentarze żydowskie w Polsce – otwieranie, likwidacja, remonty, 242–254.

Table 2. Selected Buildings Constructed
on Jewish Cemeteries in Poland

Town or village	Object	Year of construction
Annopol	clinic, kindergarten	the 1970s
Babimost	apartment blocks	the 1960s
Barczewo	wooden pigsties	after 1976
Bełżyce	the old cemetery, a community centre, the new cemetery, a depot for the local "Farmers Self-Help" cooperative	no date available
Będzin	bus terminus	the 1960s
Biała Podlaska	cinema	1972
Białobrzegi	apartment blocks	no date available
Białystok	market hall, Social Insurance Office	1964, 1986
Bielsko-Biała	sports equipment production plant	around 1967
Błaszki	factory	1967
Bogoria	pharmacy	around 1963
Brzostek	Agricultural Circle Cooperative	no date available
Bytom	apartment block	the 1960s
Chmielnik	kindergarten	no date available
Czarne	apartment block	no date available
Czerwińsk	apartment blocks	no date available
Drobin	warehouses	the 1950s
Głogów	Cooperative	around 1968
Gryfino	school	1974
Jasło	veterinary clinic	around 1955
Kalisz	apartment blocks, school, education centre, ambulance station	around 1960

Town or village	Object	Year of construction
Kałuszyn	town council office	no date available
Kamień Krajeński	local cooperative	no date available
Kamieńsk	shooting range and barracks for the Warsaw Road Works	after 1978
Kętrzyn	bus terminus	1970
Koło	community centre	probably the 1970s
Kościerzyna	factory	the 1970s
Lelów	shop	no date available
Leszno	housing estate	the 1970s
Lipno	veterinary clinic	the 1950s
Lubycza Królewska	housing estate	the 1980s
Lubin	square and playground	the 1970s
Lublin	warehouses	the 1960s
Lubliniec	driving school	the 1970s
Łask	school	around 1962
Łaszczów	veterinary clinic	no date available
Maków Mazowiecki	bus station	no date available
Mielec	post office	1960-1962
Międzyrzec Podlaski	District Sanitary Transport vehicles depot, furniture warehouse	no date available
Mińsk Mazowiecki	school	1964
Mogilno	housing estate	no date available
Mrągowo	laundry	the 1980s
Mysłowice	housing estate	no date available
Nowa Słupia	fire station, municipal agricultural services building	before 1964

Town or village	Object	Year of construction
Nowy Korczyn	warehouses of the "Farmers Self-Help" Municipal Cooperative, furniture shop, cinder block production plant	no date available
Opatów	community centre, garages, auditorium, outdoor concert stage	1962
Opole	horticultural sales point, car repair workshop	around 1960
Ostrołęka	school, orphanage, housing estate	the 1970s
Ostrów Wielkopolski	school, transformer station	the turn of the 1960s and 1970s
Pacanów	fire station, community centre	1965
Pińczów	school, abattoir	no date available
Pleszew	housing estate, kindergarten	no date available
Płock	school	the 1960s
Płońsk	car parts shop, vehicle service station	1966, 1976
Poznań	the Poznań International Trade Fair	no date available
Prabuty	garages	no date available
Przeworsk	bus station	1969
Puławy	Factory, Municipal Economics Enterprise	the 1960s
Pułtusk	factory	1963
Radzyń Chełmiński	store	the 1960s
Recz	residential buildings	no date available
Ryn	latrines for workers	no date available
Sanok	restaurant	1967
Secemin	agricultural cooperative	the 1950s
Sejny	housing estate	no date available

Town or village	Object	Year of construction
Siedlce	office block	no date available
Siemiatycze	car service pavilion	no date available
Słońsk	sawmill	the 1950s
Słubice	tourist inn, in the 1990s used by the tenant for an escort agency business	1978
Sokoły	clinic	no date available
Sokołów Małopolski	the old cemetery: warehouses for the Municipal Cooperative, the new cemetery: a petrol station	the 1960s
Stopnica	the old cemetery: an agricultural fertilizer warehouse –the new cemetery: 15kV transformer substation	the 1960s–1970s
Stryków	builder's yard	no date available
Szczekociny	the cemetery on Konopnicka Street: public toilets, the cemetery on Lelowska Street: an abattoir and cattle purchasing depot, a feed warehouse	the 1960s–1970s
Środa Śląska	kindergarten	no date available
Tarnobrzeg	department store	no date available
Tarnogród	state farm depot	the 1970s
Tczew	ambulance service station	no date available
Tuchola	transport cooperative	no date available
Wałcz	culture centre	1960-1962
Wąbrzeźno	Services and Production Cooperative	no date available
Wolbrom	school	no date available
Wrocław	school playing field, apartment blocks, garages, electrical switchboard station	1968 and later

Town or village	Object	Year of construction
Września	housing estate	the 1970s
Wysokie Mazowieckie	public toilets	no date available
Wyszogród	fruit processing plant	around 1960
Zamość	District Telecommunications Office, District Community Centre	the 1950s-1970s
Ząbkowice Śląskie	housing estate marking the 20th anniversary of the Polish People's Republic	around 1966

In at least two cases, buildings were erected without permission being obtained to use the cemetery for other purposes. In 1953, the Presidium of the Municipal Council in Lipno allocated a cemetery plot for the construction of a veterinary clinic. The application to close the cemetery set the proceedings in motion two years later.[66] Similarly in Puławy, the delay in settling the legal status of the cemetery amounted to about eight years.[67]

Relatively often, cemeteries were converted into city parks, squares and playgrounds. In the case of parks, such conversions were paradoxically facilitated by the lack of care for cemetery foliage—the failure to clear self-seeding vegetation meant that cemeteries turned into copses. Some of the cemeteries had old stands of trees dating from before the war. In 1971, the town authorities of Tczew, seeking to liquidate five cemeteries of various denominations, including the Jewish cemetery, emphasized that some of them "feature a high degree of tree cover" and, as such, are suitable for "recreation and sports" purposes.[68] Such situations arose in, among other places, Biała Podlaska, Bełchatów, Bydgoszcz (Fordon), Chojnice, Chorzów, Dynów (where public toilets were also built), Giżycko, Głogów Małopolski, Goleniów, Kołobrzeg, Konin, Lębork,

---

66 Urban, *Cmentarze żydowskie, synagogi i domy modlitwy w Polsce w latach 1944–1966*, 484–486.

67 AP Lublin, Prezydium Powiatowej Rady Narodowej i Urząd Powiatowy w Puławach, ref. no. 746/39, Wydział Gospodarki Komunalnej i Mieszkaniowej, 35.

68 AAN, Ministerstwo Gospodarki Terenowej i Ochrony Środowiska, ref. no. 1/24, Decyzje o zamknięciu cmentarzy i przeznaczeniu ich na inny cel w województwie gdańskim, 16.

Lipsk, Lubartów, Nowa Sól, Opatów, Ostrowiec Świętokrzyski, Parczew, Police, Przysucha, Radzymin, Rzeszów, Włodawa, Strzelce Opolskie, Szczecin, Świnoujście, Toruń, Ząbkowice Śląskie, Zwoleń (the planting of vegetation in the Zwoleń cemetery was in preparation for the TV program "Tournament of cities").

In the 1960s, the Culture Department of the Presidium of Lublin's Provincial Council prepared a project to establish an open-air museum of rural architecture on the grounds of the cemetery on Sienna Street. At one end of the cemetery, outbuildings were erected, the wall was knocked down and part of the area was levelled to accommodate a parking lot. Eventually, the open-air museum was established elsewhere. In the 1970s, the cemetery was used as a nursery for rare plants.[69] In Lesko, plans were made to establish a garden of flora native to the Bieszczady Mountains in the Jewish cemetery.[70] An arboretum belonging to the Institute of Dendrology of the Polish Academy of Sciences was established at the cemetery in Kórnik. The Presidium of the Sandomierz National Council allocated plots in the cemetery on Tatarska Street, inactive since around 1829, as allotments for trade union members. The same happened to the cemeteries in Inowrocław, Przemyśl, and Sosnowiec.

Afforestation of cemeteries was common. It can be assumed that the intention of the officials making such decisions was to "clean up" the area and at the same time to ensure the possibility of obtaining timber in the future. This often meant ploughing cemeteries up and removing gravestones, which were an obstacle to forest management. Just how the work involving afforestation of cemeteries proceeded can be learnt from the account of Marian Górski from the village of Dzierżbotki:

> Back in 1972, I planted trees where a Jewish cemetery once was. I remember it exactly, because I planted them myself, as I was working for the Forest District at that time. There was only sand there. They'd ploughed it all up with horse drawn ploughs, but they didn't plant anything at the very summit. There was nothing but quicksand there. What you see growing now is self-seeding. Under my leadership, some 60 men planted that forest. Because money was short and they came to earn.

69   Trzciński, Świadkiem jest ta stela, 65–66.

70   Andrzej Trzciński and Marcin Wodziński, Cmentarz żydowski w Lesku. Część 1. Wiek XVI i XVII (Kraków: Księgarnia Akademicka, 2002), 8.

They were the ones who dug up those graves, because they thought they would find gold. Dogs later scattered the bones.[71]

Creating green areas on cemeteries was a solution officially recommended by the Ministry of Municipal Economics in Circular No. 2 dated December 4th 1971. However, the previously presented cases of cemeteries being built upon in the seventies and eighties show that these recommendations were repeatedly ignored.[72]

School sports fields were created on the cemeteries in Drobin, Kalisz, Kazimierz Dolny, Klimontów and Wrocław, and in Sokołów Podlaski a sports and recreation centre with a swimming pool was created. The construction of an outdoor swimming pool on the grounds of the cemetery in Koło was planned. Cemeteries were also used for entertainment purposes. In Łosice, the cemetery was converted into a park commemorating the 20th Anniversary of the Polish People's Republic, which included a stage and a playground. In Serock, the cemetery became part of a recreational centre built in the early 1970s—at the beginning of the 21st century, there were swings and picnic shelters still in place. A travelling circus periodically pitched its tents on the cemetery in Sochaczew. Circus shows were also held in the cemetery in Kcynia and a travelling "funfair" likewise used the site. In 1962, the cemetery was the site chosen to celebrate the town's 700th anniversary; a stage was set up, on which bands performed music.[73] Firing ranges were installed in cemeteries in Błędów, Grójec, Chociwel, and Kamieńsk, and driving schools were established on the cemeteries in Człuchów and Lubliniec. Local produce markets were organized on the grounds of the cemeteries in such towns as Białystok, Chmielnik, Dobra, Nowe Miasto nad Pilicą, Ostrów Mazowiecka, Parczew, Suwałki, and Tykocin. Ewa Wroczyńska, former director of a Jewish museum in Tykocin, recounted how the cemetery was used as a marketplace: "This wretched market was relocated from in front of the Party Headquarters to the Jewish cemetery. Stalls were positioned between the graves. The graves were levelled. There, in the oldest part, dating from

---

71 Paweł Janicki, "Eksterminacja Żydów w powiecie tureckim w latach 1941–42," *Kwartalnik Historii Żydów*, no. 1/241 (2011): 86.

72 AP Otwock, Urząd Miasta i Gminy Karczew, ref. no. 78/193/50, Likwidacja cmentarza żydowskiego w Karczewie, ul. Otwocka, 1–5.

73 Correspondence with Justyna Makarewicz of Town Council Offices in Kcynia on October 5, 2020. The letter in Krzysztof Bielawski's possession.

Figure 5.2. Baruch Safier, the last Jewish resident of Leżajsk at a destroyed local cemetery, 1961. Author unknown, collection of the Archives of New Records in Warsaw.

the 16th century, trading was conducted in pigs, cows and every other type of goods. It was awful to behold. Such desecration!"[74]

In the 1960s, the Vladimir Lenin Avenue was routed through the central part of the Jewish cemetery in Lublin. In the next decade, part of the Jewish cemetery in Siewierz became a strip of the Warsaw-Katowice expressway. A similar fate befell the cemetery in Chojnice (around 1975, Kilińskiego Street was constructed along one edge of its grounds), in Ustroń (in the 1970s the Katowice-Wisła highway was built on it) and in Wiślica, where in 1984 the cemetery was cut in two by the town's new ring road.

Damage to cemeteries was also caused by the erection of electricity pylons and telephone poles, as well as the siting of communal heating pipelines and sewers, with other underground installations also being routed through them. This happened in, among other places, Boćki, Brzostek, Kcynia, Klimontów, Krasnystaw, Kraśnik, Kuźnica, Mielec, Mława, Orla, Sandomierz, Sanok, Skoczów, Sokółka, Stoczek, Tyczyn, Tykocin, Wiślica, and Zabłudów.

Facilities that had been installed in cemeteries by the Germans during the war also continued to be used, for example sports fields and stadiums in

---

74   POLIN, Oral History Collection, ref. no. 1032, Ewa Wroczyńska's testimony.

Gniewkowo, Kleczew, and Lublin (Wieniawa), a horticultural works in Ostrów Wielkopolski, and a warehouse in Mielec.

Cemetery buildings were also put to other uses. People occupied and inhabited some pre-funeral buildings (for example in Augustów, Brzostek, Ciechocinek, Łomża, Międzyrzec Podlaski, Oława, Pruszków, Sandomierz, Szczuczyn, Tuchów, Warsaw's Izbicka Street, Żabno, and Żyrardów), while others were requisitioned as service facilities. A carpentry workshop was established in Chojnice, a warehouse in Cieszyn, workshops in Gorzów Wielkopolski (in the 1980s), a presbytery of the Evangelical community in Gubin, a pattern workshop of the 22 Lipca Labour Cooperative in Kielce (around 1956), a garage of the Water and Land Drainage Works in Nakło (in 1955, a bulldozer was kept there, then later the building was adapted for residential purposes),[75] a state archive in Olsztyn, a chapel of the Pentecostal Church in Prudnik (in 1985), a warehouse for the Conservation of Monuments Studio in Słupsk (since the 1980s), a chapel of the Evangelical-Augsburg church in Szczecinek, a dissection lab (then later a warehouse) in Tarnowskie Góry,[76] a raw materials recycling depot in Wrocław, a cowshed (and since 1965 a car repair workshop) in Zielona Góra, and a refrigeration warehouse for confectioners in Żory. The Municipal Council in Rzeszów rented the pre-funeral building on Rejtana Street to be used as a cow shed, and terminated the lease in 1961 following the intervention of Maciej Jakubowicz of the Kraków Jewish Congregation, explaining that "the buildings were completely destroyed and they had not been aware of their original purpose."[77] The cemetery administration building on Kraków's Abrahama Street was requisitioned as council housing. The new users often took little care of the properties thus occupied, permitting themselves to make various adaptations (in Łomża for example, a neo-Moorish style avant-corps was removed) and eventually leaving the buildings in ruins.

Several Jewish cemeteries—including those in Chojnów, Golczewo, Inowrocław, Kętrzyn, Lubaczów, Skarżysko-Kamienna, and Słupsk—were converted into municipal cemeteries. In Koronowo in 1955, the idea of changing the nature of the cemetery was abandoned, fearing "the prejudices of worshippers, who

---

75   AAN, Urząd do Spraw Wyznań, ref. no. 22/434, Sprawa przebudowy kostnicy, 1–9.

76   Ryszard Bednarczyk, *Gliwicka 66. Inwentaryzacja kirkutu w Tarnowskich Górach* (Tarnowskie Góry: Tarnogórska Fundacja Kultury i Sztuki, 2018), 14–15.

77   Urban, *Cmentarze żydowskie, synagogi i domy modlitwy w Polsce w latach 1944–1966*, 537–538.

would not wish to bury their relatives there, which in turn might contribute to having to give up the idea of municipal cemeteries altogether."[78] The cemetery in Miłakowo was taken over by the Catholic parish. The cemeteries in Kluczbork, Pieniężno, and Wodzisław Śląski were designated as war cemeteries for soldiers of the Red Army. Deceased Evangelists were buried in the unoccupied section of the Jewish cemetery in Tarnowskie Góry.[79] The cemetery in Nowe Warpno was used as a burial place by Poles who settled in this former German town after 1945. In 1976, the town council in Piotrków Trybunalski also intended to requisition the Jewish cemetery as a municipal cemetery, an idea that met with protests by members of New York's Piotrkow and Vicinity Society.[80]

According to official statistics of the Ministry of Municipal Economics, in the years 1961–1965 "urban planning" affected 67 cemeteries, including 23 that were Roman Catholic, 20 that were Evangelical, 17 that were Jewish, and 7 of other denominations, these being mainly requisitioned for housing, municipal and industrial construction. Although the figures quoted may seem understated with regard to Jewish cemeteries (especially in light of the fact that right up to the end of the existence of the Polish People's Republic, the authorities never managed to compile a complete list of Jewish cemeteries in Poland), the above list shows that the cemeteries of other faiths were also closed and destroyed.[81]

State administrative authorities and enterprises used cemeteries as a source of building materials, selling gravestones, bricks and other materials, or using them for their own needs. The rules governing such sales were regulated by periodically updated circulars issued by the Ministry of Municipal Economics containing a price list specifying rates depending on the type of stone, its thickness, and the presence or absence of inscriptions.[82]

In 1961, during expansion of its aerodrome in Nowy Targ, the Tatra Aero Club removed the gravestones that had been used in 1945 to pave the runway, and then sold them to Józef W., a Kraków based stonemason. The Congregation

---

78   AAN, Urząd do Spraw Wyznań, ref. no. 24/686, Przekazanie cmentarza w Koronowie, 4.

79   Bednarczyk, *Gliwicka 66. Inwentaryzacja kirkutu w Tarnowskich Górach*, 14–15.

80   AAN, Urząd do Spraw Wyznań, ref. no. 132/305, Obiekty judaizmu województwa piotrkowskiego, 34–35.

81   AIPN, Ministerstwo Spraw Wewnętrznych w Warszawie, ref. no. IPN BU 1585/7150, Mniejszość żydowska – cmentarze wyznania mojżeszowego w Polsce, 83.

82   Katarzyna Sanocka-Tureczek, "Cmentarze na obszarze obecnego województwa lubuskiego w latach 1945–1975," *Ziemia Międzyrzecka* IV, (2008): 118–119.

of the Judaic Faith in Kraków became interested in the case and for at least the next twelve months corresponded with the Presidium of the Provincial Council in Kraków, the Provincial Prosecutor's Office, and the Office for Religious Affairs. Stefan Pachołek, head of the Department for Religious Affairs at the Presidium of the Provincial Council in Kraków, claimed that from a legal point of view a monument placed over a grave is movable property and thus does not belong to any grave or cemetery, so the transaction between the aero club and the stonemason's workshop was legal. Stefan Pachołek argued: "If, under these conditions, gravestones extracted from a drainage ditch, their inscriptions in any case filled with dirt, cannot be replaced over the proper graves [. . .], there should be no objection to treating these slabs (monuments) as stonemasonry material." It is not clear from the files what the final outcome of the dispute was. On October 18th 1962, the Department for Religious Affairs suggested the Congregation should take the case to court.[83]

Worth noting is the arrogant attitude of officials from Bielsko-Biała who, during the liquidation of the cemetery in 1966–1967 and the construction of the Polsport Sports Equipment Plant on that site, refused to hand over the gravestones to the local Congregation of the Judaic Faith. They agreed only "to hand over a few worthless monuments to the Congregation [. . .], stipulating at the same time that only those monuments selected by a representative of the Sports Equipment Plant could be removed." A significant number of the gravestones were used to pave the company's yards.[84]

In 1979, the Religious Association of the Judaic Faith in the Republic of Poland intervened in the matter of the demolition of a wall belonging to the cemetery in Tomaszów Mazowiecki. The wall was "supposedly" demolished by soldiers, and the bricks were taken away in military vehicles and used to build officers' villas. The Tomaszów Mazowiecki town council was ordered by provincial officials to investigate the case, but ultimately gave an evasive answer, claiming that participation by the military was "unlikely."[85]

Gravestones from the cemetery in Warsaw's Bródno district were used to build walls and arbours in the 'September 13th 1944' Park (since 2005 called

---

83 AAN, Urząd do Spraw Wyznań, ref. no. 45/476, Sprawa nagrobków cmentarnych, woj. krakowskie, 1–15.

84 Proszyk, Cmentarz żydowski w Bielsku-Białej, 132.

85 AAN, Urząd do Spraw Wyznań, ref. no. 132/305, Obiekty judaizmu województwa piotrkowskiego, 55–57.

Figure 5.3. A building materials depot at the cemetery in Rawa Mazowiecka, 1985.
Photo: Andrzej Siwiec, collection of the National Institute of Heritage.

the "Leśnik" Col. Jan Szypowski Park), a wall in the Red Army soldiers' quarters in the Bródno Cemetery, and as kerbstones in the zoological gardens, close to a cage containing monkeys. During the droughts in 2012 and 2015, as a result of lowered water levels, fragments of matzevahs mixed with paving slabs could be seen in the middle of the Vistula riverbed. In Szczecin, gravestones from Jewish and Protestant cemeteries were used to build walls around squares and frames for sandboxes in playgrounds.[86]

Sandstone slabs were a suitable material for the construction of monuments, for example in Bielsko-Biała, Łowicz (Monuments of Gratitude to the Red Army), and Kępno (a monument dedicated to officers of the Civic Militia, the Public Security Office, and soldiers of the Internal Security Corps), but probably also in Tarnobrzeg (a Monument to the Heroes of the Allied Nations, which in 2018 the authorities refused to demolish). In 1959, by order of the Ministry of Municipal Economics, some of the gravestones from the Ślęźna

---

86 Łukasz Baksik, *Macewy codziennego użytku* (Wydawnictwo Czarne: Wołowiec: 2012), 98–99.

Street cemetery in Wrocław were used "for the construction of war graves for Warsaw."[87] In Toruń, in 1963, a committee of the Presidium of the Municipal Council applied for the allocation of gravestones from the Jewish cemetery to the Union of Fighters for Freedom and Democracy in order to erect a monument to airmen who died in the September 1939 Campaign. In 1967, a certain "former resistance activist of the underground organization Polish Uprising Army from the Pomeranian District and ordinary member of the Toruń Branch of the Union of Fighters for Freedom and Democracy" likewise asked for a gravestone from the cemetery, intending to place it on the grave of her husband, a participant in the Silesian Uprisings, in the Garrison Cemetery.[88] According to some Toruń residents, a commemorative plaque dedicated to the activist of the Polish Communist Party Julian Nowicki had originally been a gravestone. And although no signs of a Hebrew inscription were found during its removal in 2012, it cannot be ruled out that the stone actually came from a Jewish cemetery (where a stonemason's workshop operated after the war), and that the original inscription had been chiselled away. It is also likely that the four columns in the form of a broken tree trunk decorating a monument to Home Army soldiers at the intersection of St. Wincentego Street and Oszmiańska Street in Warsaw previously stood in the Jewish cemetery in Bródno, just 100 meters away.

It is worth mentioning that Jewish organizations also reused damaged gravestones for initiatives related to the commemoration of cemeteries and sites of martyrdom. In 1953, the Presidium of the Socio-Cultural Society of Jews in Poland asked its Lublin branch to "obtain appropriate marble slabs from devastated cemeteries, which could be used to build a monument to fallen Jewish partisans buried in Lublin."[89]

Cemeteries also became sand pits. In Brzeziny, gravel mixed with bones from the local cemetery was used in the production of prefabricated panels used for, among other things, the construction of apartment blocks.[90] In Nowy

---

87   AAN, Ministerstwo Gospodarki Komunalnej, ref. no. 9/20, Cmentarnictwo – korespondencja dotycząca zamknięcia cmentarzy żydowskich i ewangelickich, 6.

88   Niedzielska, *Cmentarz żydowski*, 39–40.

89   AŻIH, Towarzystwo Społeczno-Kulturalne Żydów w Polsce, ref. no. 217/325, Towarzystwo Społeczno-Kulturalne Żydów w Polsce, no pagination.

90   "Brzeziny: zaniedbane dziedzictwo," Joanna Leszczyńska, accessed June 30, 2020, http://www.dzienniklodzki.pl/artykul/96658,brzeziny-zaniedbane-dziedzictwo,id,t.html.

Wiśnicz, the County Roads Administration dug sand from the cemetery.[91] In Inowłódz, a section of the Jewish cemetery was occupied and destroyed by an opencast chalcedonite mine, established in 1970.

In the event of cemeteries being reused within 40 years since the last burial, the Office for Religious Affairs required that they be formally closed and exhumations carried out. Activists of the Socio-Cultural Society of Jews in Poland and the Religious Association of the Judaic Faith in the Republic of Poland protested against this, although on several occasions (including in Białystok and Bielsko-Biała) they were forced to give their consent. Religious people in particular were outraged by these exhumations and use of cemeteries. The opinion obtained in 1975 by Rabbi Zew Wawa Morejno[92] from Rabbi Moses Feinstein, chairman of the Association of Orthodox Rabbis of the United States of America and Canada, stated:

> "As pertaining to the question, whether the laws of the Torah permit, in any manner, the relocation of graves of decedents to other cemeteries, or to other places in the same cemetery, due to a city ordinance or request by a head of government, [...] I must respond that according to the laws of the Torah it is unequivocably forbidden. It is even forbidden to remove the deceased or any remains of a deceased from his present grave to a more respectful grave, even though it be an honor for the decedent. Most certainly it is forbidden to exhume for other reasons. Moreover, it is certainly considered a great desecration and defilement to relocate a cemetery [...]. The site of the grave is forbidden to be used, for whatever purpose [...]. It is thus prohibited to convert former grave sites into promenade places such as parks, or build thereupon structures, or any other form of construction such as roads, high-ways, viaducts or to set up there any other things as market places, etc."[93]

However, this opinion was in no way binding on officials in Poland.

Source materials show that exhumations were carried out in various ways, often involving gross negligence. In Chorzów, preparations took two years, during

---

91   Piotr Szlezynger and Iwona Zawidzka, *Żydowski Wiśnicz* (Kraków: Piotr Szlezynger and Iwona Zawidzka, 2016), 96.

92   In 1973, Rabbi Zew Wawa Morejno emigrated from Poland to the United States, where he lived until his death in 2011.

93   AAN, Urząd do Spraw Wyznań, ref. no 131/520, Związek Religijny Wyznania Mojżeszowego, 32.

which time meetings of representatives of municipal services were held, and attempts were made to find the pre-war register of burials, the new burial place of the exhumed bodies was agreed with the Congregation of the Judaic Faith and the Socio-Cultural Society of Jews in Poland (in the end, the Jewish cemetery in Bytom was chosen) and an inventory was made of the preserved gravestones. The exhumation itself was carried out in 1973 with Civil Militia officers and a Representative of the town's Sanitary and Epidemiological Station in attendance.[94] However, most often no such efforts were taken. Apparently, there was no professional exhumation in Radzyń Chełmiński, where a local Farmers' Self-Help shop was erected in the cemetery in the mid-1960s. According to Kazimierz Z.'s account, a local labourer was commissioned to dig the foundations:

> When we were digging there, because my father was digging, and I was helping, as the eldest son, there were fragments of bones, already spread around, yellowish, crumbling. As this was in the 1960s, those graves must have been 40 or 50 years old [. . .]. I remember there were bones, a fragment of a skull, because the earth was claylike there, so very compacted [. . .]. We then buried those bones elsewhere.[95]

The "exhumation" at the cemetery in Opatów took place under strange circumstances. In 1961, the authorities began the procedure for its early liquidation (sooner than 40 years since its last burial) in connection with the "implementation of national economic plans," arguing as follows: "The working population suffers a lack of space for recreation, which in all cities is provided by parks. Opatów as yet has no park; it has only two small squares [. . .]. The world of workers and young people must be provided the opportunity to relax outdoors." Initially, they intended to establish a park without exhuming the bodies. On January 27th 1962, the Minister of Municipal Economics issued permission to use the cemetery for another purpose, and the Presidium of the Provincial Council in Kielce instructed officials from Opatów concerning the method of conducting the exhumation, including the need to make such plans public and the rules governing reburial. The exhumation took place on October 21st 1962. From

---

94   Renata Skoczek, "Cmentarz żydowski w Chorzowie. Okoliczności związane z jego likwidacją," in *Żydzi na Górnym Śląsku w XIX i XX wieku*, ed. Barbara Kalinowska-Wójcik, Dawid Keller (Rybnik–Katowice: Muzeum w Rybniku, Instytut Historii Uniwersytetu Śląskiego w Katowicach, 2012), 395–403.

95   An interview with Kazimierz Z. on May 28, 2018. The recording in Krzysztof Bielawski's possession.

a cemetery that had existed since at least the 16th century and occupying a plot of more than 3 hectares, the remains of only 25 people were excavated and buried "in three packages" at the edge of the park. At the same time, the last matzevahs were removed. Aleksandra Gromek-Gadkowska, a researcher into the history of Opatów, provided the following description of the work carried out:

> In front of the first row of matzevahs, a horse hitched to a plough made a deep furrow to make it easier to extract the gravestones from the ground. Then a looped chain ending with a hook was thrown over each matzevah. This was attached to a small tractor that pulled it to the ground and dragged it to a spot marked out near the northwest corner. Then the tractor returned to the site and dragged away the next matzevahs.[96]

At the cemetery of the former Jewish community in Biała (Bielsko-Biała since 1951), there were about 1,700 graves. In 1966, in connection with plans to expand the "Polsport" Sports Equipment Plant, the authorities began liquidating the cemetery. They initially intended to exhume only 10 graves, the costs to be borne by the Plant, with charges for the remaining exhumations (2,000 zloties per grave, when the average monthly wage amounted to 1934 zloties) to be borne by the families concerned. Following negotiations with the Congregation of the Judaic Faith, "Polsport" eventually financed the exhumation of about 130 bodies. Twenty other graves were exhumed at the expense of the families. The remaining approximately 1,500 gravesites containing human ashes were set aside for construction. It should be emphasized that the plans to liquidate the cemetery were announced in May 1966, giving families 14 days in which to apply for exhumation, and after numerous appeals, this deadline was extended to May 30th 1966.[97] Considering the means of communication available in the 1960s and the scattering of Bielsko Jews around the world, this was far from sufficient time.

Also in the 1960s, a section of the Wrocław cemetery on Gwarna Street was built upon: "Its area was levelled, with only the remains that were found during earthworks being removed. It is not known whether these were then re-buried in some mass grave, for example on the outskirts of this necropolis, or thrown in

---

96 "Likwidacja cmentarza żydowskiego w Opatowie," Aleksandra Gromek-Gadkowska, accessed June 30, 2020, http://gadkowski.pl/publikacja/likwidacja-cmentarza-zydowskiego-w-opatowie.

97 Proszyk, *Cmentarz żydowski w Bielsku-Białej*, 129–131.

the garbage." Evidence pointing to the lack of exhumation work back then was the discovery of numerous corpses during the construction of a hotel in 2017.[98]

In Puławy, the exhumation carried out on March 28th 1968 involved only part of the cemetery plot—a few years earlier, buildings had been erected on the remaining area, without any cemetery liquidation procedure, and another section had been taken over by the construction of Kilińskiego Street. Due to difficulties in finding a company specializing in exhumations, the task was carried out by employees of the Wood Products Cooperative, who dug up the cemetery to a depth of 1.5 metres. The bones were then transported to the Jewish cemetery in Lublin.[99]

Wojciech Kubiatowicz observed the construction of the Provincial Culture Centre on the grounds of the cemetery in Wałcz:

> I remember the Jewish cemetery and, like other young people in those years, I also more than once roamed this area. There I found not only human bones, but also skulls. At one time I kept these in a cardboard box, but unfortunately today I don't remember what happened to them. However, I well remember the construction of the Provincial Culture Centre. The cemetery was liquidated by the Municipal Communal and Housing Enterprise, this being achieved using heavy plant, with excavators used to lever up and remove the gravestones; no exhumations were carried out. Those slabs that were fit for use were collected by one of the local funeral parlours [. . .], after polishing, they probably ended up somewhere on Polish graves. On the other hand, the remaining fragments of damaged gravestones and the cracked sections of tombs were used to, among other things, reinforce the shoreline of Lake Raduń and strengthen the present-day banks of the Młynówka River. It was also said that some of the crushed stone was used as paving material for today's Królowej Jadwigi Street, then called Bieruta Street. As I said, no exhumations were carried out, and it's difficult for me to say what happened to the remains in the ground. One of the employees of the Municipal Communal and Housing Enterprise, now deceased, hearing me recall those events and my remark, once told me just this: 'A lot of those remains were buried in the grounds of today's Provincial Culture Centre.'[100]

---

98 Grażyna Trzaskowska, "Cmentarz żydowski przy ul. Gwarnej we Wrocławiu w świetle zachowanych materiałów archiwalnych" (Unpublished manuscript, Wrocław, [date unknown]), 5; Kichler, "Agonia cmentarza, czyli rzecz o wrocławskim kirkucie," 35–38.

99 AP Lublin, Prezydium Powiatowej Rady Narodowej i Urząd Powiatowy w Puławach, ref. no. 746/39, Wydział Gospodarki Komunalnej i Mieszkaniowej, 27.

100 Dariusz Dymarczyk, "Profanacja czy tchórzostwo," *Wiadomości Wałeckie*, May 27, 2014.

The Jewish cemetery in Brodnica was occupied by a furniture production plant. The workers who built it were not given any instructions on how
to deal with the corpses. When they found any bones and coffins while
digging the foundations, they buried them elsewhere within the factory's
grounds.[101]

When the construction of the post office began on the cemetery in Mielec
in 1960, Maciej Jakubowicz, chairman of the Congregation of the Judaic Faith in
Kraków, sounded the alarm: "A considerable number of human bones were excavated and treated as ordinary fertilizer or rubbish."[102] In 1965, Maciej Jakubowicz, based on the testimony of the gravedigger Antoni Skiba, described the
method of carrying out "exhumations" in Mielec:

> Dumper trucks or horse-drawn carts took the soil from the excavations
> to a so-called mound, where human bones were sorted out and placed
> in a wooden crate. On the other hand, a second crate was filled with hu-
> man bones found at the construction site, i.e. the cemetery. Then these
> crates were transported by horse-drawn cart for burial in the Catholic
> cemetery. According to the gravedigger's assessment, the crates weighed
> about 200 kilograms each.[103]

Likewise probably no exhumation took place in Iława, where in the mid-
1970s, soil mixed with bones was used in the building of a stadium. The process
of the cemetery's destruction was remembered by Iława resident F.R.:

> The bulldozers divided up the entire hillock and took it away, along with
> bones and the cemetery's soil, to the restored former German stadium,
> today the Jeziorak Iława Sports Club. [. . .] In 1975–1978 I witnessed
> the removal of the cemetery's soil from the escarpment to the present
> stands, on which seats were mounted. I saw how a bulldozer unloaded
> earth along with a well-preserved human skeleton. I found it all quite
> horrific.[104]

---

101 Piotr Grążawski, accessed June 30, 2020, https://www.facebook.com/piotr.grazawski.7.

102 Urban, *Cmentarze żydowskie, synagogi i domy modlitwy w Polsce w latach 1944–1966*,
257–258.

103 AAN, Urząd do Spraw Wyznań, ref. no. 75/32, Związek Religijny Wyznania Mojżeszowego,
vol. I, 145.

104 "Iława," Krzysztof Bielawski, accessed June 1, 2020, http://cmentarze-zydowskie.pl/
ilawa.htm.

In 1973 or 1974 in Chojna, a bulldozer was used to level the cemetery, and as it removed the gravestones it brought bones and coffins to the surface.[105] According to an entry in the Tuchola cemetery's records, during construction of the Rural Transport Cooperative's depot, "numerous metal coffins were dug up."[106]

In 1972, Zbigniew Ostapiuk made similar observations in Biała Podlaska, when the construction of a cinema began in the cemetery grounds. Bones began to turn up in the trenches being dug. One of the skulls was taken to the biology lab at the Primary School.[107]

Neither were the bones of the deceased exhumed from the cemetery in Płońsk. Archaeologist Marek Gierlach witnessed graves being dug up in 1976: "I heard that they were destroying the Jewish cemetery. When I arrived there, I saw heaps of bones and an exposed grave with a padlock[108] typical of Jewish burials. I wanted to photograph it, but when I came back with my camera, fresh concrete was bubbling in the grave."[109]

A housing estate was built on the cemetery in Września. As Tomasz H. recalled, "in the seventies we moved to newly built blocks of flats on Piastów Street. Earthworks connected with the construction of a shop were in progress. We found skulls, bones, coins and scraps of clothes there."[110]

Numerous cemeteries survived the war in relatively good condition and were devastated only later. Such was the situation for cemeteries in those areas that before the war were within the borders of the Third Reich. In the western and northern provinces, an additional impulse to liquidate them came from the increased tourist trade between Poland and the German Democratic Republic. Visitors from Germany found neglected and partially devastated Protestant and Jewish cemeteries. The Presidium of the County Council in Zielona Góra reported: "The unsatisfactory condition of cemeteries and their appearance is

---

105 Robert Ryss, "Dziedzictwo niczyje," *Gazeta Chojeńska*, July 3, 2007

106 Narodowy Instytut Dziedzictwa (hereinafter: NID), M. Grabowska, *Karta cmentarza nr 3634* ([no place]: 1992).

107 "Biała Podlaska," Krzysztof Bielawski, accessed June 1, 2020, http://cmentarze-zydowskie.pl/bialapodlaska.htm.

108 Putting a padlock into a grave was a common Jewish custom in Poland.

109 Agnieszka Krzemińska, "Tam, gdzie dusze wiecznie czekają," *Polityka*, October 24, 2017.

110 "Września," Krzysztof Bielawski, accessed June 1, 2020, http://cmentarze-zydowskie.pl/wrzesnia.htm.

an exceptionally sensitive matter and provokes unnecessary and unfavourable, albeit justified comments from tourists."[111]

Fears of criticism from tourists were one of the arguments for the early closure of the Rzepin cemetery. In 1972, the Presidium of the County Council in Słubice stated in the application for its liquidation: "Due to increased tourist traffic following the opening of the border crossing in Słubice, we consider it necessary to immediately close this cemetery."[112] In 1965, in the Zielona Góra province alone, which in the years 1950–1975 covered an area of 14,580 square kilometres, there were 875 closed and abandoned cemeteries, with Jewish cemeteries accounting for about 5% of this number. Party activists, however, had no intention of tidying up any cemeteries—including Jewish ones—located in former German territory. A simpler solution that would not require many years of investment was to just remove them from the country's landscape.[113] One such object was the Jewish cemetery in Słubice, in existence since at least 1399. From the reminiscences of its former gardener we know that in the autumn of 1945 this site was in relatively good condition, apart from the damage caused by two bombs. Over the following years, the area gradually became overgrown, monuments were stolen and graves were dug up. In 1975 the authorities proceeded to raze the cemetery—its wall was pulled down and the gravestones were taken away. Three years later, construction of the "Zajazd Staropolski" motel began on the site of the former cemetery. During earthworks, soil mixed with human bones was removed. All above ground traces of the five hundred-year-old necropolis were obliterated.[114]

When dealing with the liquidation of cemeteries, officials often claimed that no Jews were living in the area. This was often true, but it should be remembered that after 1945, for reasons of safety, many Jews in Poland concealed their identity. But even the presence of Jews in the town was no obstacle to the closing of the Jewish cemeteries in Włocławek in 1953 and Szczecin in 1982.

The work of liquidating cemeteries was mainly undertaken by municipal management companies, water boards, state-owned engineering centres and "non-socialist" contractors. A popular solution was to use the labour of the local

---

111 Kirmiel, *"Żydowskie ślady na Ziemi Lubuskiej,"* 225.

112 AAN, Ministerstwo Gospodarki Terenowej i Ochrony Środowiska, ref. no. 1/33, Decyzje o zamknięciu cmentarzy i przeznaczeniu ich na inny cel w województwie zielonogórskim, 82.

113 Kirmiel, Żydowskie ślady na Ziemi Lubuskiej, 225.

114 Reiss, "Makom tov – der gute Ort – dobre miejsce," 46–53.

Figure 5.4. Workers during the removal of matzevahs from the cemetery in Kielce, 1962. Photo: Janusz Buczkowski, collection of the Kielce History Museum.

population as part of their so-called volunteer civic activities. Such was the case in Kielce, where in 1966 employees of the "Iskra" Precision Instruments Works were involved in removing the gravestones on one such weekend of volunteer work. This was documented by Janusz Buczkowski, who took a series of photos that day. These show the cemetery covered with numerous gravestones, most of them overturned and their removal by at least several dozen workers, equipped with crowbars, pickaxes, spades and shovels. The gravestones were lifted onto a lorry with the aid of a crane and taken away. One of the photos shows six elegantly dressed men knocking over a matzevah—as it turns out, members of the management staff and the company's Polish United Workers' Party Committee.[115]

Young people too were sometimes involved in these volunteer civic activities. In Słubice, these included members of the Union of Rural Youth.[116] On April 27th 1968, students in Wrocław—including young athletes from the "Lokomotiv" football team—"tidied up" the cemetery on Gwarna Street before Labour Day, laying out a playing field on it. An enthusiastic report of their work was broadcast by Polish Radio.[117]

---

115 Janusz Buczkowski, *Tak było. . .* (Kielce: Biuro Wystaw Artystycznych w Kielcach, 2015), 8–9.

116 Sanocka-Tureczek, "Cmentarze na obszarze obecnego województwa lubuskiego w latach 1945–1975," 121.

117 Kichler, "Agonia cmentarza, czyli rzecz o wrocławskim kirkucie," 36.

The Polish Army too participated in the destruction of cemeteries. In addition to the previously mentioned cases, this included the occupation of the cemetery in Bydgoszcz by a military unit, the use of matzevahs to construct the airport in Nowy Targ, demolition of the cemetery wall in Tomaszów Mazowiecki, and the construction of an exercise yard on the cemetery in Oleśnica. Soldiers were also purported to have removed the gravestones from the cemetery in Kielce.[118] It is not known under what circumstances the matzevahs, unearthed on the premises of the military unit in Nowy Dwór Mazowiecki in September 2018, found their way there.

Until the 1980s, in correspondence regarding the liquidation of cemeteries, the question of their commemoration appeared very rarely, and if mentioned at all, was met with disapproval by the decision-makers. In Łódź, in connection with plans to route Zachodnia Street through the cemetery, an agreement was concluded with the Socio-Cultural Society of Jews in Poland, under which a commemorative mound was to be built. However, this commitment was withdrawn when the grounds of the cemetery were handed over for the construction of a housing estate.[119]

When in 1951 the Warsaw authorities issued an order to remove the gravestones from the Bródno cemetery, the Party Team at the Socio-Cultural Society of Jews in Poland stated that "it would be wrong to completely obliterate all traces" and suggested that the rest of the matzevahs should be left, put in some order, and surrounded by a fence. Paweł Hoffman from the Culture Section of the Central Committee of the Polish United Workers' Party, in a letter to Edward Ochab, Secretary of the Central Committee of the Polish United Workers' Party, considered it "absolutely pointless to erect any mausoleum or monument," but accepted the concept of the Party Team of the Socio-Cultural Society of Jews in Poland of preserving a small, fenced-off section of the cemetery, surrounded by "a wall made of gravestones (with their inscriptions facing inwards)."[120] No such lapidarium, however, was built in Bródno, and thousands of stelae brought together in one place still lie to this day in the central part of the cemetery.

---

118 Krzysztof Kąkolewski, "Umarły cmentarz," *Tygodnik Solidarność*, December 16, 1994.

119 Wiatr, "Historia cmentarza," 30.

120 AAN, Polska Zjednoczona Partia Robotnicza. Komitet Centralny w Warszawie, ref. no. 237/XVIII/22, Korespondencja w sprawie cmentarza na Bródnie, 19–20.

Figure 5.5. Gravestones moved into heaps in the Jewish cemetery
in Warsaw's Bródno district, 2015. Photo: Krzysztof Bielawski.

In 1952, Chaim Welger, a doctor at the County Hospital in Strzelce Opolskie, appealed for the protection of matzevahs, about 100 of which were located
on the hospital premises, while about 200 others had been "dumped in one pile"
in the cemetery, where at that time youngsters played football and the townspeo-
ple grazed their goats. In August 1952, Welger raised the alarm that the National
Council had issued a decree permitting the use of gravestones for construction
purposes. In a confidential letter, the head of the Religious Affairs Department
at the Presidium of the Provincial Council in Opole commented:

> Dr. Chaim would like the Presidium of the Provincial Council to fence
> off the cemetery and better arrange its gravestones [. . .] so that the mem-
> ory of fascist barbarism could be preserved [. . .]. The position of the
> Department and political factors is negative, because these gravestones
> do not belong to Jews who died at the hands of the occupying forces,
> but resemble a very private initiative, as evidenced by the fact that, as
> Dr. Chaim himself stated, some of the families of these deceased now
> reside in Palestine.

The reluctance of officials to secure and commemorate cemeteries was consistent. On December 18th 1953, Stanisław Sroka, Minister of Municipal

Economics, approved the request of the authorities in Strzelce Opolskie to close the cemetery and use it as a green, which would be tended by the employees of the "Pionier" State Agricultural Equipment Factory adjacent to the cemetery.[121] All above ground traces of the cemetery were obliterated.

A somewhat different case was that of the so-called ghetto cemetery in Białystok, which was considered a site of martyrdom. Perhaps this, along with the protests of the Socio-Cultural Society of Jews in Poland, led to the decision in 1970, in the course of preparations for construction on the grounds of the cemetery, to develop the cemetery plot "in the form of a green area of relaxation and at the same time commemorate this site where Jews had been exterminated—with a visual accent."[122]

For the decision makers, the historical and monumental aspects of cemeteries were also irrelevant, even though it was often centuries-old objects that were destroyed. The question of the historic nature of cemeteries was rarely mentioned in official correspondence, and sometimes facts were manipulated. In a letter dated December 10th 1956, concerning the use of the oldest part of the cemetery—in use since 1806—as an extension of Anielewicza Street (former Gęsia Street), the Chief Architect of Warsaw, Adolf Ciborowski claimed that 5,400 gravestones "about 20 years old" would be relocated.[123] In 1957, the Presidium of the Municipal Council in Wrocław attempted to liquidate the cemetery on Ślężna Street, and in 1974 Marian Czuliński, the President of Wrocław demanded its liquidation in a letter to the Office for Religious Affairs,[124] writing: "As part of the comprehensive clean-up of the city, I consider it necessary to liquidate this cemetery."[125] In the end, thanks to the wealth of gravestones and the involvement of Maciej Łagiewski, in 1988 the cemetery was opened to the public as a Museum of Funereal Architecture (since 1991, the Museum of Funereal Art).

In only a few cases were selected gravestones from destroyed cemeteries saved for museums. In Barczewo in 1976, following the liquidation of the

---

121 AAN, Urząd do Spraw Wyznań, ref. no. 13/381, Strzelce Opolskie – sprawa nagrobków, 1–6.

122 "Cmentarze żydowskie, miejsca egzekucji, zbiorowe mogiły na terenie województwa podlaskiego," Dariusz Stankiewicz, accessed June 1, 2020, http://bialystok.jewish.org.pl/page5.html.

123 AAN, Urząd do Spraw Wyznań, ref. no. 24/549, Sprawa trasy ul. Komunikacyjnej przez cmentarz żydowski, 4.

124 Marian Czuliński was responsible for destroying the medieval Saint Klara's Mills in Wrocław.

125 AAN, Urząd do Spraw Wyznań, ref. no. 25/581, Likwidacja cmentarza we Wrocławiu, 1.

Jewish and Evangelical cemeteries, the Municipal Parks Board in Olsztyn donated 21 gravestones, including two Evangelical crosses free of charge to the Mazuria Museum in Olsztyn.[126] However, such practices were only sporadic. In the archived files concerning the liquidation of cemeteries, there is practically no professional documentation concerning their condition in the form of an inventory of gravestones, iconographic material or lists of those buried. Two exceptions are as follows: the cemetery in Częstochowa, where in 1970 a team of surveyors drew up a map of the location of the graves and recorded some of the personal data of the deceased,[127] and in Toruń, where in 1975, at the request of the Monuments Preservation Studio, Bohdan Horbaczewski took photographs of the gravestones that were to be removed.[128]

In the light of the above-mentioned facts, it would be a truism to say that in the years when Poland was a People's Republic, cemeteries were not provided conservation and protection. According to a listing from the Institute of National Heritage, until 1959 there was only one Jewish cemetery listed in the provincial registers of immovable monuments, with five cemeteries entered in the register in the 1960s, and eight in the 1970s. In 1975, the General Conservator of Monuments listed only 77 sites in a list of Jewish cemeteries of historic value.[129] It was not until the 1980s that a breakthrough occurred when, for purposes of propaganda, the authorities began implementing a policy of improving relations with Jewish organizations in Poland. At that time, 132 cemeteries were entered into the register of monuments. By 2020, there were a total 252 Jewish cemeteries in the provincial registers of immovable monuments throughout the country. Additionally, the register (without taking into account the entire area of the cemetery) included: the lapidarium in Opatów, a complex of gravestones in Bieruń, a former pre-funeral building in Słupsk, and several cemeteries located in a larger conservation area.[130]

---

126 Wojciech Zenderowski, "Barczewo. Macewy i metalowe krzyże," *Wiadomości Barczewskie*, no. 5 (2010): 8.

127 Wiesław Paszkowski, *Cmentarz żydowski w Częstochowie* (Częstochowa: Muzeum Częstochowskie, 2012), 9.

128 Niedzielska, *Cmentarz żydowski*, 41–42.

129 AAN, Urząd do Spraw Wyznań, ref. no. 131/518, Cmentarze żydowskie w Polsce – ochrona zabytkowych cmentarzy, likwidacje, 1–7.

130 Listing from the Institute of National Heritage.

Noteworthy is the letter sent by the General Conservator of Monuments on September 12th 1975 to the Ministry of Local Economics and Environmental Protection, which read:

> Due to the liquidation of a large number of old cemeteries in Poland, their conversion into recreational areas has ceased to be merely sporadic, and at the same time is often conducted in an improper manner [. . .], inconsistent with the standards of conduct adopted in Europe—as well as those of an ethical nature—in this respect. This matter has a particular aspect in the western and northern territories, where such cases can and are immediately used for propaganda purposes by the press of some foreign countries, and moreover, arouse negative and unfortunately justified reactions in many tourists from western countries.

However, the letter, issued 20 years too late, met with the understanding of officials from the Ministry of Administration, Local Economics and Environmental Protection, who drew the provincial authorities' attention to the way cemeteries intended for public utility purposes were being managed.[131]

Some cemeteries became the property of private individuals as a result of their usucaption (when the title to a property is gained by possession of it beyond a certain period of time) or sale.

The secondary division of many cemeteries became an additional problem. New plots marked out often encroached on smaller or larger sections of cemeteries. This was not only due to the negligence or ignorance of the surveyors who worked in cemeteries with blurred boundaries, but was also a deliberate act. This happened in, among other places, Piaseczno, where single-family buildings were built on over 90% of the cemetery, a total area of 1.7 hectares, and in Siemiatycze, where new plots were created on about one quarter of the cemetery's area.

Although the escalation of antisemitism at the end of the 1960s was not clearly reflected in any official correspondence regarding the liquidation of cemeteries, it can be assumed that due to the persecution of many Jews in Poland, and their emigration, some officials felt they could permit themselves greater freedom in activities related to the destruction of cemeteries. Their arrogance can best be seen in those cases involving the destruction of the

---

131 AAN, Ministerstwo Gospodarki Terenowej i Ochrony Środowiska, ref. no. 1/24, Decyzje o zamknięciu cmentarzy i przeznaczeniu ich na inny cel w województwie gdańskim, 148–168.

graves and monuments of Shoah victims. Previously, arguments about the necessity of treating the graves of Nazi victims with dignity had often convinced the authorities. Another significant factor was in 1967 the withdrawal from Poland of the American Jewish Joint Distribution Committee, which financed the upkeep of cemeteries. On August 10th 1967, the Ministry of Labour and Social Welfare informed the Joint Distribution Committee that it would have to suspend its activities in Poland until the end of the year, as the existing aid was deemed "sufficient."[132] That same year, the project of restoring and fencing off the cemetery in Żyrardów ended in scandal with the security services preventing this operation's initiators and sponsors, members of the Compatriots Association who came to Poland from Argentina, France, Israel, the United States, and Great Britain, from participating in the ceremony marking completion of the work.[133]

It is not entirely clear what motivated the officials who organized the demolition of the monument standing over the grave of 25 people shot in the village of Imielnica in 1940 and whose remains were exhumed after the war and reburied in the Jewish cemetery in Płock. October 23rd 1949 saw the unveiling of this evocative monument over their grave, designed by Beniamin Perelmuter. In shape it resembled a "depiction" of the Second Temple of Jerusalem, it was made of marble, and on the pediment the inscription read "For them I shed tears," while on the walls were plaques with the names of the victims, the Yizkor prayer, and a sculpture of an urn. The monument was demolished in 1967. Regional historian Jan Przedpełski described the demolition as follows:

> Stanisław Chmurzyński was the cemetery's caretaker [...]. He managed to tell me that one night a group of people came to see him. They claimed that the monument was so badly damaged that it needed to be dismantled. They showed some documents, leaving him nothing to say. They drove into the cemetery with a crane and destroyed the monument. It was not in perfect condition, had aged, and vandals had done the rest. But it could have been rebuilt, instead of destroying it, and in addition under the cover of night.[134]

---

132 Audrey Kichelewski, "'Pomóc naszym braciom z Polski....' Działalność Jointu na rzecz społeczności żydowskiej w PRL w latach 1957–1967," in Społeczność żydowska w PRL przed kampanią antysemicką lat 1967–1968 i po niej, ed. Grzegorz Berendt (Warszawa: Instytut Pamięci Narodowej, 2009), 64.

133 Jan Dołęga Szczepański, "Żyrardowiacy," Folks Sztyme, January 19, 1990.

134 Rafał Kowalski, Płoccy wypędzeni. Marzec '68 (Płock: Muzeum Mazowieckie, 2018), 34.

It is not known in which month this event took place—whether it happened just after the "Six-Day War" and Władysław Gomułka's speech on June 19th 1967, with which the First Secretary of the Polish United Workers' Party publicly launched an antisemitic campaign. Certainly as early as 1964, town officials had raised the issue of reconstructing the monument due to its poor technical condition and had presented plans to close the cemetery and include it in the town's green areas.[135]

In 1971, the cemetery on Białystok's Żabia Street was graded. In his study on cemeteries in the former Białystok Province, Dariusz Stankiewicz stated (but without providing the source of his information or developing the topic further) that the order for the cemetery's liquidation was issued by the Central Committee of the Polish United Workers' Party "on the wave of the March 1968 affair." It was one of the few cemeteries (along with those in Augustów, Czachulec, Firlej, Kielce, Legionowo, Malcanów, Warsaw, and Wyśmierzyce) established during the Second World War within or close to a ghetto. The several thousand people buried there had either died or been killed by the Germans in the Białystok ghetto, including participants of the uprising such as Icchok Malmed—a hero of the Jewish resistance movement. Between 1944 and 1947, several funerals were held at the cemetery for Jews murdered under various circumstances in the Podlasie region. After the war, Jews from Białystok who had survived the Shoah fenced off the cemetery, and several monuments were unveiled on its site, the largest of which was in the form of a magnificent mausoleum. It was the site of anniversary celebrations, described by activists of the Socio-Cultural Society of Jews in Poland as "an object of special piety and veneration" and "a national relic." Attempts to liquidate the cemetery began in the early 1950s, but were abandoned following protests by the Socio-Cultural Society of Jews in Poland and the Jewish Historical Institute.

However, on March 12th 1964, the Ministry of Municipal Economics officially closed the cemetery, and three months later the Presidium of the Provincial Council in Białystok decided to use it for other purposes. In 1970—probably due to its weakened position following the March '68 affair—the Socio-Cultural Society of Jews in Poland agreed to hand over the cemetery free of charge, provided that the bodies were exhumed and the victims were commemorated "in the form of a single grave with an artistic accent." In February 1971, the

---

135 Gabriela Nowak, "O żydowskich stelach nagrobnych w Płocku," *Nasze Korzenie*, no. 6 (2009): 97.

municipal services commenced exhuming the bodies, and then removed the gravestones, monuments and other above ground traces. The area was levelled, the exhumed remains were buried in a mass grave, and over time the outskirts of the cemetery were partially built upon.[136]

A manifestation of the "post-March '68" attitude of the authorities towards Jewish organizations is likely seen in the case involving the cemetery on Kraków's No. 55, Miodowa Street. On March 27th 1969, Jan M., the cemetery's caretaker and Jan K., who lived in the pre-funeral building, discovered numerous broken and overturned gravestones. Unidentified perpetrators had damaged a total of 279 matzevahs, including a monument over the mass grave of 195 people murdered by the Germans in Skawina and the gravestone of Józef Sare—a Member of Parliament from 1907 to 1914 and deputy mayor of Kraków in the years 1905–1929. The Civic Militia were notified about the case and as a result of an investigation, they arrested "3 boys who, having drunk 2 bottles of wine, upon arriving at the cemetery upturned (according to their testimony) 49 gravestones." One consequence of this situation was a letter sent by the Presidium of the Grzegórzki District Council in Kraków on June 23rd 1969, in which the Congregation of the Judaic Faith was categorically ordered to provide 24-hour surveillance, maintain the cemetery in a proper condition as a green area (by for example regularly removing weeds and broken or withered trees), "immediately" tidy up the gravestones, restore "without delay" the pre-funeral building to its proper condition and set it apart from the cemetery "in order to increase surveillance," as well as cease burying their dead in the avenues. Execution of the above-mentioned demands would have involved significant financial outlays. The Congregation appealed against the decision, but the Presidium of the District Council rejected the appeal and, in a letter dated March 17th 1970, upheld its decision.[137]

In the spring of 1974, the Łódź authorities ordered the seizure of a section of the cemetery on Bracka Street. According to Aleksander Zajdeman's report of December 9th 1974, about 3,500 gravestones were removed at that time (it was additionally planned to rip out a second batch of about a thousand

---

136 "Cmentarze żydowskie, miejsca egzekucji, zbiorowe mogiły na terenie województwa podlaskiego," Dariusz Stankiewicz, accessed June 1, 2020, http://bialystok.jewish.org.pl/page5.html.

137 AAN, Urząd do Spraw Wyznań, ref. no. 131/517, Cmentarze żydowskie w Polsce – otwieranie, likwidacja remonty, 25–31.

monuments), and the remains were exhumed and then re-buried in 40 coffins in mass graves.[138]

The destruction of cemeteries aroused opposition from Jewish circles. Protests were sent to the authorities by the Socio-Cultural Society of Jews in Poland and the Religious Association of the Judaic Faith in the Republic of Poland. Rabbi Zew Wawa Morejno was very active in this regard, sending numerous and extensive letters to the state authorities, demanding that the liquidation of cemeteries be halted and that they should be fenced off and constantly supervised,[139] and Poland's Primate Stefan Wyszyński was also asked to help.[140] Foreign organizations also protested. These were mainly Compatriot Associations formed by emigrants, their descendants, and rabbis. It can be assumed that these protests did have some influence on the behaviour of officials in Poland. The Presidium of the County Council in Olsztyn, which from the beginning of the 1960s undertook activities aimed at covering up any traces of evangelical and Jewish cemeteries, in a letter dated May 21st 1972 recommended:

> Special care should be taken with regard to decisions concerning the use of Jewish cemeteries for other purposes. It should be remembered that each and every use of a Jewish cemetery for a different purpose is regarded by hostile circles as a particularly malicious act of state policy towards followers of the Judaic religion.[141]

In 1974, the Office for Religious Affairs prepared a draft note concerning cemeteries which stated:

> There is an urgent need to undertake actions that: a/ would make it impossible to unleash anti-Polish campaigns abroad by Jewish nationalist and Zionist circles, b/ should eliminate economic reprisals against our country, which the above-mentioned Jewish forces are aiming for, especially in the USA. The matter of Jewish cemeteries in our country is to a great extent used in [...] anti-Polish campaigns [...]. Certain actions

---

138 AAN, Urząd do Spraw Wyznań, ref. no. 131/517, Cmentarze żydowskie w Polsce – otwieranie, likwidacja remonty, 83.

139 AAN, Urząd do Spraw Wyznań, ref. no. 131/505, Wyznanie mojżeszowe. Rabin Zew Wawa Morejno, 171–184.

140 AIPN, Ministerstwo Spraw Wewnętrznych w Warszawie, ref. no. IPN BU 00231/205/6, Materiały dotyczące Leftwich – Lewkowitza Josepha i Morejno Wawa, 363.

141 Magdalena Bartnik, „Ciche pieśni. O likwidacji cmentarza żydowskiego w Olsztynie," Borussia, no. 37 (2005): 183.

should therefore be undertaken that would indicate our goodwill and willingness to preserve particularly important cemeteries.

The author—signed with the initials TD—argued for cemeteries to be put in order as far as "political needs" so required and for such activities to be used for propaganda purposes, including the obligatory presentation of the results of such works to "Jewish tourists."[142] It is very likely that this approach was brought about by the policies of the new team headed by Edward Gierek, which was attempting to obtain foreign loans for the development of the country.

In the first half of September 1976, Poland was visited by a delegation of rabbis (including Isaac Lewin and David Lifschitz) and representatives of Jewish organizations from the United States, who raised the issue of cemeteries during meetings at the Office for Religious Affairs, with the Main Commission for the Investigation of Nazi Crimes in Poland and with the General Conservator of Monuments. The matter was also lobbied by representatives of the US Department of State, a group of senators and the dockworkers' union affiliated with the American Federation of Labour and Congress of Industrial Organizations (its chairman William Perry threatened to block Polish and Soviet merchant ships if the government of the People's Republic of Poland failed to commit itself to protecting Jewish cemeteries).[143] The result of these discussions was a note in which Kazimierz Kąkol, head of the Office for Religious Affairs, declared his intention to preserve Jewish cemeteries in Poland, with some of them to be considered historical monuments, and others to be preserved regardless of such recognition. In an internal report, the Office for Religious Affairs predicted that the meeting would "defuse unfriendly sentiments and neutralize hostile forces" and "for a long time remove the Jewish problem from the list of activities undertaken by world Jewry."[144] Consequently, on November 11th 1976, the Office for Religious Affairs issued a circular containing significant recommendations:

---

142 AAN, Urząd do Spraw Wyznań, ref. no. 131/516, Cmentarze żydowskie w Polsce – otwieranie, likwidacja, remonty, 2–4.

143 AAN, Urząd do Spraw Wyznań, ref. no. 131/511, Związek Religijny Wyznania Mojżeszowego, 39–41.

144 AAN, Urząd do Spraw Wyznań, ref. no. 131/511, Związek Religijny Wyznania Mojżeszowego, 45; AŻIH, Żydowski Instytut Historyczny, ref. no. 310/82, Akta organizacyjne, no pagination.

The state authorities of the People's Republic of Poland stand firm on the principle of preserving all existing Jewish cemeteries in Poland. In practice, this means that the existing cemeteries of this religion must not be violated, liquidated or used for other purposes, and at the same time it will be required that these cemeteries are properly tended and provided appropriate external decoration in accordance with the nature and importance of such sites.[145]

However, it wasn't until the early 1980s that a noticeable, albeit inadequate, change took place. At that time, party dignitaries, aiming to convince international public opinion about the normalization of the situation in the country after martial law, made friendly gestures towards Jewish organizations in Poland, authorizing for example the airing on Polish Radio of programmes by the Religious Association of the Judaic Faith in the Republic of Poland and renovating the Nożyk Synagogue in Warsaw.[146] August 1983 saw the establishment of the International Commission for Jewish Cemeteries in Poland, which included representatives of the Office for Religious Affairs, the Ministry of Finance, the Ministry of Culture and Art, the Ministry of Administration and Spatial Management, the Religious Association of the Judaic Faith in the Republic of Poland, the Jewish Historical Institute and seven rabbis from Belgium, Israel, the United States and Great Britain.[147] In the following years, the state allocated significant funds (in a letter dated February 13th 1989, the amount was referred to as "several hundred million zloties a year"), obtained from local budgets, the funds of the General Conservator of Monuments, the Central Fund for Culture Development, and the Church Fund.[148] This financed basic cleaning and the fencing off of cemeteries. In 1985, the authorities agreed to register the Nissenbaum Family Foundation, whose aim was to care for devastated cemeteries and synagogues.[149]

---

145 Archiwum Państwowe w Siedlcach (hereinafter: AP Siedlce), Urząd Wojewódzki w Siedlcach, ref. no. 1336, Cmentarz żydowski w Siedlcach, 10.

146 August Grabski, "Współczesne życie religijne Żydów w Polsce," in *Studia z dziejów i kultury Żydów w Polsce po 1945 roku*, ed. J. Tomaszewski (Warszawa: Trio, 1997), 154.

147 JK, "Cmentarze żydowskie – ciągła troska Związku," in *Kalendarz Żydowski 1984–1985*, ed. Ewa Świderska (Warszawa: Związek Religijny Wyznania Mojżeszowego w Polsce, 1985), 160.

148 AIPN, Główna Komisja Badania Zbrodni Hitlerowskich w Polsce, ref. no. IPN BU 3076/168, Zabezpieczenie miejsc pamięci Żydów, 6.

149 The Foundation was founded by Zygmunt Nissenbaum (July 25, 1926 Warsaw—August 11, 2001 Konstanz)—a former prisoner of the Warsaw ghetto, German Nazi concentration

The above-mentioned operations nevertheless did not completely halt the destruction of cemeteries by the administration and state enterprises; for example, in 1984 the town of Wiślica constructed a ring road that passed through the cemetery, in 1986 a high school was built on the grounds of the cemetery in Biłgoraj, in Krosno Odrzańskie an apartment block was built, and in Kalisz communal heating installations disfigured the cemetery. The operations, however, certainly limited the process of destruction. The attitude of officials regarding cemeteries where no above-ground traces had survived was problematic—such sites were usually not considered cemeteries. The scale of this phenomenon can be seen in correspondence from 1986 when, at the request of the Office for Religious Affairs, provincial governors were required to collate information concerning the condition of their cemeteries and the maintenance costs. In the case of the Kielce Province, some town and municipal council offices (including those of Daleszyce, Działoszyce, Końskie, Łagów, Nowa Słupia, Pacanów, and Włoszczowa) returned incorrect answers, claiming to have no Jewish cemeteries in their area.[150] Two years later, the Provincial Office in Toruń officially stated that in the entire Province of Toruń there were no real-estate properties of former Jewish communities, and that all the cemeteries had been destroyed in 1939.[151]

At the same time, the state tried to counteract the Social Committee for the Protection of Jewish Cemeteries and Monuments which was established in 1981. Following an appeal published by Tygodnik Solidarność in the Solidarity Weekly, information concerning 800 cemeteries was collected,[152] in an attempt draw up a complete list of Jewish cemeteries. But this was viewed by the Office for Religious Affairs as a "hostile" activity since it brought into question the government's 1974 list, which recorded 522 such sites.[153] In 1983, the Ministry of Internal Affairs considered registration of this Committee "pointless," arguing

---

camps and forced labour camps at Majdanek, Auschwitz-Birkenau, Budzyń, Flosenburg, Hersbruck and Offenburg, founder of the Jewish community in Konstanz.

150 AP Kielce, Urząd Wojewódzki w Kielcach, ref. no. 1080/1079, Cmentarze żydowskie – korespondencja ogólna, k. 1–30.

151 AAN, Urząd do Spraw Wyznań, ref. no. 132/218, Obiekty judaizmu województwa tarnowskiego, 17 (the document incorrectly assigned to Tarnow Province files).

152 Małgorzata Palester-Chlebowczyk, "Ochrona cmentarzy żydowskich," Tygodnik Solidarność, July 24, 1981.

153 Eleonora Bergman and Jan Jagielski, "Ślady obecności. Synagogi i cmentarze," in Następstwa Zagłady Żydów. Polska 1944–2010, ed. Feliks Tych and Monika Adamczyk-Garbowska

that other organizations were already involved in the protection of monuments of Jewish culture, and the establishment of another "would be of no social benefit." In view of this refusal, the Committee functioned as a commission within the structure of the Society for the Protection of Monuments. In a secret note dated March 9th 1984, officers at the Ministry of Internal Affairs pointed out that "the composition of the Committee's Management Board does not guarantee loyalty" and that "it may pose threats of a political nature." Committee members found themselves in the sphere of interest of the secret services, and in one instance on June 29th 1984, Committee member Monika Krajewska was interrogated.[154]

Until the collapse of the Polish People's Republic, the issue of protecting cemeteries was definitely political in nature, as evidenced by a letter of the Office for Religious Affairs dated February 13th 1989:

> For years, the condition of Jewish cemeteries in Poland has been the subject of severe criticism by international organizations of the Jewish Diaspora and Jewish communities in Poland and Israel. This criticism is reflected in press releases, and interventions addressed to Polish diplomatic missions and the Office for Religious Affairs, and is clearly noticeable during economic talks, making it difficult to include Jewish communities around the world in any measures aimed at improving the financial and economic situation in Poland. Recently, the subject of deteriorating Jewish cemeteries in our country has become an important element of those political forces in the world interested in diluting the dramatic impact of German-Jewish relations during the Third Reich by promoting the suggestion about the need to settle accounts regarding the negative attitude of Poles towards Jews and preserve the material and spiritual monuments of Jewish culture in our country.[155]

(Lublin–Warszawa: Wydawnictwo UMCS, Żydowski Instytut Historyczny im. E. Ringelbluma, 2011), 479.

154 AIPN, Ministerstwo Spraw Wewnętrznych, ref. no. IPN BU 1585/21506, Społeczny Komitet Opieki nad Cmentarzami i Zabytkami Kultury Żydowskiej w Polsce, no pagination.

155 AP Kielce, Urząd Wojewódzki w Kielcach, sygn. 1080/1079, Cmentarze żydowskie – korespondencja ogólna, 60.

5.3. State Policy regarding Jewish Cemeteries after 1989

The political transformation following the collapse of the People's Republic of Poland brought about radical changes in the state's attitude regarding Jewish cemeteries, the origins of which should be seen in the dialogue between the authorities and Jewish organizations in the 1980s. In 1990, the Council of Ministers sent a letter to Provincial Governors, which stated:

> The Judaic religion considers burial places of their dead as especially sacred. The cemetery remains the most venerated place, regardless of its condition and what is left of it above ground. Therefore, even those necropolises without fences and gravestones continue to remain sacred sites. In this sense, the term "cemetery" has a much broader meaning than in the colloquial and statutory sense. Judaism does not recognize the concept of liquidating a cemetery, and apart from burials of the dead, the rules of that religion do not permit any other use of an area once it has been designated a burial site. The Polish state, respecting the beliefs and traditions of all religious communities, also wishes to respect the specific status of cemeteries in the Judaic religion.

The new political system meant communization—that is, state property becoming public property owned by the community. As a consequence, in 1990 most cemeteries became the property of the State Treasury, an institution of communal ownership and the subject of perpetual usufruct rights by legal entities (state, municipal and private). The state remained the owner of the active cemeteries used by the Religious Association of the Judaic Faith in the Republic of Poland.[156]

On July 18th 1991, the Polish Parliament adopted an amendment to the act on cemeteries and burial of the dead, adding an important provision: "If a cemetery's grounds are or have previously been the property of [...] a religious association, the issuing of a decision to use the cemetery's grounds for another purpose requires consent from the competent authority of that [...] religious association."[157]

In the nineties, Jewish religious communities were reactivated. In 1992, the Religious Association of the Judaic Faith in the Republic of Poland became the Union of Jewish Communities in the Republic of Poland, and a year later it

---

156 Bednarek, *Sytuacja prawna cmentarzy żydowskich w Polsce 1944–2019*, 264.
157 Bergman and Jagielski, "*Ślady obecności*," 480.

adopted a new statute. Another key item of legislation was the Act on the State's Relations with Jewish Communities, which came into force on May 11th 1997. This act excluded the possibility of expropriating cemeteries owned by Jewish communities, and at the same time introduced the obligation of protecting Jewish cemeteries—including a ban on their sale to third parties and use for other purposes—owned by the State Treasury or local government entities. Pursuant to the Act, cemeteries remaining in the hands of Jewish communities on the day the act came into force became their property. Jewish religious communities were granted the right to apply for the return of ownership of those cemeteries or sections thereof expropriated by the State, which on September 1st 1939 had been the property of Jewish communities or other religious Jewish legal entities operating on the territory of the Republic of Poland. The same applied to those cemeteries or sections thereof constituting the property of synagogue communities on January 30th 1933 in the territory annexed from Germany in 1945 operating on the basis of the Act of July 23rd 1847 on Relations between Jews, and other religious Jewish legal entities or real estate and sections thereof, whose legal status was not established. In accordance with the intention of the legislator, in the case of Jewish cemeteries only the real estate or sections thereof can be transferred (unlike other real estate properties, where Jewish communities may receive financial compensation or substitute real estate), with the proviso that said restoration may not infringe on rights acquired by third parties.

Under this Act, the Union of Jewish Communities in the Republic of Poland became the legal successor of the pre-war Jewish communities, thus gaining rights to the restoration of property, including cemeteries, provided that these were owned by the State Treasury or local government entities. This excluded the possibility of recovering cemeteries that after the war, as a result of various legal actions, had become the property of third parties.

The state also created favourable conditions for cemeteries to come under conservation protection. The July 23rd 2003 Act on the protection and care of monuments introduced the obligation of protecting and caring for cemeteries regardless of their state of preservation.[158] On July 31st 2017, Magdalena Gawin, Undersecretary of State at the Ministry of Culture and National Heritage, sent a letter to Provincial Conservators of Monuments which read as follows:

---

158 Ustawa z dnia 23 lipca 2003 roku o ochronie zabytków i opiece nad zabytkami, art. 6, ust. 1, pkt 1, lit. f.

The Polish legislator has recognized the special status of currently functioning Jewish cemeteries in relation to other cemeteries, for example Article 23, section 1 of the Act of February 20th 1997 concerning the State's position with regard to Jewish Communities in the Republic of Poland, which provides that Jewish cemeteries owned by Jewish communities or the Union of Jewish communities are not subject to expropriation. I wish also to draw attention to the adoption of an amendment to the provisions—pursuant to article 2 of the Act dated June 22nd 2017 amending the Act on the protection and care of monuments, article 13, section 5 of the Act dated August 21st 1997 on real estate management—is to be replaced as follows: 'The sale, exchange, donation or lease of real estate constituting the property of the State Treasury or a local government entity, being any cemetery listed in the provincial register of monuments, as well as the submission of said real estate properties as in-kind contributions to companies requires a permit from the provincial Conservator of Monuments'. The obvious historical value of Jewish cemeteries as burial places results directly from the presence of human remains. The most important area within the cemetery is the burial zone; the degree of preservation of architectural forms is secondary, although important when deciding on the appropriate method of protection, for example entry in the register of monuments, consideration in local planning or entry in the register of monuments. The primary goal of conservators should be to secure the sites of Jewish cemeteries in use until August 31st 1939. The burial zone, free of any buildings, should be marked out with stones until a fence can be built.

The emphasis laid on the protection of graves (the "burial zone") was an important step in light of the earlier practice of entering in the register of monuments only those cemeteries where at least above ground relics such as gravestones or architectural objects had been preserved.

Among the important activities undertaken by the government, mention should be made of the project initiated by the Ministry of Culture and National Heritage in 2017 for marking all Jewish cemeteries in Poland, this to be carried out with the participation of the Institute of National Heritage, the POLIN Museum of the History of Polish Jews, the E. Ringelblum Historical Institute and the Union of Jewish Communities in the Republic of Poland. Part of this project was to carry out field surveys and draw up a list of all cemeteries. Since 2018, various cemeteries have been marked, including those in Bolimów, Brok, Brzozów, Garwolin, Góra Kalwaria, Janowiec, Janów Lubelski, Lublin, Łomża, Nasielsk, Oleśno, Olsztyn, Orla, Proszowice, Rzochów, Serock, Siedlce, Skarszewy,

Stepnica, Szamotuły, Szlichtyngowa, Trzemeszno, Tuszyn, Tykocin, Warsaw, and Wyszogród.

In 2017, pursuant to a parliamentary act, the government created a special fund worth PLN 100 million to supplement the perpetual capital of the Cultural Heritage Foundation. Income from interest and the investment of these funds—estimated at approximately PLN 2.5 million annually—is allocated to conservation works at the Jewish cemetery at 49/51 Okopowa Street, Warsaw.

Some cemeteries are now under the care of local authorities, which periodically remove rubbish from their grounds and cultivate vegetation. In 2007, the town of Gliwice, for a symbolic 1 zloty, took over the monumental pre-burial building from the Jewish community in Katowice and, following its restoration, turned it into the Upper Silesian Jewish House of Remembrance, a branch of the Museum in Gliwice. The town council in Czeladź has a similar plan.

Despite the legal acts and guidelines described above, there are still cases of town and community council offices commissioning investments on cemetery lands. For example, in the years 2008–2009, graves were dug up on the partially built upon area of the cemetery in Ostrołęka during the reconstruction of a street. In 2017, the mayor of Zamość, Andrzej Wnuk, despite the rabbinate's protests and citing a so-called special act, built a road through the cemetery, and in 2018 the authorities of Wysokie Mazowieckie began construction of a bus station on the so-called old Jewish cemetery. Numerous bones were dug up in May 2019 during the construction of an internal road at the Hotel and Gastronomy School Complex in Sandomierz, which occupies a large section of the cemetery. Human remains, spread over a large area, were found there for several months after completion of the works.

Also, for some officials, cemeteries without gravestones do not constitute places to be respected. This is the case in Wiżajny among other places, where the Community Council Office every year organizes a folk music festival on the grounds of the devastated cemetery.[159]

---

159 In 2021 the author and Meir Bulka from Israel sent open letters to the Wiżajny authorities, asking to stop organizing the event on the cemetery. The mayor did not answer; however, the concert was moved to a nearby park, and "only" a sports competition took place on the devastated cemetery.

5.4. Participation of the Local Population in the Destruction of Cemeteries after 1945

The end of the war should be treated as only a formal turning point with respect to local populations devastating Jewish cemeteries. Cemeteries were destroyed during the war and this process continued following the capitulation of the Third Reich, although at this time thieves plundered so-called abandoned property, and their activities could have been hindered not by a German gendarme, but by an officer of the Civil Militia or Security Services, and sometimes the activists of Jewish committees. Faced with political struggle, the massive destruction of the country, and its reconstruction, the authorities, police force and judiciary had priorities other than securing cemeteries or identifying and punishing those who stole matzevahs.

In addition to activities directly related to the destruction of cemeteries, it is also important to bear in mind the consequences of the antisemitic attitudes of some members of society, which was one of the factors forcing surviving Jews to leave the country or move from their hometowns to large cities (for example Kraków, Łódź, Warsaw) or the lands annexed from the territories of the Third Reich. Between July 1944, when the Soviet Army "liberated" the eastern part of the Lublin province, and 1946, no less than 1,088 Jews lost their lives as a result of attacks, pogroms and assassinations.[160] Within the three months following the Kielce pogrom—during which, over a period of several hours, a crowd murdered over 40 people and injured about 40 more in the town centre—over 70,000 Jews left Poland.[161] Some Poles also took an active part in the antisemitic campaign of 1967–1968. The waves of emigration caused by these events resulted in many Jewish graves being left unattended.

From the very first months after the Eastern Front passed through Poland, reports on the destruction of cemeteries by Polish inhabitants began to pour in to the Central Committee of Jews in Poland, including the theft of matzevahs, the dismantling of walls, the plundering of graves, and the use of cemeteries as arable and pasture land. Gravestones became a particularly desirable building material during this period.

---

160 Julian Kwiek, *Nie chcemy Żydów u siebie. Przejawy wrogości wobec Żydów w latach 1944–1947* (Warszawa: Nieoczywiste, 2021), 215.

161 Dariusz Stola, *Kraj bez wyjścia. Migracje z Polski 1949–1989* (Warszawa: Instytut Pamięci Narodowej, 2010), 50.

Nusyn Bałanowski wrote about the cemetery in Chmielnik in a letter sent on October 20th 1946 to the Central Committee of Jews in Poland: "Local peasants are removing stones that form the wall around the Jewish cemetery in Chmielnik without any interference from anyone. They are destroying monuments etc. [...] The old cemetery [...] has been turned into a market place."[162]

The report from the investigation conducted in 1949 says much about the situation in Gniewoszów. Roman S., accused of ploughing up the cemetery, testified as follows:

> The burial grounds of this cemetery were not only not ploughed by me, but not ploughed by anyone at all, as it was already devastated after Poland's liberation from the German occupation, only the cemetery itself was plundered of its gravestones and fence by the local inhabitants—that is Gniewoszów and the surrounding villages: among others Aleksander Sz [...] living in Gniewoszów, in the village of Sarnów, whom I saw carrying posts taken from the fence; about 20 such posts and he probably still has them, but me—I had no hand in the barbaric destruction of the cemetery, especially since my honour as a Pole wouldn't permit it, because I'm deputy mayor of the village of Sarnów and second secretary of the Municipal Committee of the Polish United Workers' Party. As for the second Jewish cemetery located in the Gniewoszów settlement, I tell you that it was also devastated by the inhabitants of the Gniewoszów settlement and the surrounding villages, but I can't name them because they devastated it mostly at night.

Józef A., confirming the testimony of Roman S., added: "I myself saw gravestones stacked up in the farmyard of Antoni Sz [...], a resident of Gniewoszów, in 1947, but I can't say whether he still has them." Czesław B. testified in turn:

> Those cemeteries were devastated, i.e. gravestones and a fence were looted by people from the Gniewoszów settlement and the neighbouring village of Sarnów, partly during the occupation and following the liberation of Poland from German occupation, and it should be added that some of the fence and gravestones were even taken by individuals from the village of Oblassy.[163]

---

162 AŻIH, Centralny Komitet Żydów w Polsce, ref. no. 303/XVI/130, Korespondencja dot. cmentarza w Chmielniku, 2–1.

163 AAN, Ministerstwo Administracji Publicznej, ref. no. 1098, Sprawa cmentarza w Gniewoszowie, 231–233. The village of Oblasy is situated 21 kilometres from Gniewoszów.

The destruction of the above-ground parts of the cemetery was carried out meticulously at the beginning of the 21st century, before its necropolis was fenced off in the years 2014–2016 by the Foundation for the Preservation of Jewish Heritage and the descendants of the Jews of Gniewoszów, when there were no traces in either cemetery of gravestones, the original fencing or cemetery buildings.

According to Kazimierz Cieślicki's records, the cemetery in Urzędów was destroyed by the local population "when there were no longer any followers of the Judaic religion in the town." The fence and wooden buildings were dismantled, and the gravestones were apparently destroyed by boys grazing their cows in the cemetery.[164] In 2013 Krystyna Palmąka placed these actions at a similar time "when there were no Jews left in Szydłów," saying: "no one dug up the graves, but people destroyed matzevahs and made grindstones out of them, or used them after the war to build roads and pavements. [...] Whoever needed a stone went and took a gravestone."[165] According to a report by the Presidium of the Municipal Council in Szydłów, in 1946 there were still 1,141 "completely neglected graves" in the cemetery."[166] Today it is just an empty meadow.

In many cases, the local population continued the process of devastating cemeteries which was initiated by the German administration or post-war communist powers. This was clearly expressed by Maciej Jan P.-B. who as a pupil at school in Sochaczew in the early 1950s and was an eyewitness to the destruction of the nearby cemetery. Its destruction began during the Second World War, when, on the orders of the Germans, some of the gravestones were used to pave the runway of the airport in Bielice. In a letter sent to the Jewish Historical Institute in 1999, Maciej Jan P.-B. wrote:

> The Jewish cemetery, being an unfenced open area, was overgrown with grass, and stood out from its surroundings due to a large number of well-preserved stone monuments, mainly sandstone, cracked in places, and in places damaged. I estimate that [...] there were then between 200 and 500 gravestones, quite well-preserved, mainly in that section adjoining the school's playground. This well-preserved section of the cemetery

---

164 AŻIH, Zbiór pamiętników Żydów ocalałych z Zagłady, ref. no. 277/302, Pamiętnik Kazimierza Cieślickiego, 8.

165 "Nasi sąsiedzi – Żydzi," 161.

166 AP Kielce, Sandomierz Branch, Akta gminy Szydłów, ref. no. 28/78, Gospodarka komunalna, 11.

constituted about a third of the entire area of the necropolis. On the remaining two-thirds stood only sporadic monuments. [...] The state of
affairs described here existed between June 1950 and spring 1952 [...].
I don't know who gave the signal to destroy the cemetery. Enough to say
that on the high bank of the Bzura River, where the first line of graves and
gravestones with inscriptions began, a few older boys stood struggling
with a gravestone. [...] When I asked what they were doing, they replied
that they were going to "send off the Jews." [...] This "send off" consisted
in breaking up or tearing out a gravestone and sending it spinning over
the edge of the riverbank. Such a heavy stone slab rolled at high speed
down the slope of the riverbank, bouncing over protrusions or gaps, to
land in the river's current far from shore. [...] Soon there were several dozen pairs of hands taking part in this extraordinary game. I believe
that between 20 and 30 monuments were destroyed in the early stages
of this destruction. The destruction of the cemetery was not the work of
just one group or one spring afternoon, as the cemetery was extensive
and contained too many gravestones for a "single act of destruction." In
the following days, new attempts were made. Some of the gravestones
turned out to be too close to the wall. In such cases, a group of three or
four boys, high school pupils, lifted a large stone already removed from
its grave site, using it to smash against another, still resistant to vandalism
and desecration. [...] I remember the cries: 'Look how the Kikes[167] fly',
while those 'Kikes' made enormous splashes in the water of the dirty,
swollen river.[168]

The destruction of the cemetery in Warsaw's Bródno district was the "work"
of the Germans during the war, and afterwards the work of the city authorities
and some local residents. The process of its destruction was observed by Tadeusz Rowicki, who lived nearby:

> In the spring of 1943, the Germans, using the labour of Jewish prison-
> ers, began to demolish the perimeter, the red brick wall surrounding the
> Jewish cemetery. This task lasted several months. The wall was pulled
> down, but all the monuments, as well as the pre-funeral building and the
> building where the Jewish cemetery's Polish caretaker lived remained
> intact. [...] Large-scale destruction of the cemetery began after the war.
> This was in 1952. I remember it clearly, because the fellow in charge of

---

167 Polish: "Żydki."
168 ŻIH, Monuments Documentation Department, Sochaczew files, M. J. P.-B., *Zagłada
cmentarza wyznania mojżeszowego w Sochaczewie*, manuscript, 1–5.

the group of labourers hired to dismantle the graves was a school friend of mine. The way it was carried out was the dismantled gravestones were thrown onto a horse-drawn platform and then transported to one area in the middle of the cemetery. They were left there. In time, most of those monuments were stolen. The local residents used them to make whetstones for sharpening knives or used the sandstone gravestones as building material. Later, a dense grove of pine trees was planted on the levelled grounds. [...]. In the mid-1970s, the work of destruction began to be conducted even more brutally. In many places, on the outskirts of the cemetery, human remains were dug up and taken to the municipal garbage dump."

A section of the cemetery was also taken up in connection with the widening of the street.[169]

As the Presidium of the Provincial Council in Kielce stated in 1958, most of the damage to the cemetery in Opatów took place in the years 1945–1948, and until 1955 there was "systematic looting of gravestones." In the autumn of 1958, the city was plastered with posters announcing an order issued by the Presidium of the Municipal Council in Opatów summoning all those "who had in any way acquired a gravestone from the Jewish cemetery" to return it to the warehouse used by the Presidium of the Municipal Council.[170]

In August 1944, Michał Leib Rudawski arrived back in his hometown of Przytoczno, where the cemetery had been ploughed up and partially occupied by neighbouring properties. The wife of Jan K., whose farm had annexed the largest area of the cemetery, explained it thus: "After the Jews [...] had been deported by the Germans, there was no one left to bury there. Well, it would have been a pity for the land to go to waste. What's wrong with that? If we hadn't done it, others would have taken it, or pigs would have grazed there."[171] On returning to their hometown, the Jews of Miechów who had survived the Shoah were also to find the cemetery ploughed up. The town authorities had leased a section containing no graves to one of the local farmers. The local Jewish Committee successfully applied for a ban to be issued on using the cemetery as arable land

---

169 Włodzimierz Susid, "Cmentarz żydowski na Bródnie," *Słowo Żydowskie*, June 2, 1995, 21.

170 AAN, Ministerstwo Gospodarki Komunalnej, ref. no. 9/32, Decyzje o zamknięciu cmentarzy i przeznaczeniu ich na inny cel w województwie kieleckim, 75–77.

171 Michał Rudawski, *Mój obcy kraj?* (Warszawa: Agencja Wydawnicza Tu, 1996), 162.

or a pasture for livestock. But despite this official ban, in December 1946 Committee activists complained that it was proving difficult to enforce.[172]

There were also cemeteries which survived the war in good condition but were destroyed later. One such case was a cemetery in Mokobody, a little shtetl not far from Siedlce where 290 Jews lived before the war. The Red Army dislodged the Germans from this region in July 1944. According to a report of the Mokobody's mayor sent in September 1944, a synagogue was destroyed but the cemetery was left intact. In December 1944, 24 survivors recreated the local religious community and appointed a rabbi. In March 1945, seven or eight Jews were killed, presumably by partisans. After this murder, other survivors left the village. In the next years the cemetery was destroyed. At the beginning of the 60. single remnants of graves were visible.[173]

The Jewish community in Sokoły owned two cemeteries. After the war, a clinic was built on one of them, and a sports field on the other. Until the 1950s, there were still gravestones in Sokoły. The gradual destruction of the cemetery was remembered by one of the residents, who in an interview with Julita Januszkiewicz for the daily paper *Kurier Poranny* said: "This cemetery was terribly neglected. But at least there was something left. Then the locals took the matzevahs somewhere. Even people from afar came for those stones. They were valuable, made of granite. They took them because they were needed for something. Cows were grazed there too."[174]

It was no different in Radziłów, one of the towns where, in 1941, some Poles conducted pogroms against their Jewish neighbours. Anna Bikont described the cemetery's destruction on the basis of conversations with the residents:

> 'They took the stone slabs to use as whetstones for sharpening axes'—
> says Stanisław S.—'I don't think there was anyone in Radziłów that
> didn't have a whetstone made of those cemetery stones. They cut down
> all the trees' [...] 'When people started to rebuild, they took away
> gravel in wheelbarrows and plastered their walls with Jews'—recounted
> Kazimierz Z. [...]—'And the new people's authorities took whatever was
> left, which the peasants hadn't stolen at night, and used it to build a road.

---

172 AŻIH, Centralny Komitet Żydów w Polsce, ref. no. 303/XVI/150, Kraków WKŻ, 10–7.

173 AP Siedlce, Starostwo Powiatowe w Siedlcach, ref. no 62/29/19, Gminy wyznania żydowskiego, 13, 39; Kwiek, Nie chcemy Żydów u siebie, 273-274.

174 "Boisko na cmentarzu – Sokoły," Julita Januszkiewicz, accessed June 30, 2020, https://poranny.pl/boisko-na-cmentarzu-sokoly/ar/5135140.

Stones from the barn are in the foundations of our house, everyone took one'—recalled Olszewski. 'After the war, kids were sent on the errand: "Go and get some sand from the graves," because the sand there was yellow, good sand for plastering. I also took sand from there. Once I found a human bone, I threw it the hell away, a friend threw a skull into the river and it floated.'[175]

The "whetstones" mentioned in the above statement were grinding discs made of gravestones. Due to the properties of sandstone, matzevahs were very often used as grinding discs after processing, which involved cutting a circle out of the stone slab, chiselling out a square hole in its centre and mounting it on an axle with a crank handle. Matzevahs were also used to make small sharpening stones for scythes and knives. This production was not only for personal use; in the 1940s and 1950s, grinding wheels made of matzevahs could be bought at country fairs.[176] In the last three decades, such grinding wheels have been discovered in many places in various parts of Poland, including: Augustów, Baranów, Błędów, Brok, Chojnów, Ciechanowiec, Dobrzyń nad Wisłą, Horodło, Izbica Kujawska, Jarocin, Kazimierz Dolny, Kock, Korycin, Krosno, Lublin, Milejczyce, Mordy, Nowy Dwór Gdański, Ostrów Mazowiecka, Otwock, Radoszyce, Radzyń Podlaski, Rybnik, Ryki, Skulsk, Stoczek Łukowski, Tarczyn, Tykocin, Wielopole Skrzyńskie, Zabłudów, and Złocieniec.

The scale on which this was practiced is attested to by an interview conducted by an employee of the Lublin Village Museum with a resident of a certain town in the Province of Lublin who, when asked about the material used by Jews to make gravestones, replied that it was a "whetstone."[177] It is worth quoting what Marianna Opałka from Chmielnik said in an interview. Describing the local cemetery in 2015, she said that the Jews "didn't have any monuments, they only had 'discs' with inscriptions." It is possible that the appearance of the cemetery (virtually stripped of its gravestones over the years) had faded from her memory, but she had more than once seen grinding discs made of matzevahs.[178]

---

175 Anna Bikont, "Mieli wódkę, broń i nienawiść," *Gazeta Wyborcza*, June 15, 2001.

176 Tomasz Wiśniewski, *Nieistniejące mniejsze cmentarze żydowskie. Rekonstrukcja Atlantydy* (Białystok: Kreator: 2009), 17.

177 Paweł Sygowski, "Cmentarze żydowskie Zamojszczyzny – stan badań, stan zachowania, uwaa gi konserwatorskie," in *Żydzi w Zamościu i na Zamojszczyźnie. Historia – kultura – literatura*, ed. Weronika Litwin, Monika Szabłowska-Zaremba, and Sławomir Jacek Żurek (Lublin: Towarzystwo Naukowe Katolickiego Uniwersytetu Lubelskiego, 2012), 287.

178 *"Nasi sąsiedzi –Żydzi,"* 273.

Figure 5.6. A grinding disc made from a matzevah in Brok, 2010.
Photo: Krzysztof Bielawski.

In Jedwabne, according to assurances by a resident who wished to remain anonymous, it was not the Germans who destroyed the cemetery. This was done by some farmers who used the matzevahs as building material: "They weren't Germans, they were our own people. They took the stones from the graves to build walls and pigsties. The perimeter was like that in our cemetery and was also demolished."[179]

A whole range of acts of destruction were listed in the letter the Presidium of the Municipal Council in Kielce sent to the Municipal Headquarters of the Civil Militia on September 15th 1964. In this letter, the Municipal and Housing Department called on the police to "provide special protection" for the Jewish cemetery, which "is subject to systematic destruction through the destruction of perimeter walls and gravestones, the grazing of cattle and chickens, destruction of foliage and activities of the local population that are unworthy of such a solemn place."[180]

---

179 An unrecorded interview with an anonymous resident of Jedwabne, conducted by Krzysztof Bielawski on July 10, 2008.

180 AP Kielce, Urząd Wojewódzki w Kielcach, ref. no. 1080/1067, Kielce – cmentarz żydowski na Pakoszu, 15. At this same time Kielce officials exchanged copious correspondence

In Nowy Wiśnicz, the local population used matzevahs as rubble to fill foundations, for building bridges and water culverts, to line a liquid manure tank and as material for secondary gravestones in the municipal cemetery.[181] In Tarnobrzeg, gravestones were used to create "sewage pits" on two private estates.[182] In Boćki, a wall of the Catholic cemetery was built of matzevahs. According to accounts repeated by the residents, this was done on the initiative of the local parish priest who supposedly wanted to "secure" the gravestones in this way. In Przedbórz, fragments of matzevahs were used as kerbstones around a roadside Catholic shrine.

Attesting to the various possibilities of using stone material from cemeteries is the case of a farm purchased in 2014 by Justyna Pietrzak-Toporek in the village of Grodzisko near Radoszyce. After its renovation began, she discovered gravestones in many places, as she recounted in an interview with Marek Kozubal from the *Rzeczpospolita* newspaper:

> The first two matzevahs we came across served as a step at the entrance to the building. Later it turned out that these stone slabs were almost everywhere: a horse's manger was made of them, the foundations of the barn were lined with them, and upon removing the plaster in the cellar, it turned out that they also lined the walls and edges of the building. The matzevahs were also on the road and in the garden.[183]

A significant role in the destruction of cemeteries was that played by the owners of stonemasonry workshops, who treated matzevahs as raw material for the creation of gravestones for the cemeteries of various faiths. The practice existed during the war and intensified following its end. Mordechaj Canin, a journalist for the Yiddish newspaper *Forverts*, who visited Poland in the years 1945–1947, wrote in one of his reports:

---

concerning plans to liquidate the cemetery, and the initial project to preserve part of it and commemorate it was suspended.

181 Szlezynger and Zawidzka, *Żydowski Wiśnicz*, 95–97.

182 AAN, Ministerstwo Gospodarki Komunalnej, ref. no. 9/10, Groby wojenne, korespondencja dotycząca cmentarzy żydowskich, 34.

183 "Macewy znalezione w żłobie dla konia," Marek Kozubal, accessed June 30, 2020, http://archiwum.rp.pl/artykul/1273416-Macewy-znalezione-w-zlobie-dla-konia.html?_= Rzeczpospolita-1273416?_=8.

> In Siedlce, for the first time during my trip to Poland, I encountered
> a wholesale trade in matzevahs. I had heard about individual cases be-
> fore, [...] but a whole transport of matzevahs arrived in Siedlce. [...]
> A stonemason and trader from Siedlce had bought a whole wagon load
> of Jewish matzevahs in Olsztyn.[184]

In Płock, a stonemason's workshop opened for business at the Jewish cemetery itself, next to the former pre-funeral building.[185] In 2013, Violetta Bachur of the Jewish Historical Institute found an obelisk with Hebrew inscriptions among dozens of old gravestones stored in an abandoned stonemason's workshop in Warsaw; the stone had previously stood over the grave of Mordechai, son of Arie, who died in 1882.

In recent years, new gravestones made from matzevahs have been discovered in the cemetery of Gołkowice (a 1963 grave in the Evangelical cemetery), Gorlice (1945 and 1975 graves in the Catholic cemetery), Harklowa (post-war gravestones of people who died in 1925, 1939 and 1943 in the Catholic cemetery), Nowy Sącz (a 1970s family tomb in the Communal cemetery), Przeworsk (a 1962 grave in the Communal cemetery), Supraśl (a 1962 grave in the Evangelical cemetery), Topczew (a 1944 grave in the Catholic cemetery), and Wadowice (gravestones of Red Army soldiers in the War Cemetery).

Reworked gravestones can also be found in Jewish cemeteries, including those in Bochnia, Bytom, Gliwice, Kalisz, Kraków, Płock, Wałbrzych, Warsaw, and Wrocław. In Warsaw, the reworking of matzevahs has been on a considerable scale. Not only new gravestones were made from them, but also steps between the various sections of the cemetery. Numerous such cases were revealed by Przemysław Isroel Szpilman, who in the years 2002–2020 was director of the Jewish cemetery on Warsaw's Okopowa Street. These involved gravestones from various periods. One of them was that of Josef O., exhumed in 1991 from an unmarked grave in a village near Warsaw. As it turned out, his gravestone was carved on the back of a 19th-century matzevah. Following intervention by the deceased's son, this stone was replaced with a new one.

Tearing gravestones out of the ground and taking them away often required the cooperation of several people, the use of cranes and some means of transport. In 1946, the Civil Militia and soldiers of the Internal Security Corps broke

---

184 Canin, *Przez ruiny i zgliszcza*, 194.
185 Nowak, "O żydowskich stelach nagrobnych w Płocku," 99.

Figure 5.7.
A matzevah used in the 1960s
for making a Catholic headstone
in Przeworsk, 2023.
Photo: Krzysztof Bielawski.

up a gang of 12 people, who were transporting marble monuments from the cemetery in Warsaw by lorry.[186] When in December 1968 thieves stole two granite slabs measuring 3.5 x 4 metres and weighing about 5 tons from the cemetery on Wrocław's Lotnicza Street, they cut down trees at the cemetery gates to gain entrance for their lorry.[187] Eugeniusz Dąbrowski from Krynek remembered lorries being used to transport stolen matzevahs.[188] In 1970, thieves used a Star crane and a Żubr lorry belonging to the Szczecin branch of the Gas Works Enterprise in Warsaw to remove monuments from a cemetery in Łódź.[189] In 1971, a man died in the cemetery in Opole, pinned down by one of the monuments while dismantling gravestones.[190]

Both unused and active cemeteries were devastated. Religious Congregations were unable to effectively prevent theft and acts of vandalism. In 1965, the Religious Association of the Judaic Faith intended to employ caretakers who were "in their prime" and dogs to guard the cemetery in Warsaw, which was "constantly being devastated."[191]

---

186 AM, "Nocna obława na hieny cmentarne. Likwidacja 12-osobowej bandy na cmentarzu żydowskim w Warszawie," *Express Wieczorny*, December 14, 1946.

187 AAN, Urząd do Spraw Wyznań, ref. no. 132/323, Obiekty judaizmu województwa wrocławskiego, 40.

188 "Krynki. Macewy żydowskie wywoziły tiry," Eugeniusz Dąbrowski, accessed June 30, 2020, https://www.youtube.com/watch?v=2Szcnb9Da0A&t=238s.

189 AIPN, Ministerstwo Spraw Wewnętrznych w Warszawie, ref. no. IPN BU 00231/205/6, Materiały dotyczące Leftwich – Lewkowitza Josepha i Morejno Wawa, 347.

190 Halina Łabęcka, Zbigniew Łabęcki, *Cmentarz żydowski w Opolu, ul. Poniatowskiego. Studium konserwatorskie rozszerzone*, manuscript (Opole: Halina Łabęcka, Zbigniew Łabęcki, 1987), 82.

191 AAN, Urząd do Spraw Wyznań, ref. no. 75/32, Związek Religijny Wyznania Mojżeszowego, 419.

It became common to see cemeteries used as pasture land. Cemeteries were also managed as arable land in, for instance, Aleksandrów Kujawski, Bełchatów, Brzostek, Bychawa, Czudec, Goworowo, Jabłonka Kościelna, Jarczów, Łaszczów, Osięciny, Pilzno, Pruchnik, Przytoczno, Pułtusk, Raszków, Stary Targ, Sierpc, Szreńsk, Tarczyn, Turobin, Wyszków and Zakroczym. This is often done unofficially, with no intervention on the part of the local administration. Such was the case, for example, in Pułtusk. In 1956, the cemetery's caretaker, Zofia Chrzanowska, informed the Socio-Cultural Society of Jews in Poland about the seizure of a section of the cemetery by Feliks P., who "illegally ploughed up part of the cemetery, without any permission from the authorities, with the intention of cultivating the entire area of the cemetery."[192] This method of exploitation involved not only the removal of gravestones and other above-ground elements that interfered with ploughing, but also the disturbance of human remains, which—in the case of graves dug in frozen ground or children's graves—were not always buried at the 1.5 metre depth required by the regulations. A good example is the cemetery in Lelów. According to interviews with the residents of that village, conducted in 2014–2015 by Agnieszka Gwiazdowicz from Warsaw University's Institute of Ethnology and Cultural Anthropology, fragments of gravestones and bones were dug up during ploughing in the cemetery: "When a field is cultivated, sometimes the odd piece is dug up and the owner of this field would always put these next to the willow tree that stood there." Another Lelów's resident said:

> There used to be a field there, and now there's a meadow, I still remember it as a field and there was one of us, dead and gone now, who dug up human remains [. . .], he dug up arm and leg bones.
> —What did he do with them?
> —Well, nothing, he just covered them up with earth.
> —And continued ploughing?
> —Yes.[193]

Today, what was once the new Jewish cemetery is an agricultural wasteland. One can occasionally still find small pieces of destroyed matzevahs on its surface.

---

192 AŻIH, Towarzystwo Społeczno-Kulturalne Żydów w Polsce, ref. no. 45/325, Towarzystwo Społeczno-Kulturalne Żydów w Polsce, 194.

193 Agnieszka Gwiazdowicz, "*Cmentarze żydowskie w Lelowie jako miejsca (nie)pamięci*" (BA diss., University of Warsaw, 2016), 42, 57.

Figure 5.8.
The pre-funeral house in Czarnków
was used as a poultry-house with
tombstones to build the stairs, 1989.
Photo: Tadeusz Baraniuk, collection
of the National Institute of Heritage.

In the 1980s, the "breeding of nutrias and chickens" was reported at the cemetery in Pruszków.[194] In Skierniewice, where a family garden was cultivated on the cemetery grounds, the residents of a nearby property began using the ohel of Tzadik Shimon Bornstein as a shed for storing garden tools.[195]

In 1973, Henryk K. from Zambrów was going to build a pigsty at a local cemetery. His application was probably rejected by the town authorities.[196]

In Bisztynek, Działdowo, Olsztyn, Płońsk, Sierpc, Sochaczew and Sokoły, local residents set up "informal" playing fields in the cemeteries.

As a result of the sale of cemetery plots by local authorities, but also the illegal seizure of land and its subsequent usucaption (that is, the title to it being gained by reason of its possession over a certain period of time), several dozen cemeteries were totally or partially built upon with single-family houses. Construction works on them and their further use usually took place without any supervision by conservators of monuments or Jewish organizations. On private properties, it is rare for cases where graves have been dug up to be disclosed. One example is the case of the cemetery in Osieczna, where in 1994 a cesspool was dug.[197] In 2014, the author of this book discovered that earthworks were being carried out at the Jewish cemetery in Wizna. Witold P., who became the

---

194 NID, J. Szczepański, *Karta cmentarza nr 10133* ([no place]: 1984).

195 Marcin Wodziński, *Groby cadyków w Polsce* (Wrocław: Towarzystwo Przyjaciół Polonistyki Wrocławskiej, 1998), 218.

196 AAN, Urząd do Spraw Wyznań, ref. no. 131/510, Związek Religijny Wyznania Mojżeszowego, 16–18.

197 Dariusz Czwojdrak, "Kłódki grobowe z cmentarza żydowskiego w Osiecznej," *Zeszyty Osieckie*, no. 17 (2009): 29.

owner of a section of the cemetery by usucaption, ordered it to be levelled and fish ponds to be dug. During a visit, numerous bones and broken up skeletons were discovered protruding from excavated graves.

Destruction of cemeteries also includes the plundering of graves. The search was for gold dental crowns and items that Shoah victims might have taken with them. The motivation behind this came from folk tales of people supposedly being buried together with "treasure" ("If a Jew dies, [...] they wash him, bleach him and bury him in a sitting position. They give him a bag of money and he keeps the sack").[198] In Warsaw, looters were additionally encouraged by the rumour of a golden brick allegedly lying somewhere in the ruins of the ghetto.

Mass graves were also plundered. Probably the perpetrators of these latter acts assumed that digging up the graves of many people would bring them more "spoils" for less work. In January 1948, unidentified perpetrators in Białystok "searching for gold teeth" twice dug up the grave in which the victims of the 1905 pogrom were buried.[199] On June 19th 1956, the caretaker of Warsaw's Okopowa Street cemetery revealed that a mass grave of people who had died or were killed in the ghetto had been plundered. The perpetrators dug down to a depth of about 2 metres and scattered the remains of the dead, their clothes and shoes. The Civil Militia prepared an ambush and reinforced patrols in the vicinity of the cemetery. In his correspondence with the Socio-Cultural Society of Jews in Poland, the Commander in Chief of the Civil Militia, General Ryszard Dobieszak noted that recently a number of cases of cemeteries being desecrated had been discovered in the country, including that of the Orthodox Church in Warsaw and a Jewish cemetery in Wrocław.[200]

"Hidden treasure" was also searched for in Wieruszów, where the practice was supposed to have ended in the 1950s.[201] In Myszyniec, the cemetery was an attraction both for children who found bones while playing there, and adults who took away sand mixed with bones in horse-drawn carts. One resident remembered that in the 1960s he found a skull on the road in front of the

---

198 Dionizjusz Czubala and Piotr Grochowski, *O tym nie wolno mówić... Zagłada Żydów w opowieściach wspomnieniowych ze zbiorów Dionizjusza Czubali* (Toruń: Wydawnictwo Naukowe Uniwersytetu Mikołaja Kopernika, 2019), 57.

199 *Biuletyn Żydowskiej Agencji Prasowej,* January 27, 1948.

200 AŻIH, Towarzystwo Społeczno-Kulturalne Żydów w Polsce, ref. no. 45/325, Towarzystwo Społeczno-Kulturalne Żydów w Polsce,, 46–45.

201 Grzegorz Szymański, "Batalia o wieruszowski cmentarz," *Słowo Żydowskie,* June 13, 1997, 4.

cemetery that had fallen out of a farm cart loaded with sand.[202] In Otwock, bones dug up in the Jewish cemetery were sold to medical students practicing in local hospitals and sanatoriums.[203] In Bolszewo near Wejherowo, local youths searched the graves until at least the 1970s. In her BA thesis, Nina Herzberg quoted two statements by witnesses: "The local youth" had "removed skulls from the graves. One of my friends made an ashtray out of such a skull." Another person tells how "the young people were looking for valuables, jewellery in those graves, apparently someone found something."[204] When in the mid-1960s the Jewish cemetery in Klimontów was earmarked for the construction of a school, according to a witness, "crowds came from all over to watch them dig in the cemetery. This is the effect that the 'Jewish gold!' rumour had on people."[205] In the second half of the 1980s, Monika Polit—today an assistant professor at Warsaw University—witnessed graves being dug up in a cemetery in Łódź and the sieving of the excavated soil.[206]

Thefts from cemeteries were part of a broader phenomenon of plundering Jewish property. Even during the war, following the extermination of the Jewish population, some of their former neighbours proceeded to appropriate property that had been left behind. The scale of the practice was enormous. Priest Tomasz Zadęcki from Klimontów wrote about the robberies committed in his parish: "After the Jews had gone, a group of so-called miners was formed. These people went around Jewish houses at night wielding pickaxes and iron crowbars [...] and knocked down walls, smashed stoves, dug in cellars and took out hidden Jewish wealth: money, fabrics, leather, etc."[207] This so-called plundering also flourished in post-war years and included the so-called Reclaimed Lands (German territory annexed to Poland after the Second World War). The cemeteries of various denominations fell prey to thieves, although it was certainly easier for them to prowl unattended Jewish and Protestant cemeteries. This is attested

---

202 An unrecorded interview between the author and an anonymous resident of Myszyniec, May 24, 2015.

203 An unrecorded interview between the author and an unnamed employee of the Otwock Regional Museum, August 10, 2008.

204 Nina Herzberg, "*Społeczność żydowska w Wejherowie i okolicach w ujęciu koncepcji miejsc pamięci*" (BA diss., University of Gdańsk, 2014), 31.

205 Radosław Januszewski, "Szkoła Tysiąclecia," *Rzeczpospolita* , October 27, 2001.

206 Correspondence with Dr. Monika Polit, January 27, 2020. The letter in Krzysztof Bielawski's possession.

207 Januszewski, "Szkoła Tysiąclecia."

to by a letter dated November 11th 1957, in which the Deputy Command-er-in-Chief of the Civil Militia Colonel F. Jóźwiak drew the attention of provin-cial militia commanders to recently observed acts of destruction and theft in "abandoned cemeteries." The following provinces saw a significant increase in this type of crime: Koszalin, Wrocław, Gdańsk, Poznań, Zielona Góra, Opole, Szczecin, and Olsztyn. Militia posts recorded numerous cases of theft of metal fences, gates and coffins, thefts of valuable gravestones and the desecration of corpses in search of valuables. The Civil Militia's headquarters ordered officers to intensify surveillance of abandoned cemeteries by for instance, more fre-quent patrolling, organizing ambushes, and monitoring transactions conducted in stonemasons' yards and jewellery shops.[208]

The looting of graves still occurs today. In recent years, the author of this book has come across fresh excavations in cemeteries, including those in Błonie, Sosnowiec, Starowola and Warsaw's Bródno district.

Littering in cemeteries has also been a serious problem. Illegal dumps were established in the cemeteries in Grodzisk Mazowiecki, Krosno, Krzywcza, Po-dole, Tarczyn, Starowola, Zaklików and many other towns. In the early 1980s, the Wrocław cemetery was littered by officers of the Motorized Civil Militia Re-serves who were quartered in a nearby dormitory and threw their empty bottles from the windows onto the gravestones.[209] In the case of Dzierzgoń, the follow-ing was entered under the heading "Existing threats" in its so-called Cemetery Card drawn up in 1985: "Destruction of the cemetery under heaps of garbage."[210] In Karczew, it was common practice to bury bones and offal left over from the slaughtering of animals. In 2002 volunteers from the "Olszówka" Association began cleaning up the cemetery in Krosno, removing several tons of rubbish.

In Karczew, the cutting down of trees growing in the cemetery contributed to the gradual transformation of the site, from a hill into a dune. The shifting sand proceeded to de-stabilize the gravestones and expose human bones.

Local populations also took advantage of those gravestones that had been used by the Germans for various purposes during the war. In Bychawa, residents took the matzevahs that had been used on the orders of the Germans to pave

---

208 AIPN, Ministerstwo Spraw Wewnętrznych w Warszawie, ref. no. IPN BU 1585/7150, Mniejszość żydowska – cmentarze wyznania mojżeszowego w Polsce, 1.

209 Correspondence with Renata Wilkoszewska-Krakowska of the Museum of Cemetery Art in Wrocław, February 18, 2019. The letter in Krzysztof Bielawski's possession.

210 NID, Jacek Gzowski, *Karta cmentarza nr 14164* ([no place]: 1985).

a street, and turned them into grinding discs.[211] In Mogielnica, the square in front of the former German gendarmerie that had been laid with matzevahs, served a dozen or so residents until the beginning of the 21st century. In Brańsk, Kazimierz Dolny, and Sobienie-Jeziory, the Germans requisitioned the monasteries and church buildings as their headquarters, and after 1945 monks and priests became the beneficiaries of these properties being lined with Jewish gravestones. When in 1984 a lapidarium was being established in the Jewish cemetery in Kazimierz Dolny, the monks refused to give up the gravestones.[212] Ultimately, the matzevahs were returned, although in 2010 fragments of gravestones with Hebrew inscriptions were still visible in the floor of the monastery's corridor and in a wall in front of the entrance. In Brańsk, the kerbstones in front of the presbytery were not dismantled until the beginning of the 1990s. Likewise in Sobienie-Jeziory, the priests were unwilling to solve a similar problem until 2003. When Father Wojciech Lemański suggested to the local parish priest that he remove the gravestones and transport them back to the cemetery, his reply was: "But what will I use to drive into my garage?"[213]

To this day, there is a secondary trade in gravestone rubble, obtained during street renovations and the demolition of houses. In 1998, on a farm in the village of Kolonia Dęba, the police discovered about 20 cubic metres of broken gravestones intended for the foundations of a residential house. Its owner claimed that he bought the rubble from a friend in Nowy Kazanów. Involved in the recovery of the gravestones was Teresa Sabat from the Kielce branch of the State Monuments Protection Service, who at the time stated that "in the villages you can buy matzevahs for half a litre of vodka."[214] A similar situation took place near Pińczów.[215] Around 2001, a resident of Żołynia Dolna built a dam using matzevahs probably bought from the company renovating the market square in Leżajsk.[216]

211 Robert Kuwałek and Marta Kubiszyn, "Miasteczko polsko-żydowskie na Lubelszczyźnie," in *Dziedzictwo kulturowe Żydów na Lubelszczyźnie. Materiały dla nauczycieli*, ed. Marta Kubiszyn, Grzegorz Żuk, and Monika Adamczyk-Garbowska (Lublin: Zakład Kultury i Historii Żydów UMCS, Ośrodek "Brama Grodzka – Teatr NN," 2003), 63.

212 Baksik, *Macewy codziennego użytku*, 21.

213 Wojciech Lemański, *Z krwi, kości i wiary. Wojciech Lemański w rozmowie z Anną Wacławik-Orpik* (Warszawa: Agora, 2013), 114.

214 Iwona Boratyn, "Nie te czasy na takie bajania," *Gazeta Wyborcza*, June 13–14, 1998.

215 Dariusz Rostkowski, "Warsztat nagrobkami wykładany," *Express Wieczorny*, May 28, 1999.

216 Beata Terczyńska, "Nagrobki w rzece," *Nowiny*, August 29, 2005.

Jewish cemeteries, increasingly overgrown with dense vegetation, constituting specific enclaves, often attracted underworld types and became the venues for various criminal acts. In the early years after the war, Warsaw's Okopowa Street cemetery was a favourite meeting place of prostitutes and their customers.[217] In 1974 the trial took place in Nowy Dwór Mazowiecki of a young fascist who, as part of his "activities," dug up a skull in the Jewish cemetery and destroyed it.[218] In view of the risk of being attacked and mugged, at the beginning of the 21st century, tourist guides have advised against visiting the cemetery in Warsaw's Bródno district, where an employee of the Jewish Historical Institute was once robbed. In 2008, several teenagers in Warka beat up a Hasid who wished to pray at the grave of tzadik Izrael Icchak Kalisz. In 2017, at the Jewish cemetery in Ożarów, the police discovered the corpse of a newborn baby wrapped in a plastic bag, abandoned by a mother subsequently found to be insane.[219]

Administrative buildings in cemeteries were also of considerable interest for thieves. In January 1992, the gatehouse to the cemetery at 49/51 Okopowa Street in Warsaw was badly damaged. The intruders smashed windows, destroyed the bars on the windows, tore out window frames, plundered the storeroom and then set it on fire, also smashing three gravestones. Numerous cases of burglaries have been reported involving buildings in a cemetery in Katowice. In 2018, the pre-funeral building in Kalisz was burgled.

Cemeteries became a venue for expressing antisemitism, neo-fascism and various xenophobic attitudes. This was probably the motivation of the perpetrator or perpetrators who in Ostrowiec Świętokrzyski in November 1945 destroyed the monument at the grave of three young women and a boy who had been murdered several months earlier following their return from a concentration camp.[220] In August 1946, a monument was blown up at the cemetery in

---

217 "Szkoła życia na cmentarzu," Maciej Piotrowski, accessed June 30, 2020, https://www.tygodnikprzeglad.pl/szkola-zycia-na-cmentarzu/.

218 AIPN, Akta spraw sądowych, ref. no. IPN BU 626/16, Akta w sprawie karnej Arkadiusza Mariana G.

219 "Co z matką noworodka znalezionego na cmentarzu?," Monika Miller, accessed June 30, 2020, http://www.radio.kielce.pl/post-73222.

220 *Biuletyn Żydowskiej Agencji Prasowej*, June 3, 1945; *Biuletyn Żydowskiej Agencji Prasowej*, November 12, 1945.

Figure 5.9. A broken tombstone on a symbolic grave of the Shoah victims in Kutno, 1946. Author unknown, collection of the Emanuel Ringelblum Jewish Historical Institute.

Biała Podlaska, unveiled on June 20th 1946 by the local Jewish Committee.[221] The fact that pyrotechnics were used may suggest that this action was carried out by members of the so-called independence underground. Following this event, Jews took to the streets. A rally was held during which Jews called on "all noble Polish residents of Biała Podlaska" to protest against the desecration of a kindred grave.[222]

In 1946, a similar event took place in Kutno, where Shoah survivors had placed a monument in the cemetery on a symbolic grave, in which ashes from the death camp in Chełmno on the Ner were laid. This matzevah, featuring an inscription in Hebrew and Polish that read: "To the eternal memory of Jews who now rest in a common grave, murdered by Nazi thugs. Your Jewish comrades honour your memory" was smashed just five days after its unveiling. As Efraim Wajkselfisz recalled, the Civil Militia claimed that the destruction was the work

---

221 Leon Pakman, "A binel zichronot," in *Sefer Biala Podlaska*, ed. Moses Joseph Feigenbaum (Tel Aviv: Kupat Gmilut Hesed a»sh kehilat Biala Podlaska, 1961), 463.

222 *Biuletyn Żydowskiej Agencji Prasowej*, August 28, 1946.

of Red Army soldiers, whereas an officer of a Red Army unit attributed it to Poles.[223] According to a report by Mordechaj Canin, the monument in Kutno was in fact devastated twice.[224]

The daubing of antisemitic slogans and symbols on gravestones, walls and cemetery buildings became a common occurrence. There are numerous examples of such behaviour in the archives. In 1961 in Warsaw, unidentified perpetrators desecrated the graves of Jewish soldiers of the Polish Army who died in September 1939, daubing their graves with swastikas and the slogans "Jude Raus."[225] Much more information about this type of occurrence is available thanks to research and the monitoring of antisemitism conducted on a broader scale since the 1990s. Swastikas, stars of David drawn hanging from gallows, inscriptions such as "Jude Raus," "Jews to the gas," "Jews get out," "Time to bomb Israel," "Soap from Jews," "There's no room for Jews here," "Heil Hitler," "Poland for Poles," "Rudolf Hess," and "SS" have been found in many cemeteries, including those in Augustów, Białystok, Bielsko-Biała, Brzesko, Brzeziny, Chełm, Cieszyn, Czeladź, Częstochowa, Gdańsk, Gorlice, Góra Kalwaria, Grójec, Jasło, Kalisz, Koło, Kołobrzeg, Kozienice, Kraków, Kutno, Kuźnica, Legnica, Leżajsk, Lublin, Łańcut, Łódź, Łomża, Łosice, Małogoszcz, Mielec, Mińsk Mazowiecki, Mszczonów, Myślenice, Nowy Sącz, Olsztyn, Oświęcim, Ożarów, Pasłęk, Płock, Przysucha, Radom, Radomsko, Radzyń Podlaski, Rajgród, Skwierzyna, Sobienie-Jeziory, Sopot, Starachowice, Staszów, Suwałki, Szczytno, Tarnów, Tomaszów Mazowiecki, Tuliszków, Tyczyn, Ulanów, Urzędów, Warka, Warsaw, Wasilków, Wieliczka, Wiślica, Wrocław (devastated on the eve of the opening of the renovated synagogue in 2010), Wysokie Mazowieckie, and Zduńska Wola. In the light of Alina Cała's research, such acts are particularly frequent during election campaigns, and since 1991 "most, if not all, existing monuments and active objects of Judaism have been damaged or desecrated with antisemitic inscriptions," including Jewish cemeteries.[226] Inscriptions of a satanic nature also appeared at the cemeteries in Mogielnica (2009), Mysłowice (2013), Olkusz (2015), Pyskowice (in or before 2008), Ulanów (before 2009), Warsaw

223 "In Liberated Kutno," Efraim Wajkselfisz, accessed June 30, 2020, https://www.jewishgen.org/yizkor/kutno/kut401.html.

224 Canin, *Przez ruiny i zgliszcza*, 155–156.

225 AIPN, Ministerstwo Spraw Wewnętrznych w Warszawie, ref. no. IPN BU 0296/134, vol. 1, Mniejszość żydowska w PRL, 319–343.

226 Cała, *Żyd – wróg odwieczny?*, 604–606.

(2012), and Zduńska Wola (date unknown). In Gliwice, Satanists set up a so-called black mass altar made from matzevahs.[227] Desecrators also used Christian themes: for example, in August 1993, a cross and the inscription "I.N.R.I." were painted on a monument to Shoah victims at the Tarnów cemetery; in the spring of 2015, "John Paul II" inscriptions were found on gravestones in Olkusz; in February 2019 in Wrocław's Lotnicza Street cemetery, an unidentified perpetrator painted "Jesus is king" on the cemetery wall, the inscription measuring a dozen or so metres in length. (After its removal by local volunteers, the inscription reappeared.)

Anti-Muslim and anti-immigrant sentiments have also been reported in recent years. At the twice-devastated cemetery in Sochaczew (in 2015 and 2018), swastikas, the image of Adolf Hitler, and the slogans "Shoah never happened" and "F[. . .] Jews" were found, along with: "Islam will dominate," "Allah bless Hitler," "Islamic state was here," and "ISIS," which were painted on the ohel of the Bornstein tzadiks and on monuments in memory of the Shoah[228]. The cases of cemetery destruction in 2018 in Dąbrowa Białostocka, Mysłowice, and Płock can probably be ascribed to an increase in social tensions of an antisemitic nature after the Polish Parliament introduced an amendment to the Act on the Institute of National Remembrance—the Commission for the Prosecution of Crimes against the Polish Nation.

A lack of surveillance and perimeter fencing invites various acts of profanation. In 1952, the Socio-Cultural Society of Jews in Poland, in its report on cemeteries in the Łódź Province, specifically in Tuszyn, reported: "Bathers from the nearby swimming pool use the cemetery as a kind of place to cool off."[229] Due to its location on the banks of the river Poprad, the cemetery in Piwniczna became an unofficial beach. In 1974, Bogdan Łopieński took a series of photos there, showing young people dressed in swimwear, sunbathing and playing

---

227 Walerjański, "Zatarty ślad – historia cmentarzy żydowskich w Gliwicach," 157.

228 In the 2015 parliamentary election campaigns, Polish right-wing parties built their popularity among other things on scaring the society with a potential influx of immigrants and refugees from Africa and the Middle East. In the following years this thread plus antisemitism were present in the media subordinated to the state authorities. It contributed to increasing xenophobic, nationalist, anti-Muslim and antisemitic sentiments. One of their indications were acts of vandalism in Sochaczew, where on December 14-15, 2015 a masked man painted patriotic, nationalist, antisemitic and quasi-Muslim slogans and symbols on cars, buildings, as well as at a Jewish cemetery. Similar case took place in the same cemetery in November 2018.

229 AAN, Urząd do Spraw Wyznań, ref. no. 13/377, Uporządkowanie cmentarza, 3.

Figure 5.10. The desecrated cemetery in Sochaczew, 2016. Photo: Krzysztof Bielawski.

ball among the matzevahs.[230] Sixteen years later, Stanisław Śmierciak wrote in a *Gazeta Krakowska* article on July 19, 1990:

> The Jewish cemetery on the river Poprad in Piwniczna is [...] desecrated. Some people use the gravestones as sun loungers. Others find them useful picnic tables on which a half-litre of vodka and bottles of beer can conveniently be placed. There are still others who in the evening and in the darkness of night turn the gravestones into love nests. Sometimes, one can hear until late at night, the drunken singing of people partying by a bonfire in the former cemetery.

In 2009, the cemetery in Mogielnica was a meeting place for drug users, who—as attested to by the traces they left behind—smoked marijuana in one of the ohels of the local tzadiks, and used another ohel as a latrine. The desecration of cemeteries also includes, as revealed in recent years, erotic photo sessions, with naked models being photographed in Łódź (2011) and Chęciny (2013). The photo session in Chęciny became particularly famous. In July 2013, Łukasz Sz., a photographer from Kielce who takes wedding pictures for a living, posted photos on Facebook showing the disrobed model Justyna J. at the Jewish cemetery in Chęciny. In one of them the girl, dressed in just shorts, with a large cross

---

230 Archiwum Ośrodka Karta, Kolekcja Bogdana Łopieńskiego, ref. no. OK 1600 0098 0001, OK 1600 0176 0003, OK 1600 0193 0001.

between her bare breasts, sits facing the photographer with her legs spread apart. In another photo, in a topless outfit, she leans against a matzevah and kisses the cross hanging around her neck. News about this event appeared in Polish and foreign media. Since July 25th 2013, photos from the session at the cemetery have been published on Łukasz Sz.'s private Facebook profile. Over the course of two weeks, the photographer's friends posted a dozen or so comments under the pictures, mainly regarding the technical aspects of the photos and the beauty of the model. The photographer took part in these discussions. However, when the media became interested in the matter, Łukasz Sz. suddenly began to claim that by taking erotic photos he meant to draw attention to the condition of Jewish cemeteries. It is worth adding that for his open air photo shoot, he chose a cemetery that is regularly tended by the Chęciny authorities.

Representatives of Jewish Communities in Poland strongly condemned the photographer from Kielce. The opinions of recognized artists have also appeared. Andrzej Borys, president of the Świętokrzyskie branch of the Association of Polish Artistic Photographers, described the photos by Łukasz Sz. as "lousy." Remarks by graphic artist and art theoretician Marek Sobczyk were of a similar vein. The case gained notoriety, but the proceedings initiated by the Kielce-East District Prosecutor's Office were discontinued. A statement published on the website of the public prosecutor's office in Kielce read:

> The decision was made to discontinue the investigation into the July 2013 desecration in Chęciny, in the Świętokrzyskie province, of the graves of unidentified individuals buried in the 17th-century Jewish cemetery by holding a photo session there with the participation of a half-naked model. The basis for this decision was the conclusion that the action in question did not involve any elements of a criminal offence. As part of the proceedings, the public prosecutor analyzed the legal aspect of the photographer's and model's conduct in terms of whether their actions were iconoclastic, aiming to disrespect the resting place of people of Jewish origin, or whether it was merely a controversial artistic undertaking. Following an analysis of all the evidence gathered in the case, the conclusion reached was that the photographer and the model did not intend to insult the people buried in the cemetery. Because their actions were accompanied by elements indicating a desire to achieve only an artistic goal, as demonstrated by the appropriate characterization of the model, the processing of the photos by their author, and the deliberate selection of a secluded place, so as not to expose outsiders to a view of a half-naked woman that perhaps might shock them. It is also

important that in none of the photos are there any gestures that would express contempt for deceased persons of Jewish origin. The legal and criminal assessment of the incident did not miss the fact that the creators of the photos recognized that they had elicited extreme aesthetic feelings, but it was established that these people did not intend to desecrate the burial place of people of the Jewish faith. In analyzing the facts of the case, the public prosecutor considered the cultural definitions of art and, through this prism, assessed the event, recognizing [. . .] that art may shock the viewer, may disrupt his entrenched and well-established sense of harmony and beauty, and impose the artist's perception of reality or artistic creation.

Shortly thereafter, the model Justyna J. sued a local newspaper for infringement of her personal rights in connection with its publication of an article about the session at the cemetery.

Roma feasts have repeatedly been held at the cemetery in Mikołów. A resident of the town, who wished to remain anonymous, wrote about it thus:

> A large family lived for years in the gravedigger's house, or rather cell. The father of the family was a Gypsy and several times he invited whole clans, arriving in their traditional wagons, with hundreds of people celebrating special events (weddings?) for days at a time. As children, nothing could stop us from going there and taking a peek, we were always welcomed and served with food baked on the fire, although we always shivered in fear, as we didn't understand the language and were well aware that this was all happening in a cemetery.[231]

In many cases, the perpetrators of the destruction were not detected. This was largely due to the secluded location of some of the cemeteries, the lack of surveillance and delays in the disclosure of vandalism and theft. It is possible that some events were not documented by law enforcement agencies or they failed to take appropriate steps to apprehend the perpetrators. A good example is the story of Lucjan Wilanowski, who twice found his mother's grave dug up in a Warsaw cemetery, but the Civil Militia refused to accept notification of this crime, because—as they explained—"it would spoil their statistics. They had

---

231 "Mikołów," Krzysztof Bielawski and Małgorzata Frąckowiak, accessed June 30, 2020, http://www.cmentarze-zydowskie.pl/mikolow.htm.

a bad record of detection results due to the Jewish cemetery, where people were constantly stealing something, and constantly smashing something."[232]

In at least a few cases, the very people employed in the cemeteries or there to guard the graves contributed to the destruction. In 1955, Alfred Borensztejn, in a letter to Polish Radio, complained about the grazing of animals in the cemetery in Płock: "Is it right that people are permitted to graze cows, chickens and ducks in cemeteries [. . .] and I, as the son of my parents, visiting their destroyed grave, must step over cow pats." The Department for Religious Affairs at the Presidium of the Provincial Council in Warsaw determined that the Płock branch of the Socio-Cultural Society of Jews in Poland was to blame for the situation, by allowing Stanisław Ch. to graze his animals in return for taking care of the gravestones. The officials banned the grazing of cattle in the cemetery.[233]

In 1959, Stanisław K., a former member of the Chevra Kadisha burial society in Kraków, reported on the activities of a certain K., who from 1948 was manager of the Jewish cemetery on Kraków's Miodowa Street, and allegedly sold gravestones to stonemasonry companies, including stonemason W. According to Stanisław K., the following persons assisted in the practice: cleaner woman Ł., her son Władysław Ł., "Julek—an old cemetery worker," and his son.[234]

In 1961, Marian J. and Jan Ł., employees of the Jewish cemetery in Warsaw, were among seven individuals suspected of painting ten swastikas and three inscriptions reading "Jude Raus" on the gravestones of Jewish soldiers killed in September 1939. Civil Militia officers interrogated the suspects and took handwriting samples from them, installed a telephone wiretap in the cemetery's administration building, and introduced a secret collaborator code-named "Wyga." Despite the extensive documentation of the proceedings now in the archives of the Institute of National Remembrance, no information is available concerning the results of the investigation.[235]

In 1961, the Civil Militia took an interest in one Franciszek K., caretaker of the Jewish cemetery in Łódź. He was suspected of desecrating graves for the

---

232 USC Shoah Foundation, Visual History Archive, ref. no. 6642, Lucjan Wilanowski's testimony.

233 AAN, Urząd do Spraw Wyznań, ref. no. 24/552, Sprawa dewastacji cmentarza w Płocku, 1–12.

234 AIPN, Ministerstwo Spraw Wewnętrznych w Warszawie, ref. no. IPN BU 1585/7150, Mniejszość żydowska – cmentarze wyznania mojżeszowego w Polsce, 44–46.

235 AIPN, Ministerstwo Spraw Wewnętrznych w Warszawie 1956–1990, ref. no. IPN BU 0296/134, vol. 1, Mniejszość żydowska w PRL, 319–343.

purpose of robbing them and the theft of gravestones, intending to alter and sell them.[236]

The trade in stolen gravestones involved the Warsaw cemetery at No. 49/51 Okopowa Street. At the end of 1956, the Congregation of the Judaic Faith in Warsaw made it a priority to "investigate and explain the taking of some gravestones for the building of new monuments."[237] The Civil Militia became interested in the case. Quite a lot of information about this practice was provided in the 1960s by one of the cemetery's employees, who was also a so-called secret informer collaborating with the Militia, codenamed "Wileński." On October 16th 1965, an officer of the Civil Militia, M. Karolak, in a report written on the basis of information provided by "Wileński" about the finding of two reworked marble slabs, noted:

> This is not an isolated case of G [...] and B [...] using old slabs to create new gravestones at the Jewish cemetery. [...] Such scams were also pulled off by previous Jewish cemetery employees—N [...] and J [...]. Should any member of the public visiting the cemetery discover that the gravestone on the grave of their relative or loved one is missing, the cemetery staff explain it away as the activity of 'cemetery hyenas' or marauding hooligans.

1965 saw the destruction of earlier burial sites—the grave for a distinguished activist in one of the Jewish organizations was dug "in a place where lay the remains of people buried much earlier than twenty years previously."

On October 21st 1967, "Wileński" sent the following report to the Civil Militia:

> The engineers K[...] and W[...] have designed the use of old gravestones for the perimeter wall of the Jewish cemetery in Warsaw. Due to the fact that among the graves to be demolished there are dead whose relatives or families are still alive, two cases of objection to the above matter have been noted. [...] Last Wednesday, F[...] and Ś[...] from Nowogrodzka

---

236 AIPN, Wojewódzki Urząd Spraw Wewnętrznych w Łodzi [1945] 1983–1990, ref. no. IPN Ld PF10/522 vol. 1, Meldunki sytuacyjne komendanta miejskiego MO ds. bezpieczeństwa w Łodzi, 102.

237 AAN, Urząd do Spraw Wyznań, ref. no. 131/503, Związek Religijny Wyznania Mojżeszowego, 259.

Street[238] arrived at the cemetery and despite the reservations of the labourers working there, ordered them to continue removing gravestones and put them aside for construction of the cemetery's perimeter.[239]

It cannot be ruled out that "Wileński" also profited from the trade in matzevahs. This can be attested to by the report of Captain J.S. from Division IV of Department III at the Ministry of Internal Affairs, concerning a visit by "Wileński" to the Headquarters of the Polish Scouting Association on February 11th 1969, during which he allegedly offered the scoutmasters a chance to participate in the sale of gravestones from the Jewish cemetery, with some of the proceeds to go to funding their activities, since "Wileński's" two sons belonged to that Association. Captain J. S. described the case as a "disgusting provocation."[240]

When in 1969, some 247 gravestones were damaged in the cemetery in Kraków, the authorities arrested three teenagers who confessed, but only to some of the damage. The Religious Affairs Department suspected that the destruction of the remaining monuments was the work of Władysław L. and Jerzy K.—tenants living in the cemetery's pre-funeral building. The Department's memorandum stated:

> The two of them solicit Jewish citizens visiting the cemetery in order to extort money from them for tending to and watching over the graves of deceased relatives. As it has recently been stated, those graves paid up and thus cared for by these individuals survived the destruction that took place on March 26-27th 1969. It is suspected that following the destruction caused by the 3 minors (who during the investigation confessed to damaging only 49 monuments), the two tenants, constantly in attendance in the cemetery, could most likely have been the perpetrators of the remaining destruction, in order to extort remuhneration from the families affected for repair of the graves. The aforementioned tenants are middle-aged pensioners, unemployed alcoholics.[241]

---

238 The offices of the TSKŻ (Socio-Cultural Society of Jews in Poland) were at No. 5 Nowogrodzka Street in Warsaw.

239 AIPN, Ministerstwo Spraw Wewnętrznych w Warszawie, ref. no. IPN BU 00170/429, Teczka pracy ps. "Wileński," 30–162.

240 AIPN, Ministerstwo Spraw Wewnętrznych w Warszawie, ref. no. IPN BU 00945/2713/J, [...], 23–24.

241 AAN, Urząd do Spraw Wyznań, ref. no. 131/517, Cmentarze żydowskie w Polsce – otwieranie, likwidacja remonty, 52–55.

In 1977, the Congregation of the Judaic Faith in Katowice accused the former caretaker of the local cemetery of devastating the caretaker's apartment and the pre-funeral building, which was caused by "installing a bathtub without our knowledge and draining the water from it through a hole in the floor directly into the basement, which resulted in damp walls, and the chopping up of a doorframe (during arguments or drunken orgies)." The caretaker's children were alleged to have treated the cemetery as a playground and written "various antisemitic slogans" on the gravestones.[242] In 1985, a court case was pending in Gliwice for the eviction of the janitor living in the pre-funeral building at No. 14 Poniatowskiego Street who, according to the Congregation of the Judaic Faith, had "instead of guarding the grounds [. . .], led to their systematic destruction."[243]

The State Archives in Katowice contain a certified copy of a letter dated 1983, in which Feliks Lipman, Chairman of the Congregation of the Judaic Faith in Katowice, asked the mayor of Mysłowice for permission to liquidate the cemetery:

> We draw your attention to the fact that the Jewish Cemetery in Mysłowice is completely devastated and unserviceable. We consider it our duty to completely liquidate the cemetery, and therefore ask for your consent to the transportation of the remaining gravestones to the warehouse of the Jewish Cemetery in Katowice, and also undertake to fully restore order on the site following the cemetery's closure.

Feliks Lipman undertook to carry out the work at his own expense and declared his intention to erect a monument to victims of the Shoah on the site of the liquidated cemetery.[244] It is not known what motivated such a surprising application.

In several cemeteries, some gravestones were found to have been buried, which led to the ground being disturbed and the matzevahs again being removed. In Drobin, following the intervention of Jewish emigrants living in the United States, the town authorities took apart a pavement that had been formed using matzevahs after the war. All these gravestones were then placed in a pit

---

242 AŻIH, Związek Religijny Wyznania Mojżeszowego w Polsce, ref. no. 360, no pagination.

243 AP Katowice, Urząd Wojewódzki w Katowicach, ref. no. 1/714, Cmentarze żydowskie, 37.

244 AP Katowice, Urząd Wojewódzki w Katowicach, ref. no. 1/714, Cmentarze żydowskie, 200.

dug in the cemetery, which was filled in and planted with bushes.[245] In 1997, during the construction of a lapidarium at the cemetery in Hrubieszów, 25 unused matzevahs were buried in a pit.[246] A similar event happened in Kcynia at the end of the nineties with the gravestones being transferred from in front of the "Orzeł" cinema to the local Jewish cemetery—three of them subsequently being used to commemorate the cemetery, while the remainder were buried. Jan Kurant prepared documentation of the matzevahs and submitted this to the town council.[247]

After 1989, as a result of political changes, the participation of private entrepreneurs in the process of cemetery destruction increased. Most often this involved the implementation of investment plans. In 1995, Jadwiga C. purchased a plot of land that included the Jewish cemetery in Ryn, previously owned by the "Las" Suwałki Forest Production Enterprise, planning to build a holiday resort there. Her application to the town authorities for permission to remove the gravestones was rejected. Four months later, Jadwiga C. sold the property to a company called Jocz. Shortly thereafter, its labourers removed the last seven matzevahs, dug up five graves and pulled down the cemetery's perimeter fence. According to the testimony of an employee of the company wishing to remain anonymous, the gravestones were taken to a rubbish dump.[248] The cemetery in Płońsk, covering an area of 3.3 hectares also fell prey to investors. In the years of the Polish People's Republic, a shop and a car service station were built on part of this cemetery. After 1990, a shopping mall was built on the cemetery. In 2013, the company City Star Ltd signed a perpetual lease agreement for the site of the former cemetery with the district manager in Płońsk. On February 24th 2016, the company dismantled and removed a set of monuments commemorating the cemetery and the local Jewish community.

In 2012, a private entrepreneur purchased part of the cemetery on Wrocław's Gwarna Street, where garages had been built in the years of the Polish People's Republic. These were dismantled between July 9th and August 9th 2013. At the

---

245 AAN, Urząd do Spraw Wyznań, ref. no. 132/306, Obiekty judaizmu województwa płockiego, 18.

246 Andrzej Trzciński, *Cmentarz żydowski w Hrubieszowie. Nagrobki niewykorzystane do pomnika-lapidarium i zakopane obok lapidarium*, manuscript (Lublin: Andrzej Trzciński, 1997).

247 Correspondence with Jan Kurant, December 2, 2007. The letter in Krzysztof Bielawski's possession.

248 Konrad Zbrożek, "Cmentarza już nie ma," *Gazeta Warmia i Mazur*, January 11, 1996.

same time, a fresh heap of earth mixed with human bones was discovered in the city. According to the assumptions of some residents, this soil could have come from the excavations underway on Gwarna Street. The new owner of the plot ordered archaeological research to be carried out. The work resulted in a report which found no trace of "grave [...] forms." The archaeologists issued an opinion that there was no need to conduct archaeological supervision during earthworks for the planned development of the site. In 2015, the investor sold the plot to Gwarna Wrocław Sp. z o.o., which intended to build a Best Western hotel on the site. In February 2017, during construction of the hotel, it turned out that on a plot measuring 18x38 metres, beneath the ground there were over one hundred boxes containing bones (probably moved to that place following exhumation connected with the decommissioning of the opposite side of the cemetery in the 1930s), along with two sarcophagi, skeletons and numerous individual bones and about thirty gravestones or their fragments.[249]

In 2017, another private businessman destroyed the cemetery in Maszewo. The neglected, overgrown cemetery plot was levelled using bulldozers. The work was carried out in connection with his investment activities.

In just the last decade, construction has been planned on several cemeteries: in Biłgoraj (a shopping mall, in 2016), Poznań (a multi-storey car park for the Poznań International Fair, in 2018), Przeworsk (a communications and commercial centre, in 2015), Siemiatycze (a mast for a mobile phone network, in 2013) and Swarzędz (a hotel, in 2017). As a result of protests by Jewish organizations and local social activists, these investments were ultimately not carried out.

Worth noting is the phenomenon of trading in items from Jewish cemeteries, treated as collectible Judaica and decorative elements. In Kazimierz Dolny, a fragment of a matzevah featuring a bas-relief of a lion and a tree was embedded in the wall of a single-family house, serving as a decoration for the building.[250] The owner of a property in Warsaw placed a matzevah brought from the Węgrów area as a decoration for his garden. At least several times, offers to buy matzevahs have been submitted to the E. Ringelblum Jewish Historical Institute. At a scrap yard in 2006, a certain antiquarian bought a cast-iron matzevah, previously

---

249 Kichler, "Agonia cmentarza, czyli rzecz o wrocławskim kirkucie," 36–38.

250 Monika Krajewska, *A Tribe of Stones. Jewish Cemeteries in Poland* (Warszawa: Polish Scientific Publishers Ltd, 1993), 12.

stolen from the cemetery in Krzepice.[251] That same year, a resident of Lubartów tried to sell about 20 matzevah fragments via Allegro, the most popular Polish online auction website. In 2010, an antiques dealer from Nurzec-Stacja offered a grinding wheel made from a matzevah. As it turned out, he had several other such stones on his property, purchased from residents of Podlasie. An online auction of another matzevah converted into a grinding wheel took place in 2015; this time the seller was a resident of the village of Kopytowa in Podkarpacie. Thanks to the involvement of social activists, all of these auctions were blocked. However, it is not known how many other, similar auctions have been carried out.

In 2012, an engraved copper plaque appeared on Allegro with a fragment of an inscription in Hebrew reading: "A woman is buried here, Ms. Chava Dvo[ra]." According to information obtained from the seller, "the plaque came from a scrap yard in a small town in the province of Podlasie" and was bought at a flea market. Following the author's intervention, this artefact was donated to the collection held by POLIN Museum of the History of Polish Jews.

5.5. Archeological Operations in Jewish Cemeteries

Since 1945, archaeological work has been carried out in at least several dozen Jewish cemeteries in Poland. These operations were undertaken by way of research into the medieval fortified settlements, on which those cemeteries had been later established, or as part of so-called rescue works, for example following a landslide on an escarpment in Wyszogród. The question of archaeological work in Jewish cemeteries reveals different attitudes among some archaeologists and historians on the one hand, and representatives of Jewish religious organizations on the other. In the opinion of the former, archaeological research can provide valuable information concerning the history of a cemetery and the history of the local Jewish community and its funeral customs. Majer Bałaban—a historian, but also a rabbi—wrote in 1929: "Our home-grown researchers fail to take into account the fact that the cemetery they have in front of them may not be the first in a given town and that they ought to closely examine where the former cemetery was located, and dig and look there." In the case of the oldest cemetery in Krakow's Kazimierz district, Bałaban suggested: "One should take

---

251 Michał Bojanowski, "Czy mury runą?," *Chidusz*, no. 2 (2019): 9.

a trowel and dig in this area, and then we would find out just who was buried there.[252]

Paweł Fijałkowski of the E. Ringelblum Jewish Historical Institute[253] also pointed out that "the greatest opportunity, although unfortunately one not taken advantage of" to increase our knowledge about the history of Jews in Poland is through archaeological research. The results of the research have been studies on the dating and organization of cemeteries, the method of conducting burials, the equipping of graves, and funeral customs in general. For the guardians of these monuments, archaeology provides an opportunity to unearth funerary monuments of significant historical and artistic value that have over time become submerged beneath ground level.

From the point of view of Halacha, invasive archaeological research, due to the violation of graves, the removal of bones and the objects that were deposited with the deceased, constitute acts of destruction and desecration. In 2022, the matter was comprehensively presented by Dariusz Rozmus in his book *Prawne i badawcze wyzwania archeologii żydowskiej* (The legal and research challenges of Jewish archaeology),[254] noting in the summary that the primacy of Jewish religious laws should be recognized and invasive research in Jewish cemeteries should be refrained from.

In 1946, employees of the Marie Curie-Skłodowska University's Department of Anthropology were engaged in securing human remains that had been scattered in Lublin's destroyed Jewish cemeteries. Following their conservation, the bones were handed over as scientific material to the Marie Curie-Skłodowska University. One of the finds was the skull of a seventy-year-old woman, recovered after cutting off the rest of the skeleton from the wall of a trench that had been dug during the Second World War in the eastern part of the cemetery on Kalinowszczyzna Street. Dissection of the skull revealed the presence of seven coins dating from the 11th, 17th and 18th centuries, attached to the parietal bone by means of hardened scalp with traces of hair.[255] Archaeologists returned to the

---

252 Bałaban, *Zabytki historyczne Żydów w Polsce*, 110–111.

253 Paweł Fijałkowski, "Obrządek pogrzebowy Żydów polskich w świetle badań archeologicznych. O potrzebie badań archeologicznych nad historią i kulturą Żydów w Polsce," *Biuletyn Żydowskiego Instytutu Historycznego w Polsce*, no. 3/151 (1989): 25.

254 Dariusz Rozmus, *Prawne i badawcze wyzwania archeologii żydowskiej* (Sosnowiec: Wyższa Szkoła Humanitas, 2022), 297.

255 Krystyna Modrzewska, "Czaszka z monetami z XVIII w. z Lublina-Kalinowszczyzny," *Wiadomości Archeologiczne* 22, no. 2 (1955): 214–215.

Lublin cemetery three more times: in 1968, 1974 and 1976, this time conducting invasive research aimed at finding relics of a fortified settlement dating from the early Middle Ages, above which Jews had buried their dead no later than the sixteenth century. In the first phase of this research, 38 graves were discovered, and 138 in the second phase, unearthing such relics as coffin nails, boards, padlocks, a ceramic fragment and coins.[256] This research led to the discovery of the remains of Slavic buildings from the tribal period, and wooden structures which were associated with the defensive fortifications of the settlement.

In the years 1949-1955, archaeologists attempting to unearth an eleventh century fortified settlement in Lutomiersk, discovered about 1200 graves in a cemetery that had been established on that site by the kahal (Jewish community) in the mid-eighteenth century. This was the largest archaeological study of a Jewish cemetery in Poland.[257]

In 1959, during conservation work in the Remuh synagogue and the adjacent cemetery, over 700 matzevahs and their fragments, the oldest of which dated to the second half of the sixteenth century, were unearthed under a layer of earth, rubble and turf.[258] These headstones were used to assemble a lapidarium, which today is one Krakow's main tourist attractions.

In 1959, archaeological research was carried out at the cemetery in Grodzisk Mazowiecki, where graves from the early Iron Age and the period of Roman influence had been discovered during the construction of outbuildings. So-called archaeological rescue operations at the cemetery in Wyszogród were carried out for the first time in 1963, after an approximately 20 metre wide stretch of the Vistula escarpment collapsed. Work continued in 1971 and 1973 with the exploration of 49 graves, in which skeletons, relics of boards for shoring up graves, ceramic fragments and padlocks were found.[259]

During archaeological operations in Brześć Kujawski, 200 skeletons of adults were discovered. In Dobrzyń nad Wisłą, work was carried out in the years 1971

---

256 Paweł Fijałkowski, "Obrządek pogrzebowy Żydów polskich w świetle badań archeologicznych," 26–28.

257 Paweł Fijałkowski, "Obrządek pogrzebowy Żydów polskich w świetle badań archeologicznych," 29.

258 Kazimierz Radwański, "Odkrycie renesansowych i barokowych nagrobków żydowskich na cmentarzu Remuh w Krakowie, *Biuletyn Krakowski* 2 (1960): 64.

259 Marek Piotrowski, "Próba rekonstrukcji obrządku pogrzebowego ludności żydowskiej na podstawie badań archeologicznych cmentarza w Wyszogrodzie," *Rocznik Mazowiecki* 9 (1987): 216–221.

and 1988-1991 in connection with a landslide of the Vistula's escarpment, on which a cemetery was located. The research, encompassing 35 graves, served as the basis for two anthropological studies. In the years 1988-1989, archaeologists unearthed 11 graves in Krasiczyn, in which they found bones, relics of wooden boards for shoring up graves and ceramic fragments, which were handed over to the National Museum of the Przemyśl Region. Invasive archaeological work was also carried out in other cemeteries that had been established on former early medieval hill forts and settlements: in Oborniki, Rogoźno and Śrem.[260]

In 2014, a search began for mass graves of prisoners of a branch of the German Nazi concentration camp Gross-Rosen at the Jewish cemetery in Kamienna Góra, whose destruction had left it with no headstones remaining. The aim of these operations was to determine the exact location of the graves, to identify the course of the exhumation of 1946 and conduct an anthropological study of the remains of the prisoners buried there. In 2015, 68 wells were drilled, after which three pits to a depth of up to 1.6 metres were dug. When in 2016 the Rabbinical Commission for Cemeteries learned about the dig, it demanded that no further work be conducted. Following intervention by Poland's Chief Rabbi Michael Schudrich and the Jewish Community in Wrocław, the Kamienna Góra town council in January 2017 promised that no further archaeological work would be carried out at the cemetery,[261] a decision that sparked antisemitic remarks in the right-wing media.

A growing threat to Jewish cemeteries is the increasingly popular phenomenon of amateur research conducted by so-called detectors, i.e. non-professional seekers of various artefacts using electronic metal detectors.

Not all invasive operations by archaeologists must lead to the destruction of graves and thus the violation of halachic principles (Jewish law and jurisprudence, based on the Talmud). Noteworthy is the work being conducted at the Jewish cemetery in Gniezno. All the above ground traces of its existence were destroyed during the Second World War and in later years. When in 2006 construction of an Emergency Rescue Centre at the District Headquarters of the State Fire Service in Gniezno began, bones appeared during the excavations. Due to the nature of the investment and the funds that had been raised, at the

---

260 Małgorzata Hajduk, "*Cmentarze żydowskie w badaniach archeologicznych. Podsumowanie dotychczasowego stanu badań*" (MA diss., University of Warsaw, 1993), 49, 73–80.

261 "Naczelny rabin w Kamiennej Górze," accessed June 30, 2020, http://www.kamiennagora. pl/pl/aktualnosci/naczelny-rabin-w-kamiennej-gorze.html.

request of the city authorities, Poland's Chief Rabbi Michael Schudrich agreed to the construction continuing, provided that the facility was so constructed as not to contribute to any further destruction of the graves. The task of archaeologists was to gradually expose layers of earth and precisely determine the location of burial sites, without violating them. This enabled the construction plan to be successively modified by relocating foundations and finally pouring them between the graves, without disturbing the human remains. The excavations were secured with concrete strip footings, and the excavated soil, possibly containing human ashes, was left on site as an integral part of the cemetery. The work was carried out in close cooperation with the Rabbinical Commission for Cemeteries.

In Węgrów, archaeological research caused further new building on the cemetery to be halted. In 2011, the owner of a business located within the boundary of the cemetery intended to erect a building for the needs of his business operations. The investor, after consulting the Rabbinical Commission for Cemeteries, ordered surveys of the area to be conducted using GPR, which failed to provide a clear answer as to the location of graves. The Commission then issued approval for archaeological research, which revealed human remains at a depth of 0.75–1 metre. Due to the requirements of the Rabbinical Commission for Cemeteries, exploration was limited to a level that would enable the presence of bones in the burial pit to be determined. The excavations were filled up, and the entrepreneur abandoned the investment after being refused a building permit.[262]

In Warsaw, at the request of the Cultural Heritage Foundation, archaeologists in 2020 began exploring the oldest part of the cemetery at 49/51 Okopowa Street. This work was carried out under the supervision of the Rabbinical Commission for Cemeteries and the State's Conservator of Monuments with the consent of the Jewish Religious Community in Warsaw, and was limited to removing a layer of earth investigating the effects of the decomposition of leaves. The result was the discovery of destroyed matzevahs, the frameworks of graves, a cobbled avenue, numerous empty food and medicine bottles dating from the second half of the nineteenth century and the first half of the

---

262 Wojciech Bis and Wiesław Więckowski, "Cmentarz żydowski w Węgrowie w świetle sondażowych badań archeologicznych," *Rocznik Liwski* 9 (2016–2017): 110–111; Correspondence with Marcin Natan Dudek-Lewin, March 18, 2020. The letter in Krzysztof Bielawski's possession.

twentieth century, and an unexploded shell from the Second World War. A year later, archaeological work began at a second Jewish cemetery in Warsaw—on St. Wincentego Street, during which a road overgrown since 1945 and the outlines of grave sections were unveiled. The Jewish community in Warsaw hopes that the research will make it possible to determine the location and thus commemorate the grave of Szmul Zbytkower—a merchant, banker and the cemetery's founder, who died in 1801.

Chapter 6

Destruction of Cemeteries as Perceived by the Jews

The desecration and destruction of cemeteries, forcing the Jewish population to participate in this practice, to walk on pavements made of matzevahs or—as in Plaszow—to live in cemeteries, were severe forms of repression. The cemetery was the burial place for family members, friends, respected rabbis and tzadiks, and other members of the community. For religious people it is a sacred place, but also ritually unclean. This is especially important for the Kohanim, who adhere to strict rules of ritual purity. Breaking up stone matzevahs, walls and buildings as well as operations related to their use (carrying, transporting, and installing them) was very hard physical work. Also important to bear in mind were cases of forcing Jewish labourers to excavate graves, digging up the remains of the dead and searching them for gold dental crowns or other valuables. These were therefore extremely traumatic experiences, causing emotional, moral, and physical suffering.

Frank Dobia (born Icek Jakub Dobraszklanka), along with other prisoners of the Hasag camp in Skarżysko-Kamienna, was forced to bolster the foundations of the school, which the Germans were converting into a hospital. Gravestones from the local cemetery were used for these works. In his 1996 account, Frank Dobia recounted: "We had no option. We felt terrible that we have to destroy our own cemeteries. There was nothing that we could do or refuse. If we refused, we would be shot." The prisoners were also tormented by a growing sense of hopelessness—they witnessed the killing of people and the destruction of their burial places.[1] Mordechai Friedel, who had to dig out bones from the oldest Jewish cemetery in his family town of Łask, was also scared and helpless: "They [the Germans] told us to bring shovels. They took us to the old cemetery to take all bones out of the cemetery. I remember, my shovel hit a bone. It scared

---

1   USC Shoah Foundation, Visual History Archive, ref. no. 20367, Frank Dobia's testimony.

me, I jumped out [sprang aside]. Right away I had a revolver almost on my head. A German [said]: "Back to clean [work]."[2]

As early as the first half of 1941, Rabbi Szymon Huberband claimed that the destruction of heritage materials—including cemeteries—had never before been undertaken on such a massive scale as following the outbreak of the war. He drew attention to the fact that the destruction of synagogues, cemeteries, religious utensils and manuscripts would make it impossible to study the history and culture of the Jews, and called for the creation of copies of gravestone inscriptions as soon as possible.[3] The authors of the June 1942 Oneg Shabbat Report, aware of the scale of the practice, perceived the destruction of cemeteries, even their being ploughed up, as a desire to "remove all traces of the Jews."[4] This practice ("annihilation of all traces of the Jews in this land") was viewed similarly by Henryk Makower, who was additionally outraged by the use of the Warsaw cemetery as an illegal point of transfer for food and animals.[5] In January 1943, an anonymous correspondent in *Wiadomości*—the underground newspaper and publishing house of the Coordination Commission of the Jewish National Committee and the Bund—wrote:

> Blow after blow that time and again have fallen and struck at the Jewish nation and torn away entire parts of the national body with a thoroughness that has spared not even the cornerstones of prayer houses and monuments in Jewish cemeteries, has led to us becoming increasingly accustomed to the idea of children in their cradles and women being mass murdered.

The Nazi forced labour camp in Plaszow, from 1944 a concentration camp, was established on the grounds of two Jewish cemeteries. In mid-1942, Jakub

---

2   USC Shoah Foundation, Visual History Archive, ref. no. 22839, Mordechai Friedel's testimony.

3   Szymon Huberband, "Memoriał w sprawie ratowania zabytków kultury żydowskiej," in *Archiwum Ringelbluma. Konspiracyjne Archiwum Getta Warszawy. Pisma rabina Szymona Huberbanda*, vol. 32, ed. Eleonora Bergman, Anna Ciałowicz (Warszawa: Żydowski Instytut Historyczny im. E. Ringelbluma, 2017), 254–257.

4   "06.1942, Warszawa-getto. Raport 'Oneg Szabat'. Gehenna Żydów polskich pod okupacją niemiecką" in *Archiwum Ringelbluma. Ludzie i prace "Oneg Szabat,"* vol. 11, ed. Szymon Morawski, Beata Jankowiak-Konik (Warszawa: Żydowski Instytut Historyczny im. E. Ringelbluma, 2013), 322.

5   Henryk Makower, *Pamiętnik z getta warszawskiego. Październik 1940 – styczeń 1943* (Wrocław: Ossolineum, 1987), 182–183.

Stendig was "horror struck" to discover that the Plaszow camp was to be located directly over cemetery plots. "This is really too much. After all, we cannot possibly live with the dead, among their graves in a cemetery" he commented on the German plans to build the camp.[6]

There were about 150,000 prisoners in Plaszow, mainly Jews from southern Poland, Slovakia and Hungary. Some of them were forced to dig up graves, tear up gravestones, and use them to line the camp's roads and paths. One of the prisoners at Plaszow was Irene Hirschfeld, who in 1995 recounted: "The stones were from the Jewish cemetery, the monuments. . . Part of Plaszow Concentration Camp was on the Jewish cemetery that existed before the war even. As a matter of fact, my mother and my father were buried in that cemetery." In the recording made over 50 years after her ordeal in the Plaszow camp, one can clearly feel the trauma of this witness, whose voice cracks while recounting the story of her life on the graves of her ancestors.[7] Likewise shocked by this experience was thirteen-year-old Erna Spagatner, whose father had been buried there just a year earlier, in February 1942. Shortly after the war, she wrote:

> They built barracks on the cemetery. They ploughed the earth with tractors, knocked down the monuments, and a camp was erected on those graves. Even the dead were not left in peace. I can't convey what I felt like walking on the very ground where my daddy was buried. The people who worked here in the barracks told us how they found bones everywhere. I didn't want to hear about it, I blocked my ears. I couldn't believe something like that was possible.[8]

Salomon Sultanik perceived walking on the graves, "perhaps the graves of my grandparents," as a "truly terrible situation."[9] The exhumation of human remains traumatized Lydia Steindler for the rest of her life. When she spoke about it in an interview in 1996 ("I remember the first time I dug up a skull, it just fell apart [from the skeleton]"), she covered her face with her hands.[10] The prisoner Zygmunt Müller smashed the matzevah of his mother Róża into pieces as small as

---

6   AŻIH, Relacje. Zeznania ocalałych, ref. no. 301/1792, Jakub Stendig's testimony, 3.

7   USC Shoah Foundation, Visual History Archive, ref. no. 7556, Irene Hirschfeld's testimony.

8   Esther Friedman, *Daleka droga do domu* (Kraków: Ambrozja, 1997), 54.

9   USC Shoah Foundation, Visual History Archive, ref. no. 27274, Solomon Sultanik's testimony.

10 USC Shoah Foundation, Visual History Archive, ref. no. 23991, Lydia Steindler's testimony.

possible, hoping that this would prevent her gravestone being used in construction works.[11]

Following the conversion of the pre-funeral building into a stable, Jakub Stendig viewed Amon Göth, the commandant of the Plaszow camp, as "a criminal executioner, because with one wave of his hand he desecrated the majesty of death and stabbed a dagger into Jewish hearts, wounding their most sacred feelings of worship for the dead." When the building was blown up in 1944, J. Stendig, forced to deploy the explosive charges, decided to hide in the barracks to avoid watching the explosion. In his deposition after the end of the war, he wrote:

> For the German swine, this was a wonderful spectacle; they revelled in the act of destroying the achievements of Jewish civilization and culture. For us it was a day similar to Tischa Beaw, when with sadness we recall the destruction of the temple. In our hearts, one more chamber was filled with a desire for vengeance.

He suffered pangs of guilt for his participation in the destruction of the building and these were not allayed by the fact that he was forced to do so:

> I don't know how history will judge us regarding our technical role [...]. Were I to take this matter to court, it would not be to seek absolution. I can't seek that, and perhaps will not find it, since I am fully aware that this act will weigh on my conscience for the rest of my life. I accuse myself of this crime, although a mitigating circumstance may be the fact that my wife and daughter were with me in the camp, and by refusing I would undoubtedly have been also sentencing them to death. [...] How could I risk three human lives as the cost of my avoiding any part in the demolition of the building?[12]

The necessity of living in a cemetery caused fear among the prisoners of the Plaszow camp; it was a form of humiliation and at the same time deprived them of any hope for survival. Mila Hornik expressed it thus in her account: "The first impression was terrible, all around us a cemetery, gravestones and a pre-funeral building [...]. We were terribly depressed, we told ourselves: there's no coming

---

11   Stella Müller-Madej, *Dziewczynka z Listy Schindlera*, ed. Aleksander Bartłomiej Skotnicki (Kraków: Wydawnictwo AA [no date]), 8.

12   AŻIH, Relacje. Zeznania ocalałych, ref. no. 301/1349, Jakub Stendig's testimony, 1, 7–8, 11.

back from a cemetery."[13] Erna Spagatner, quoted earlier, had a feeling of communing with death—at night she would sit on the doorstep of her barrack and secretly "converse" with her dead father.[14]

Izaak Grynbaum, who was hiding in the cemetery in Chęciny, was also shocked. Before the war, he claimed, he would never even have dared enter a cemetery at night. He was terrified at having to take gravestones from the dead to build himself a hideout.[15]

The planned but ultimately abandoned idea of constructing a crematorium in the cemetery on Miodowa Street in Kraków would have destroyed or exhumed about 400 graves, including those in the Kohen sectors. This intention caused a great stir among the board members of the pre-war Jewish community. Rabbis were consulted. Jakub Stendig described the atmosphere of the conference as follows:

> The mood was funereal, pale emaciated faces, trembling hands pulling at grey beards; how were they to find a way out of such a dire and exceptional situation. How to reconcile sanitary regulations with the requirements of the Talmud? Where were the bodies to be buried? How were they to be taken?[16]

Desecration of the graves of rabbis and tzadiks contributed to stories of a hagiographic nature being recounted. Their authors attributed miraculous properties to the remains of the deceased, such as the amazingly good condition of the bodies or their open eyes, with which the deceased were to stare at and deter those who thought to exhume them. It seems that in view of their helplessness, faced with this desecration of graves, such myths—apart from their hagiographic themes, particularly characteristic of Hasidic Judaism and folk religiosity—were aimed at "reversing" in a sense the negative message and introducing positive elements into it, while at the same time restoring reverence for the desecrated corpses.

Two such stories were recorded by Rabbi Szymon Huberband. During the destruction of the oldest cemetery in Drobin, the grave of Rabbi Chaim Chajkel

---

13 AŻIH, Relacje. Zeznania ocalałych, ref. no. 301/188, Mila Hornik's testimony, 6.

14 Friedman, *Daleka droga do domu*, 54.

15 Szynowłoga-Trokenheim, *Życie w grobowcu*, 66–67.

16 AŻIH, Archiwa Wojewódzkich Komisji Historycznych, ref. no. 303/XX/558, Kraków, WŻKH, Jakub Stendig, Cmentarz żydowski, ul. Miodowa 55, 50.

was dug up. Despite the passage of 70 years since his demise, his body was said to be "whole and intact." The Jews moved the body to another Jewish cemetery and reburied it.[17] In Ciechanów, a group of Jews, anticipating the Germans, who had decided to install a latrine in the ohel of Tzadik Awraham Landau, exhumed the body and buried it in one of the courtyards. They too claimed that "not only the body, but also the shroud and the boards on which the deceased was placed were perfectly preserved."[18] A similar account came from Płock where, due to the boggy ground, "some of the bones had rotted away," but the excavated skeleton of Rabbi Zysze Płocker was still in good condition.[19]

Three legends relate to the grave of Rabbi Moshe Isserles Remuh in a cemetery in Kraków. One tells of German officers who were supposed to dig up the grave on the anniversary of his death, but instead of the treasures they expected to discover there, they found the body of a famous rabbi who looked "like a living man, merely asleep." As a result, when the Germans "saw this, they took fright and ran away." In turn, the desecration of Remuh's grave was believed to have been foretold in the old Kehilla community chronicles as an event that would protect Jews from being expelled from Kraków.[20] According to another story, the Germans failed to destroy Remuh matzevah because the tree growing above it bent its branches and covered the gravestone so that it was impossible to find.[21]

In the case of Tzadik Elimelech of Leżajsk, two narratives collide. One is of a hagiographic nature, in which the issue of the body's condition reappears. The Tzaddik, removed from his grave, was supposed to look so menacing that the Polish workers and the German gendarmes guarding them all fled in terror, and soon after became ill and suffered greatly.[22] The second story, however, tells about the Tzadik's grave being dug up and the bones being thrown beneath

---

17 Huberband, "Zagłada bożnic, bejt ha-midraszy i cmentarzy," 224–225.

18 Szymon Huberband, "Dziennik 9–19.05.1942," 58.

19 Rafał Kowalski, *Raz jeszcze. Żydzi – Płock – Polska* (Płock: Muzeum Mazowieckie w Płocku, 2016), 120.

20 "Folklor," in *Archiwum Ringelbluma. Konspiracyjne Archiwum Getta Warszawy. Utwory literackie z getta warszawskiego*, vol. 26, ed. Agnieszka Żółkiewska, Marek Tuszewicki (Warszawa: Żydowski Instytut Historyczny im. E. Ringelbluma, 2017), 741.

21 Henryk Halkowski, *Żydowski Kraków. Legendy i ludzie* (Kraków – Budapest: Austeria, 2009), 50–51.

22 Beata Gładyś, "Rozwój chasydzkiego ośrodka pielgrzymkowego w Leżajsku," *Peregrinus Cracoviensis* 17, (2006): 189.

a tree. One of the local teenagers was said to have taken Elimelech's skull, jammed it on a stick and used it to scare passersby.[23]

It is hard to tell whether one should classify as manifestations of superstition or black humour the comments concerning the revenge of the dead, which were bandied about in the Łódź ghetto in December 1942, following a fire at the wooden products factory, which several months earlier had been built on the Wesoła Street cemetery. In his diary for December 23rd 1942, Józef Zelkowicz noted: "In the ghetto it is said that the dead have taken their revenge on the authorities. Instead of leaving them in peace, a timber yard was set up in the cemetery."[24]

It is estimated that about 300-350 thousand Polish Jews survived the Shoah, constituting about 10% of the pre-war community. Most of them found their way to territory belonging to the Soviet Union during the war. These were refugees from territories occupied by the Germans and residents of the eastern provinces of the Second Polish Republic, which after September 17th 1939 were conquered by the Red Army.[25] Those who returned to their home towns after the summer of 1944 were usually aware that most of their family members had not survived. No more than a dozen or several dozen Jews returned to those towns where Jewish communities had numbered several thousand or more before 1939. Some of them hoped to put their lives back together. In those towns, however, they often found their homes occupied by new tenants, and met with hostility and physical violence.[26] Their life in the ruins was dominated by feelings of emptiness, alienation and fear.

Those returning also directed their steps to the cemeteries, only to discover that the gravestones and graves of their family members had been desecrated and destroyed, and that the destruction was the work not only of the Germans, but also some Poles. Often mentioned in their accounts of that period is the issue of courtyards laid out with matzevahs. Some of these were located on properties seized by the Germans during the war, and later moved into by Poles

---

23 *"Święta Kuczek już nie będzie. Żydzi w Leżajsku,"* Juliusz Ulas Urbański, accessed June 30, 2020, http://ulas2.republika.pl/ulas.htm.

24 Józef Zelkowicz, *Notatki z getta łódzkiego 1941–1944* (Łódź: Wydawnictwo Uniwersytetu Łódzkiego, 2016), 304.

25 Stanisław Krajewski, *"Powojnie, od 1944 do dziś,"* in *POLIN. 1000 lat historii Żydów polskich,* ed. Barbara Kirshenblatt-Gimblet, Antoni Polonsky (Warszawa: Muzeum Historii Żydów Polskich POLIN, 2014), 358.

26 Cała, *Żyd – wróg odwieczny?,* 453–456.

who had no intention of demolishing pavements featuring Hebrew inscriptions. Other such yards were laid out by the Poles themselves, trusting that no one would ever come asking for the gravestones of their ancestors.

Such was the experience for example, of Rosa Goldstein, who survived the occupation in Poland and returned to Sochaczew at the end of January 1945:

> Our first steps were directed to the cemetery to attend the graves, since there was no longer anyone alive there. But what we saw was horrible [. . .]. Terrible desolation, broken monuments, devastated graves, while nearby houses had their backyards lined with marble slabs from the cemetery.[27]

Feigele Peltel (Vladka Meed) was unsuccessfully looking for her father's grave in the Warsaw cemetery. Wherever she turned, there were overturned tombstones, desacrated graves and scattered skulls. Feigele Peltel wrote in her book: "Was one of these desectated skulls that of my father? How would I ever know? Nothing. Nothing was left me of my past, [. . .] not even my father's grave."[28]

In the spring of 1945, Aleksander Wajselfisz, on furlough from the army, found the cemetery in Radom being used as grazing land. His first instinct was to shoot the cows. A sense of being surrounded by hostility must have been felt by the people featured in five photographs taken in the same cemetery and included in Łukasz Krzyżanowski's book, *Dom, którego nie było. Powroty ocalałych do powojennego miasta* (The house that wasn't there. The return of survivors to their home towns after the war). The people immortalized in the photos are standing over the shattered gravestone of Ludwik Gutsztadt, shot in his own apartment on June 19th 1945. According to the handwritten description, two other photographs depict a group standing over the grave of "victims of the post-war pogrom in Radom."[29] At that time, the cemetery was visited by Serka Cygielman, who after the war made a long journey from the German concentration camp

---

27 ŻIH, Monuments Documentation Department, Sochaczew Files, Rosa Goldstein's letter to Jan Jagielski.

28 Vladka Meed, *On both sides of the wall: memoirs from the Warsaw ghetto* (New York: Schocken Books Inc, 1999), 262–263.

29 Łukasz Krzyżanowski, *Dom, którego nie było. Powroty ocalałych do powojennego miasta* (Wołowiec: Wydawnictwo Czarne, 2016), 91, 97– 98. In 1945, several murders of Jews took place in Radom, as a result of which no less than seven people lost their lives. See: *Biuletyn Żydowskiej Agencji Prasowej* August 23, 1945 and November 12, 1945.

in Bomlitz to Radom. What made her decide to emigrate to Germany was this visit to the cemetery where, instead of her father's matzevah, the 24-year-old saw cows and pigs grazing and the grave of five Jews killed after the war.[30]

In the summer of 1945, Jekutiel Cwilich barely recognized the cemeteries in Zamość. The sight of the oldest cemetery reminded him of a "shaved head." He only recognized the second Zamość cemetery, where the gravestones had also been removed and the fence pulled down, mainly thanks to the preserved pre-funeral building, which was now inhabited by a Polish gravedigger. He also found the graves of Jews murdered after the Eastern Front had passed through the area.[31]

Szmul Niciński came from Łódź back to his hometown of Złoczew with the intention of visiting his mother's grave. Walking through the town, he saw a street paved with matzevahs. On reaching the cemetery, he discovered not only excavated graves; it turned out that the resting place of his relatives was being used by some residents of the town to bury dead dogs and horses.[32]

Leo Engel arrived in Jaworzno in 1945. After visiting his family home, now occupied by Poles, he decided to go to the cemetery. There he found the ransacked grave of his grandfather, people searching for gold teeth, and human bones lying scattered on the ground. Years later, he described the condition of the cemetery as "one more Holocaust."[33] In turn, Mojżesz Jakubowicz in 1946 came across a pavement made of matzevahs laid by the Germans in front of his friends' house in Nowy Sącz. Among them he found his great-grandfather's gravestone, and felt "as if he was walking on hot coals."[34]

Feelings of bitterness, grief, emotional breakdown, hatred, anger, lust for revenge, sadness and a desire to flee not only from the town, but also from

---

30 USC Shoah Foundation, Visual History Archive, ref. no. 28548, Shirley Zaidman's (Serka Cygielman's) testimony.

31 Monika Adamczyk-Garbowska, "'Pan/Pani żyje?'. Zamość po Zagładzie w wybranych wspomnieniach, relacjach i reportażach z języku jidysz," in *Żydzi w Zamościu i na Zamojszczyźnie. Historia – kultura – literatura*, ed. Weronika Litwin, Monika Szabłowska-Zaremba, and Sławomir Jacek Żurek (Lublin: Towarzystwo Naukowe Katolickiego Uniwersytetu Lubelskiego, 2012), 331.

32 A. Jachimek, "Geshendet oych nochn toyt," in *Sefer Zlochev*, ed. Yaakov Freund (Tel Aviv: Ha-Vaad ha-Tsiburi Shelyad Irgun Yotsei Zlotsev ba-Arets uva-Tefutsot, 1971), 408.

33 USC Shoah Foundation, Visual History Archive, ref. no. 6655, Leo Engel's testimony.

34 USC Shoah Foundation, Visual History Archive, ref. no. 29827, Mojżesz Jakubowicz's testimony.

Poland, were mentioned in an extensive account given by Leibe Fershtenberg. In April 1946 Fershtenberg arrived in Sochaczew for the first time in seven years and walking "through the ruins" also arrived at the town's devastated cemetery:

> An image appears before my eyes that has remained in my memory forever after and will always arouse anger and hatred for those who desecrated the graves of so many generations of Sochaczew Jews. I see before me a grassy field, no traces of graves, no matzevahs, not a single brick from the ohels of the great tzadiks of Sochaczew, but this place is not desolate, empty... On the contrary, it is loud and cheerful, horses are gambolling, cows and goats are grazing, desecrating the sacred soil in which the bones of our beloved rest.

This bitterness was heightened by the sight of the gravestone of Pinchas Weinberg—husband of the previously quoted Rosa Goldstein, the post-war deputy mayor of Sochaczew and the chairman of the local Jewish Committee, murdered by unidentified perpetrators on May 20th 1945. Following his murder, most of the Jews who survived the Shoah left Sochaczew.[35] In fact, according to iconographic material and witness' accounts stored at the E. Ringelblum Jewish Historical Institute, at that time there were still many fragments of smashed gravestones in the cemetery. Those would disappear over the years. Certainly, however, the pre-war image of a large cemetery where at least several thousand people had been buried since the 17th century, compared to this view of a pasture filled with broken matzevahs, would have been associated by Lejbel Fersztenberg with emptiness.

The journalist Mordechaj Canin was also to experience a shock. Following a visit to Międzyrzec Podlaski in 1947, he wrote:

> All the villages around were full of Jewish gravestones: in stables, barns, and in the farmyards of peasants. They were literally underfoot. [...]. Go to the yard where the tzadik from Biała used to live, maybe you'll recognize your mother's or father's matzevah there, maybe you'll even read the names of your grandparents!"

---

35 Leib Fershtenberg, "Oyf di hurbus," in *Pinkas Sokhatshev*, ed. Avraham Shmuel Shtein and Gabriel Weissman (Jerusalem: Irgun Yotsei Sokhatshov be-Israel: 1962), 552-553.

On the other hand, in Białystok's ghetto cemetery, Canin found "grazing goats and pigs roaming over the graves of our heroes and martyrs," and in Lublin, a shepherd whittling a human bone into a handle for his knife.[36]

The condition of the cemeteries, awareness of their destruction being the work of some of their Polish neighbours, and the difficulties in recovering gravestones, caused survivors severe psychological pain. It was one of the factors that led to emigration from Poland—a country that for many now symbolized a cemetery for millions of Jews from Poland and other European countries. The fate of Jewish cemeteries inflicted a permanent wound for the survivors and the relatives and descendants of Polish Jews living in the Diaspora. Evidence of this can be seen in an excerpt from the introduction to the *Yizkor Book of Kurov*, published ten years after the war. In this town, the gravestones from two cemeteries were used on the orders of the Germans to pave the roads,[37] and by Polish farmers for various practical purposes. On the first pages of this book, Moshe Grossman wrote:

> Not only were our nearest and dearest murdered, cut to pieces and de-stroyed, but their graves were also swept away. Those who were shot, gassed, burnt and violated—they have no graves. In Kurov, the graveyard of our forefathers was also destroyed. For long centuries, they had passed away and been brought for burial; until the year 1939 and the advent of Hitler. But the Christians of Kurov and the surrounding countryside took the tombstones of the Jewish cemetery and used them as grind-stones or as lintels and doorsteps for their homes. They ploughed up the bones that lay in the graves and mixed them with the soil; and on the site of the graveyards they sowed wheat and oats; and there they planted po-tatoes. The graves and tombs of the ten preceding generations were torn out by their roots and reduced to nothing. And all those of our brethren who were tortured and tormented by the Germans, with the aid of Poles and Ukrainians, now lack that place of rest which is the ultimate borne of all mortals. Even their bones were ground up and used as manure, in a last shameful and total annihilation.[38]

---

36 Canin, *Przez ruiny i zgliszcza*, 75, 180, 258.

37 Adam Kopciowski, Marta Kubiszyn, Andrzej Trzciński, and Marzena Zawanowska, *Śladami Żydów. Lubelszczyzna* (Lublin: Stowarzyszenie Panorama Kultur, 2011), 221.

38 Moshe Grossman, "A Burial Place and a Memorial," in *Yizkor-Buch Kurov. Sefer Yizkor. Matzevot zikaron Laayaratenu Kurov*, ed. Moshe Grossman (Tel Aviv: Irgun yotsei Kurov be-Israel, 1955), no pagination.

News about the condition of the cemeteries reached Jewish emigrants and their compatriot associations living thousands of miles from Poland. In the years that Poland was a People's Republic, visiting the country was a difficult undertaking for most of them, restrained by so many odious memories, including the image of Poland as an antisemitic country, but also the fear of travelling to a communist state, difficulties in obtaining visas, and the costs of travel. Some of them undertook to fence off and tidy up their cemeteries or transferred funds to Poland for such work to be carried out. Many tried to intervene by sending letters to the authorities, various organizations and the media.

In late 1957, six rabbis from the United States sent letters to Warsaw, to the Socio-Cultural Society of Jews in Poland regarding the cemetery on Lublin's Sienna Street. One of them was the rabbi of the Lublin compatriots association in New York, Wadia Ber Farbiarz, who wrote:

> Presently, hyenas devoid of any human conscience have made this cemetery a subject of trade. The cemetery where so many bones of ancestors and relatives, fathers, brothers, sisters and children are buried—has been leased to a gardener who is desecrating the remains of our loved ones, ploughing them up and throwing them away. It has come to our notice that this gardener is even intending to start building a house on this cemetery. This is unheard of in the history of humanity, and the Jewish Code under the name Yoreh De'ah, Chapter 368, paragraph 1 clearly states: 'It is forbidden to desecrate a cemetery by using it for one's natural needs, or to eat there or keep certain accounts. Nor is it permitted to graze cattle on it, direct waterways through it, walk from one end to the other (using the cemetery as a shortcut) mow the grass for hay, or dig up the soil for one's own use.' [. . .] We kindly request you oust this gardener immediately and establish some kind of custodial care for this cemetery, which is an old cultural monument of Lublin.[39]

The administrative authorities were also approached for help by Rabbi Izaak Jedydia Frenkel of Tel Aviv, who in April 1963 on a trip to Poland to commemorate the 20th anniversary of the Warsaw Ghetto Uprising, visited Łęczyca. There he found a devastated cemetery—scattered bones and farm wagons being driven over them. In a letter sent to the Chairman of the town council, the rabbi asked for the construction of a fence, promising to cover the costs. The reply of the local authorities was negative, however, because the town planning had

---

39   AŻIH, TSKŻ, ref. no. 325/217, TSKŻ w Lublinie, no pagination.

designated the cemetery as a future green area and a new street. Faced with this situation, the rabbi attempted to intervene at the government level by writing directly to Prime Minister Józef Cyrankiewicz. The rabbi was not only a diplomat, but also a determined operator. In his letter he wrote:

> In my heart there are deep feelings of good will to Poland and I have therefore decided to ask you kind sir, to intervene. I have not yet informed my compatriots, not only in Israel but all over the world about the above request. If this matter comes to light and is reported in the world press, it will undoubtedly shock public opinion [...]. Liquidation of this cemetery, which is located outside the town limits, is probably not a necessity in life [...]. Is it possible that after the complete extermination of the Jews, the local inhabitants are still disturbed by the existence of Jewish remains in the cemetery, or is this an act by individuals who still live with memories and under the influence of the Nazi occupation?[40]

The rabbi's efforts proved ineffective—today there is a housing estate on the site of the cemetery. There is not even a modest commemorative plaque marking the spot, the installation of which was suggested in a letter to rabbi Frenkel by the Chairman of the Municipal Council in Łęczyca, Wiesław Pawłowski.

Compatriot associations also undertook to intervene. In 1993, the World Association of Sochaczew Jews in Israel was notified that one of the town's residents had dismantled a section of a recently erected cemetery fence and that garbage containers had been placed in the cemetery. In a letter dated August 4th 1993, members of the Association's Management Board—Szlomo Frydman, Josef Grundwag and Lejb Fersztenberg—appealed to the mayor to demand the residents repair the fence and remove the garbage container.[41]

The disastrous condition of Jewish cemeteries and their progressive destruction was a frequent topic of the so-called Yizkor Books (commemorative books) published by Shoah survivors and articles in the foreign press. Photos of overturned matzevahs, bones in excavated graves, and animals grazing in

---

40 AIPN, Ministerstwo Spraw Wewnętrznych w Warszawie, ref. no. IPN BU 1585/832, Cmentarz żydowski w Łęczycy, 6.

41 ŻIH, Monuments Documentation Department, Sochaczew files, Letter from the World Association of Sochaczew Jews in Israel, August 4, 1993, no pagination.

cemeteries were an important feature of the album with the meaningful title *Polish Jews: The Final Chapter*, published in the United States in 1977.[42]

The closing of cemeteries by the administrative authorities meant that Jews were forced to bury their dead in communal cemeteries or those of other denominations, or else transport the bodies to the nearest—often distant—cemeteries run by the Congregation of the Judaic Faith. In Częstochowa, due to plans to build a steel mill, access to the cemetery was restricted in the mid-1960s. In the case of the last people to be buried there—Dawid Albert and Lena Milowarf who died in 1970—at least until January 1978, their families could not obtain permission to install headstones. Closure of the Jewish cemetery forced local Jews to use the Kule Christian cemetery (at that time there was no communal cemetery in Częstochowa). Between 1971 and 1977, seven such funerals were held there.[43]

The nearby presence of Jewish graves in communal cemeteries could cause conflicts. This was the case in Żary where, as a result of the municipal cemetery being expanded, the Jewish cemetery became one of its sectors. In 1957 the Presidium of the Provincial Council in Zielona Góra reported the "hooligan antics of Catholics" and "frequent insults and offensive language used against Jews and dead Jews being cursed."[44]

In Tarnów, the threat of vandalism led to the cessation of burials being held in the depths of the cemetery. A new burial sector was opened closer to the cemetery gates, using an as yet unoccupied avenue.[45] In other places, some families were afraid to bury their dead in Jewish cemeteries, or even exhumed the remains of their relatives. The necessity of such exhumation caused family members psychological pain. In 1958, the body of Rabbi Meir Szapira was moved from Lublin to a cemetery in Jerusalem. In 1964, the same happened with the graves of the Bernsteins, Naftali Herz and Izrael Akiba, who had been

---

42 Earl Vinecour and Chuck Fishman, *Polish Jews: the final chapter* (New York: New York University Press, 1977).

43 Paszkowski, *Cmentarz żydowski w Częstochowie*, 9; AAN, Urząd do Spraw Wyznań, ref. no. 132/283, Obiektu judaizmu woj. częstochowskiego, 11–12.

44 AAN, Urząd do Spraw Wyznań, ref. no. 25/579, Profanowanie cmentarza żydowskiego – Świdnica i Żary, 23–27.

45 Adam Bartosz, *Cmentarz żydowski w Tarnowie. Przewodnik* (Tarnów: Komitet Opieki nad Zabytkami Kultury Żydowskiej w Tarnowie, 2019), 36–37.

buried in Tarnów.[46] Several exhumations were also carried out in Strzegom, the last one probably taking place in 1992.[47] In Sopot in 1963 and 1976 the bodies of Frejdel Skibielska and Aron Beresin were moved to the municipal cemetery.[48] In Częstochowa, in 1971, at the request of the Rebbetzin Alte Fejga Teitelbaum of the Satmar Hassidic dynasty, the Office for the Care of the Graves of Foreigners exhumed the remains of Tzadik Avidgor Szpiro and his family members, Nechuma and Rywka Matel Szpiro, who were finally laid to rest in New Jersey. That same year, in a secret report by the Civil Militia in Częstochowa, there was mention of an entry visa being refused a United States citizen named Krępska, who intended to exhume the body of her father Jakub Rozensztejn.[49] In the 1970s, several exhumations took place in Kłodzko, with the remains being transferred to the Jewish cemetery in Berlin and to the municipal cemetery in Wrocław.[50] In 1979, the remains of Tzvi Henoch Ha-Kohen Levin, the rabbi of Będzin who was buried in Czeladź, were transferred to a cemetery in Jerusalem. In 2003, an exhumation was carried out in Łomża. The cases listed above are only a small part of all exhumations carried out.

Fear of graves being destroyed accompanied those people forced to emigrate after the antisemitic campaing in 1968. One such situation was described in 2012 by Róża Król from the Socio-Cultural Society of Jews in Poland while conducting a guided tour of the Central Cemetery in Szczecin for employees of the Polin Museum of the History of Polish Jews:

> This gravestone belongs to friends of mine from Israel. They were leaving for Israel, were already packed, when their father died. He suffered a heart attack from all of this hostility, and the antisemitic campaign at the time was such that they buried him in a Polish cemetery because they were afraid that the Jewish cemetery would be destroyed.[51]

---

46 Leszek Hońdo, *Cmentarz żydowski w Tarnowie* (Kraków: Wydawnictwo Uniwersytetu Jagiellońskiego, 2001), 28.

47 Leszek Leo Kantor, "Płonące zboże i czerwone porzeczki," *Gazeta Wyborcza*, November 21, 2012.

48 Hanna Domańska, *Kamienne drzewo płaczu* (Gdańsk: Krajowa Agencja Wydawnicza, 1991), 77–79.

49 AIPN, Wojewódzki Urząd Spraw Wewnętrznych w Częstochowie, ref. no. Ka 010/75 vol. 2, Sprawa obiektowa kryptonim "Omega," "Babel," 151.

50 Einhorn, Jamróg, and Włodarczyk, *Dzieje społeczności żydowskiej w Kłodzku w XIX–XX w.*, 83.

51 POLIN, Oral History Collection, ref. no. 311, Róża Król's testimony.

When Symcha Klamra died in Warsaw in 1982, the family decided to hold the funeral at a communal cemetery, because at the Jewish cemetery "gravestones were routinely being stolen."[52] When in 1994 the pre-funeral building in Czechowice-Dziedzice was demolished, destruction of the cemetery intensified. The drunks and drug addicts who gathered there made the family members of the deceased afraid to visit their graves. In order to protect them against destruction, in 1997 and 2016 two gravestones (without the bodies being exhumed) were moved to the cemeteries in Bielsko-Biała and Wilamowice.[53]

Other evidence of the concerns of families is the inscription on the plaque attached to the gravestone of J. P. Gross at the Stalowa Street Jewish cemetery in Sosnowiec, which reads: "Here lies a Polish citizen who served in the Polish army and perished in the defence of Poland. Leave his resting place alone. There are many religions, but only one God." The original's spelling mistake in Polish suggests that the plaque was made abroad. The fear of holding burials in Jewish cemeteries accompanies some Polish Jews to this day.

Visiting destroyed cemeteries is a moving experience for those who return to Poland after years in exile. This was the case for Nimrod Ariav from Israel, looking for the cemetery in Bełżyce, where he buried his father, murdered by the Germans in 1942. During a visit in 1963, he couldn't find a place he knew so well. Asking about the cemetery in the town council offices, he was met with verbal aggression. It was not until 1988 that Ariav, with the help of another, friendlier official, established the location of the cemetery. Ariav almost suffered a heart attack on discovering that the cemetery was completely devoid of gravestones, was now a children's playground, and on Fridays the site of a cattle market.[54]

Similar experiences awaited the Israeli Dorit R., who in 2017, together with the author of this book, visited Radzymin, her mother's birthplace. Most of the buildings in the former Jewish district—including her family's house—had been destroyed during the tank battles at the end of July and early August 1944. But the most bitter experience was a visit to the cemetery, which the local authorities had converted into a park in the late 1960s and early 1970s. All above-ground traces of the graves had been obliterated, the only thing being left at one end was the ohel of the town's tzadik Shlomo Yehoshua David Guterman,

52   Kowalski, *Płoccy wypędzeni. Marzec '68*, 115.

53   Sławomir Pastuszka, *Cmentarz żydowski w Czechowicach-Dziedzicach* (Kraków: Wydawnictwo Jak, 2019), 42.

54   USC Shoah Foundation, Visual History Archive, ref. no. 55570, Nimrod Ariav's testimony.

rebuilt in 2015–2016. The condition of the cemetery, with cars parked on it and teenagers sitting on the tzadik's grave caused Dorit R. to tremble and cry. She did not want to enter the cemetery as it would entail trampling on unmarked graves. After just a few minutes, she asked to be taken back to her hotel in Warsaw.

Awareness of the destruction of cemeteries is something that helps to give Poland an image as a place marked by the Shoah and antisemitism. Ilana Szlachter expressed this in her memoirs, written in Holon in 1994. Citing the reasons preventing her from visiting Poland, she mentioned, among other things, "fear of a concealed hatred of Jews" and the fear that she would have to "tread on the Jewish monuments used to pave the market square in Raciąż."[55]

---

55 Ilana Szlachter (Wojtkowska), "Zwykłe życie," *Biuletyn Żydowskiego Instytutu Historycznego w Polsce*, vo. 1/2 (185/186) (1998):116.

Chapter 7

Reactions
of Poles to the Destruction
# of Cemeteries

If we assume that most of the approximately 1,200 Jewish cemeteries in Poland were devastated by local populations, and that over the last 80 years the destruction and profanation of each of them can be attributed to a varying degree to several dozen people, then—without attempting precise statistics—the number of Poles involved in this practice should be estimated to be at least tens of thousands.

Certainly, digging up cemeteries and smashing gravestones was an unpleasant experience for many of those forced to do so by the Germans. Bronisław Matuszewski, as a prisoner of the German camp for juveniles in Bydgoszcz in 1940, took part in the demolition of a cemetery and on June 7, 2006, in an interview with Małgorzata Wąsacz from the newspaper *Gazeta Pomorska*, confessed: "It was heartbreaking for us to destroy those gravestones. We were well aware that all the time there were people lying beneath them." In 1940, Franciszek Musiolik from Rybnik, on the orders of the priest, participated in filling in the church pond with earth taken from the Jewish cemetery. Years later, he stated that for him, a 12-year-old boy at the time, the sight of those bones and skulls was "literally ghastly."[1]

Many bystanders did and still do view this practice with indifference. A surprising fact worth noting here is that Jewish cemeteries are often treated as not having the same rights as other burial places. This was what Sławomir Kapralski discovered during his sociological research: "For Poles, Jewish cemeteries are not cemeteries. As long as I talked about such sites in that way, I had serious problems finding out where they were located. People simply didn't understand me. The problem was solved as soon as I started using local

---

1   "Opowieść o likwidacji cmentarza żydowskiego w Rybniku," Franciszek Musiolik, accessed June 30, 2020, https://www.youtube.com/watch?v=UP866a8uXpI.

terms, such as *kirkut* or *okopisko* (ethnic: trench). For those people, these were not cemeteries; they were places of a different order."[2]

The Catholic Church, the highest authority for millions of Poles, took a passive attitude to the destruction of thousands of graves of its "older brothers in the faith." Yet a single Episcopal letter, read out in thousands of churches in Poland, could have reduced the destruction of cemeteries and encouraged the public to care for them. This did happen, but it was rare. In August 1946, at the request of Jewish organizations, bishop of Lublin Stefan Wyszyński pleaded with his flock to respect the cemeteries of all faiths, including Jewish ones.[3] Pope John Paul II during a sermon in Kalisz in 1997, said:

> Polish-Jewish history is still very real in the lives of both Jews and Poles. [. . .] Jewish cemeteries, of which there are so many on Polish soil, also tell of this common past. There is just such a cemetery here in Kalisz. These are places of a particularly profound spiritual, eschatological, and historical significance. May these places unite Poles and Jews, for together we await the Day of Judgment and Resurrection.[4]

It was only in January 2015 that the Committee for Dialogue with Judaism of the Polish Episcopal Conference issued a statement saying:

> We call on priests to take the initiative of commemorating the Jewish community in those places where they lived, and we call on the faithful and local authorities to help in this work. Let us not shrug our shoulders in indifference, saying: 'It's none of our business.' It is a duty of conscience! Perhaps a former synagogue, Jewish cemetery, or the graves of Shoah victims are not completely forgotten and something can be done to restore them. Let us not allow these signs of life and faith to disappear from the face of the earth.[5]

---

2   Bogdan Białek, *Cienie i ślady* (Kielce: Znak, 2013), 64.

3   Stefan Wyszyński, "Biskup Lubelski do Przewielebnego Duchowieństwa w sprawie cmentarzy, mogił i miejsc straceń," *Wiadomości Diecezjalne Lubelskie*, no. 8 (1946): 293–297; AIPN, MSW, Teczka pracy "Krystyna," 00170/52/3, 252–253. The author wishes to thank Prof. Bożena Szaynok for access to this document.

4   "Homilia kaliska Ojca Świętego," John Paul II, accessed: May 25, 2022, https://info.kalisz.pl/pope/index.htm.

5   "Apel o upamiętnienie," accessed June 30, 2020, https://jewish.org.pl/opinie/apel-o-upamitnienie-ydow-6850/.

The appeal was never renewed, nor is it to be found on the website of the Polish Episcopal Conference.

Some Poles reveal superstitious attitudes—the conviction that the perpetrators of destruction face punishments of a supernatural origin, including disease and death. This is manifested in the stories repeated by the non-Jewish population about the excavation of the graves of rabbis and tzadiks and about the tenants of houses erected on former cemeteries who have suffered various misfortunes in their lives. Some residents of Ryki believe that car accidents in this town are a consequence of using sand from the Jewish cemetery to build roads. In Grajewo, stories abound about ghosts haunting the apartment blocks built on the site of the cemetery.[6] In Pułtusk, a local rumour has it that the engineer who ordered the removal of the last gravestones was kidnapped and murdered by unidentified perpetrators. Barn fires in Gniewoszów have been viewed as a punishment for the destruction of the cemetery. In Pacanów, horses grazed in the cemetery were supposed to have "gone loco." The phenomenon was documented by Alina Cała at the turn of the seventies and eighties when recording statements by the inhabitants of towns and villages who spoke of ghosts appearing in a cinema built on the site of a cemetery, flashes of light scaring peasants when tearing up grass on graves, or car accidents on a road that led through a cemetery.[7]

A duality of attitudes can be noticed in the case of converting cemeteries into housing estates. For some people, this fact was irrelevant. Some took advantage of the bargain price of new, "post-cemetery" plots. Others definitely had no desire to live over graves.[8]

The takeover and use of cemetery grounds, and the buildings and gravestones standing on them, caused conflicts between neighbours. This is attested to by a letter from a resident of Szczuczyn, sent to the Socio-Cultural Society of Jews in Poland in 1956:

---

6   Mirosław Tryczyk, *Drzazga. Kłamstwa silniejsze niż śmierć* (Kraków: Znak, 2020), 83.

7   Alina Cała, *Wizerunek Żyda w polskiej kulturze ludowej* (Warszawa, Wydawnictwo Uniwersytetu Warszawskiego, 2005), 111.

8   Mariusz Koper, "Zapomniane sztetl – Lubycza Królewska. Śladami nieistniejącego," in *Żydzi w Zamościu i na Zamojszczyźnie. Historia – kultura – literatura*, ed. Weronika Litwin, Monika Szabłowska-Zaremba, and Sławomir Jacek Żurek (Lublin: Towarzystwo Naukowe Katolickiego Uniwersytetu Lubelskiego, 2012), 247; Tryczyk, *Drzazga*, 83.

I address the above named Society concerning case No. 1546/45, because I have not received the annex to the reply of the copy of the letter. I can only assume that this letter was stolen by the head of the local Post Office, K[. . .] Edward, because he is currently grazing his cow on the cemetery grounds and it is most important for him to be able to continue using it. [. . .] Currently, the head of the Post Office and the chairman are threatening me, and especially my wife, that he will hold me accountable for the fact that I too previously used this cemetery. Indeed I did, but the Presidium forced me to do so, as it demanded 500 zloties a year in tax [. . .]. I used it because many farmers applied for cemetery grounds to be allocated to them.[9]

There have also been witnesses for whom the destruction of cemeteries caused sincere outrage and opposition. Some remained passive, while others tried to intervene by, for example, writing letters to local authorities, newspaper editors, radio stations, the Religious Association of the Judaic Faith in the Republic of Poland, the Socio-Cultural Society of Jews in Poland, and the Jewish Historical Institute. Correspondents were not always familiar with the structure of Jewish organizations—for example, a letter from Połaniec was sent to the Congregation of the Judaic Faith in Łódź. One can imagine the determination of the correspondents in establishing the addresses of the relevant appeal bodies and their searches in telephone directories or telephone number services.[10] In the first words of his letter, Tadeusz M. of Praszka apologized to the Chairman of the Religious Association of the Judaic Faith in the Republic of Poland that he was writing to him directly (perhaps to a private address, the envelope has not survived), but "I found only this address in the phone book and I don't know anyone else I could contact regarding this matter."[11] Reports concerning destruction of cemeteries were also sent to the media, rightly defining them as the "fourth power." The authors of these letters often wished to remain anonymous. They were probably equally afraid of conflict with the authorities, those individuals causing the destruction, and the ostracism of their neighbours. This was experienced by, among others, Marian Górski of Dzierżbotki, who in the seventies decided to bury remains he found scattered in the nearby cemetery. Years

---

9   AŻIH, Towarzystwo Społeczno-Kulturalne Żydów w Polsce, ref. no. 325/45, Towarzystwo Społeczno-Kulturalne Żydów w Polsce, 165.

10   AŻIH, Związek Religijny Wyznania Mojżeszowego w Polsce, ref. no. 360, no pagination.

11   AŻIH, Związek Religijny Wyznania Mojżeszowego w Polsce, ref. no. 360, no pagination.

later, he recalled: "People back then started laughing at me and calling me a 'Jewish gravedigger.'"[12] Even greater problems were the fate of Ireneusz Socha, who in 1981 lived in an apartment block built next to the Jewish cemetery in Dębica. Outraged by the use of the cemetery as a playground and a place for drunken revelry, Socha tried to intervene with the town authorities, the Civil Militia and the Judaic Congregation. His involvement led to conflict with other residents: "By defending the cemetery, I became a public enemy among my neighbours. People wrote letters denouncing me. I began being visited by undercover officers who tried to dissuade me from my intention. But I didn't give up."

On August 6th 1951, Iwaniska residents Stanisław B., Józef C. and Leonard K. informed the Łódź branch of the Socio-Cultural Society of Jews in Poland about the destruction of the cemetery in their town: "There were such individuals, i.e. cemetery hyenas, who carried out robberies from that Jewish cemetery, taking all the monuments and the gravestones that serve as this cemetery's perimeter." In the letter, they included the names and addresses of two people who had used matzevahs as foundations for cottages and barns, demanding that the Socio-Cultural Society of Jews in Poland notify the public prosecutor's office and emphasizing: "we cannot stand to see this destruction of a dead people's culture." The letter resulted in proceedings being conducted by the Religious Affairs Department at the Presidium of the County Council in Opatów. The signatories of the letter and the accused were questioned. The latter pleaded not guilty, claiming that the cemetery was destroyed by the Germans during the Second World War. During the proceedings, the senders of the letter, perhaps in the face of this direct confrontation with the perpetrators and fearing mob rule repercussions at the hands of their neighbours, stated that they "cannot provide any explanations, because the cemetery is about 2 kilometres from town and they don't know anything about this matter at all."[13]

An anonymous correspondent from Warta who, on July 17th 1954 sent a letter "on behalf of interested citizens" to the editorial office of the radio program *Fala 49*, was well aware of the power of the mass media. He was outraged by the destruction of the Jewish cemetery by some local residents—the gradual dismantling of the perimeter wall and the grazing of cows, goats, horses and pigs in the cemetery. He pointed out that the graves of Shoah victims were located in the cemetery. From the rather awkwardly written letter (of which only a copy

12   Janicki, *Eksterminacja Żydów w powiecie tureckim w latach 1941–1942*, 86.
13   AAN, Urząd do Spraw Wyznań, ref. no. 9/357, Iwaniska – profanacja cmentarza, 2–5.

of the first page has survived), one can guess that the author hoped to publicize the matter over the air and thus admonish the vandals. The editors of *Fala 49* forwarded this correspondence to the Office for Religious Affairs in Warsaw and a few weeks later, the Presidium of the Municipal Council in Warta appointed a cemetery caretaker.[14]

Intervention via the *Fala 49* program was also the means chosen by Stanisław D. from the village of Gęś, who wrote with indignation about the setting up of a produce market in the cemetery in Parczew. In his letter of April 26th 1955, he pointed out that "everyone says that it's wrong" and explained:

> Whatever a person may be—Jew or any other, he is a human. I myself am impartial, no one in my family is Jewish, but I hear a lot of people say and rightly so, that we don't know where we ourselves are going to rest, and who knows, they might do the same to us, we can't tell where our graves await us.

The letter of a simple farmer and, at the same time, someone aware of his rights as a citizen (the letter ends with a note that the sender is waiting for an explanation) resulted in a positive settlement of the matter. The editors of the *Fala 49* program this time too notified the Office for Religious Affairs and on July 15th 1955 a decision was taken to move the market to another place, fence off the cemetery and plant trees on it.[15]

In 1959, Jan M. from Opoczno wrote to Polish Radio—this time to the program *Fala 56*. In a letter several pages long, he described the condition of Jewish cemeteries in his hometown. For their destruction and an attitude of indifference he boldly blamed the national council and the local committee of the Polish United Workers' Party, noting that "the old Jewish cemetery existed as far back as the times of the Polish Republic of the Nobility, existed during the interwar period, existed during the German occupation, and ceased to exist when the Polish People's Republic came into existence." He pointed out that this was not only Opoczno's problem, but that "there are hundreds of such towns."[16]

The painter and graphic artist Zdzisław Lachur of Katowice, who in 1959 visited his family living in Nysa, was not afraid of confronting either the perpe-

---

14   AAN, Urząd do Spraw Wyznań, ref. no. 19/482, Opieka nad cmentarzem w Warcie, 1–8.

15   AAN, Urząd do Spraw Wyznań, ref. no. 22/447, Korespondencja, 4–5.

16   AP Kielce, Urząd Wojewódzki w Kielcach, Wydział ds. Wyznań, ref. no. 1080/1071, Cmentarz żydowski w Opocznie – zamknięcie cmentarza 1955–1959, 30–35.

trators of the cemetery's destruction or the authorities. While walking with his mother and sister, he noticed that in the Jewish cemetery a group of men were tearing out the gravestones using a tractor. Since he failed in his attempt to stop the vandals, he took several photographs of the men and reported them to the mayor of the town and the Civil Militia, whose officers then went "to the place of such barbaric activities." Next he sent a letter to Dawid Sfard at the Warsaw branch of the Socio-Cultural Society of Jews in Poland.[17]

In 1961, Zofia T. of Połaniec, living near the cemetery, informed the Congregation of the Judaic Faith in Łódź about plans to build an agricultural depot and garages on the grounds of the cemetery. In a brief and pointed letter, she stressed that "your ancestors' bones should rest in peace" and requested they intervene as soon as possible.[18]

In 1966, Father Tadeusz Lisiecki, pastor of the local Roman Catholic parish, protested against the liquidation of the cholera and Jewish cemeteries in Sobota. With regard to the latter, in a letter to the Presidium of the Provincial Council, he noted that "there are graves here under the care of relatives residing in Israel, who come to this cemetery, and thanks to their efforts, these graves are properly tended and this cemetery is still in operation, and in the event of any Jewish families living in the vicinity, this cemetery will be the place where their dead will be buried and so should not be liquidated."[19] The priest's efforts, however, did not bring about the expected results.

A letter concerning the planned construction of a bypass road through the cemetery in Ropczyce was delivered in 1973 to the Kraków branch of the Socio-Cultural Society of Jews in Poland. It was sent by Jakub G. of Dębica, but was signed by "Interested parties." The letter began with the words: "Honouring the memory of your ancestors resting in the cemetery in Ropczyce." The authors asked Socio-Cultural Society of Jews in Poland to intervene with the authorities and block construction of the new road.[20]

Less courage and confidence in the authorities was shown by the anonymous author of a letter to the Office for Religious Affairs, probably sent in 1979

---

17 AŻIH, Archiwum Towarzystwa Społeczno–Kulturalnego Żydów w Polsce, ref. no. 325/55, TSKŻ. Zarząd Główny, 472–473.

18 AŻIH, Związek Religijny Wyznania Mojżeszowego w Polsce, ref. no. 360, no pagination

19 AAN, Ministerstwo Gospodarki Komunalnej, ref. no. 9/39, Decyzje o zamknięciu cmentarzy i przeznaczeniu ich na inny cel w województwie łódzkim, 104–105.

20 AIPN, Ministerstwo Spraw Wewnętrznych w Warszawie, ref. no. IPN BU 1585/7150, Mniejszość żydowska – cmentarze wyznania mojżeszowego w Polsce, 141–142.

when, in connection with the expansion of a street, the authorities of Tarnów intended to "reduce" the Jewish cemetery by 22 metres. In the letter he wrote: "Strange things are happening here in our great town of Tarnów, the Jewish cemetery is being destroyed with Catholic ferocity [. . .]. This is a blurring of the traces of imperialism and fascism, which brings death and destruction to nations."[21] That same year, Adam Penkalla from the Monument Conservation Studio in Radom published an extensive appeal in the pages of *Fołks Sztyme*[22] to save and document Jewish cemeteries.[23]

The condition of the cemetery in Zakroczym distressed Antoni K., who on July 3rd 1980 wrote a letter to the Warsaw branch of the Religious Association of the Judaic Faith in the Republic of Poland:

> I am asking you to take care of our Jewish cemetery. I live near this ceme-
> tery and I can't bear to look at it. In this cemetery, people graze cattle and
> horses, and the cattle leave their dung on the graves. People empty out
> their toilets and take their rubbish to the graves. They also dig graves up
> and leave bones lying on the surface. I appealed to the mayor, but he said
> he didn't care. Please, come and see for yourselves.[24]

Probably many correspondents felt powerless in the centralized reality that was the People's Republic of Poland. They expected action from Jewish organizations and administrative authorities. There were also people with the conscience of social activists, who themselves made efforts to protect and commemorate cemeteries. That was the idea of Tadeusz M. of Praszka, who in 1981, after four years of observing the destruction in the cemetery and battling hooligans, wanted to organize a committee for the construction in the cemetery of a monument to those who had been shot dead. The project collapsed due to a lack of funds and, in addition, the initiator of this idea heard (perhaps in the town council offices) that it was none of his business. In a letter to the Religious Association of the Judaic Faith in the Republic of Poland, Tadeusz M. asked for

---

21 AAN, Urząd do Spraw Wyznań, ref. no. 132/318, Obiekty judaizmu województwa tarnowskiego, 204.

22 *Fołks-Sztyme* was a bilingual magazine published in Yiddish and Polish in Poland between 1946 and 1991.

23 Adam Penkalla, "Cmentarze żydowskie – postulat najpilniejszy," *Fołks Sztyme*, November 3, 1979.

24 AŻIH, Związek Religijny Wyznania Mojżeszowego w Polsce, ref. no. 360, no pagination.

help, and in a post scriptum added: "Maybe it would be possible to fence off the cemetery area."[25]

Some people put their words into action. Since 1973, the cemetery in Warsaw has been tended by people associated with the Catholic Intelligentsia Club as part of Jewish Culture Week.[26] The 1980s saw the first non-Jewish social initiatives to protect cemeteries. In 1981, the Social Committee for the Care of Cemeteries and Monuments of Jewish Culture in Poland was established. It included Jews as well as people of non-Jewish origin, including: Jerzy Bandowski, Marian Marek Drozdowski, Zygmunt Hoffman, Jerzy Hryniewiecki, Jan Jagielski, Danuta Kaczyńska, Monika Krajewska, Eryk Lipiński, Antoni Marianowicz, Teresa Prekerowa, Aleksander Wallis, and Henryk Zimler. Despite the unfavourable attitude of the state authorities, the Committee received financial support from the Conservation Office, the Polish National Lottery and private donors. By 1987, thanks to the efforts of this Committee, several dozen gravestones were restored in the Warsaw cemetery at 49/51 Okopowa Street. The committee organized readings, film screenings, conducted publishing activities, and initiated the drawing up of a list of Jewish cemeteries in Poland. The committee operated mainly in Warsaw, but soon attracted many social activists from all over the country. In their brochure, the committee's activists wrote:

> We also call on the residents of cities, towns and villages: right around the corner from you, on a neighbouring street, on the outskirts of your town, the ruins of a synagogue or cemetery matzevahs are falling into disrepair. It is you who can help the most, take care of them, secure them, and protect them from theft or destruction. [. . .] Join us in saving the monuments of Jewish culture in Poland![27]

In 1981, the Inter-company Trade Union Committee of NSZZ "Solidarność" in Przemyśl appealed for protection of the "cemeteries of the Jewish people" in the pages of the Solidarity newspaper *Tygodnik Solidarność*,[28] and shortly thereafter applied to the Ministry of Culture for recognition of the cemetery

---

25 AŻIH, Związek Religijny Wyznania Mojżeszowego w Polsce, ref. no. 360, no pagination.

26 Krzysztof Śliwiński, "Nasz cmentarz żydowski," *Więź*, no. 4/294 (1983): 58.

27 Monika Krajewska, "'Świadkiem niech będzie ten kamień' (Genesis 31:52)," in *Kalendarz Żydowski 1986–1987*, ed. Ewa Świderska (Warszawa: Związek Religijny Wyznania Mojżeszowego w Polsce, 1987), 206–209.

28 "Apel o pamięć," *Tygodnik Solidarność*, May 29, 1981.

in that town as a heritage site.[29] In 1984, the Kórnik Cultural Society exhibited matzevahs in the former passageway to the synagogue. In 1986, the Society for the Protection of Monuments in Kazimierz Dolny built a lapidarium in the local cemetery, and in the following years similar projects were carried out by the Society of Friends of Przasnysz (1986) and the Society of Maków Mazowiecki Enthusiasts (1987). In Krośniewice, preservation of the cemetery was pursued by Józef Jędrzejczak and after two years his efforts led to the construction of a bridge and a road to the cemetery.[30] At the same time, Ireneusz Ślipek took care of the cemetery in Warta. In 1987, thanks to the involvement of Jerzy Fornalik, pupils of the Special School and Educational Centre in Borzęciczki began tending the cemetery in Koźmin Wielkopolski.

A significant improvement in this respect was brought about by the democratization of life in Poland after 1989. Numerous cemeteries obtained non-Jewish guardians—both individuals (Zbigniew Romaniuk of Brańsk, Artur Cyruk of Hajnówka, Robert Augustyniak of Grodzisk Mazowiecki, Natalia Bartczak of Wińsko, Dorota Budzińska and Jolanta Konstańczuk of Dąbrowa Białostocka, Grzegorz Kamiński of Gliwice, Agnieszka Kostuch and Katarzyna Sudaj of Trzemeszno, Dariusz Walerjański of Zabrze, Bogusław Polak of Mysłowice, Damian Lewandowski of Seroczyn, Kamila Klauzińska of Zduńska Wola, Dariusz Popiela of Nowy Sącz, and others) and local social organizations (including the "Borussia" Foundation in Olsztyn, the J. Rajnfeld Volunteer Jewish Cemetery Cleanup Corps of Warsaw, Otwock's Social Committee for the Remembrance of Otwock and Karczew Jews, the Jan Karski Society of Kielce, and the Studnia Pamięci Association of Lublin[31]).

On the initiative of Łucja Pawlicka-Nowak, employees of the District Museum in Konin, including Zdzisław Lorek and Ryszard Laba, placed boulders in about 20 cemeteries in the former Konin Province. The inscriptions on them read: "Jewish cemetery. Legally protected area. Respect the resting place of the dead." They additionally secured several hundred matzevahs and their broken fragments, found in various places outside cemeteries. Particularly noteworthy

---

29 "Spotkanie w Przemyślu," *Tygodnik Solidarność*, June 2, 1981.

30 Paweł Fijałkowski, "Kamienne owoce czasu," *Fołks Sztyme*, January 6, 1989.

31 As part of the *Ogrodnicy Pamięci* (Gardeners of memory) project, the Studnia Pamięci Association has published a guide for people involved in the protection of cemeteries: Klimowicz, Sygowski, Tarajko, and Trzciński, *Cmentarze żydowskie. Podręcznik dobrych praktyk w ochronie dziedzictwa lokalnego.*

is the Committee for the Protection of Jewish Cultural Monuments in Tarnów, which in 2017, after many years of caring for the Tarnów cemetery, acquired and allocated about 3 million zloties for its renovation, and the Cultural Heritage Foundation of Warsaw, which since 2017 has been using an endowment fund worth 100 million zlotys set up by the Ministry of Culture and National Heritage for the purpose of cleaning up the cemetery in Warsaw. In 2020, the Cultural Heritage Foundation began creating a nationwide Coalition of Jewish Cemetery Guardians.[32]

Some cemeteries have been taken care of by members of Christian churches and religious associations, who regard this commitment as good deeds for the sake of "older brothers in the faith." They include, among others, the "Emaus" Pentecostal Church in Mikołajki, the "Christ the Good Shepherd" Church of God in Świdwin, the Pentecostal Church in Żywiec, and the Baptist Church Congregation in Mińsk Mazowiecki. Non-institutional priests are also involved in these activities (including Father Stanisław Bartmiński of Krasiczyn, Father Wojciech Lemański of Otwock and Jasienica, Father Henryk Romanik of Koszalin, Father Leszek Sikorski of Bodzentyn, and Father Remigiusz Stacherski of Popowo Kościelne) and members of various Protestant congregations, including Eugeniusz Kuteń of Pruszków.

Motivating these people in their work is, among other things, a desire to care for the graves of former residents of their town, concern for their cultural heritage, and an interest in Jewish culture. Activities include cleaning graves, repairing cemetery infrastructure, conservation of gravestones, recovery of matzevahs taken from cemeteries, and various forms of commemoration, documentation and popularization.

Thanks to the abolition of censorship, the emergence of the Internet, and the development of independent media, cases of cemetery destruction are now more often being detected and publicized. The subject of cemetery destruction comes up increasingly frequently in the Polish press, radio, television and book publications.

The condition of cemeteries is also a source of inspiration for artists. The album by Monika Krajewska[33] *Czas kamieni* (The Time of Stones) published in 1982, contained photographs of cemeteries taken since the 1970s. Although the main theme was sepulchral art, this was an important publication drawing

---

32   The coalition's website: https://cmentarzezydowskie.org/.

33   In 1985 Monika Krajewska converted to Judaism.

attention to decaying Jewish cemeteries. The album had also German, French and English versions.[34] In 1993 Monika Krajewska published another album *A Tribe of Stones. Jewish Cemeteries in Poland.*[35] The cemetery theme also appeared in the album *Ostatni. Współcześni Żydzi polscy* (The Last Ones. Contemporary Polish Jews) by Małgorzata Niezabitowska and Tomasz Tomaszewski, published in New York (1986), Schaffhausen (1987) and Warsaw (1993).[36] Particularly expressive was a photo showing the cemetery in Karczew with a dog running around among bones lying scattered on the ground. In 2007, Karolina Freino initiated the artistic project *Murki i Piaskownice* (Walls and Sandboxes), dealing with the problem of using Jewish and Protestant gravestones in Szczecin to build walls, sandboxes, backyard rubbish shelters and pavements. A famous project was that of Łukasz Baksik, who in the years 2008–2012 photographed matzevahs reused for various purposes—as building material, grinding wheels and paving slabs. This work resulted in an exhibition of his photographs (presented in, among other places, the Centre for Contemporary Art in Warsaw, the Stanisław Udziela Ethnographic Museum in Kraków, and the National Historical Museum of the Republic of Belarus in Minsk), an album entitled *Macewy codziennego użytku* (Matzevahs of everyday use), and numerous articles.[37] Cemeteries have also been of interest to a group of photographers and ethnologists, namely Jan Janiak, Katarzyna Kopecka, and Piotr Pawlak, who since 2015 as a part of their project *Obecnie nieobecni* (Presently absent) on destroyed cemeteries—including those that were turned into a shooting range in Kamieńsk, a race track in Łódź, and a bus station in Opoczno—take photographs of matzevahs made of transparent plexiglass. So far, exhibitions of their photographs have been presented at the POLIN Museum of the History of Polish Jews, the Marek Edelman Centre for Dialogue in Łódź, and the Polish parliament.

---

34 Monika Krajewska, *Czas kamieni* (Warszawa: Interpress, 1982); Monika Krajewska, *Zeit der Steine* (Warszawa: Interpress, 1982); Monika Krajewska, *Time of Stones* (Warszawa: Interpress, 1983), *Le temps des pierres* (Warszawa: Interpress, 1983).

35 Monika Krajewska, *A tribe of stones. Jewish cemeteries in Poland* (Warszawa: Polish Scientific Publishers Ltd, 1993).

36 Małgorzata Niezabitowska and Tomasz Tomaszewski, *Ostatni. Współcześni Żydzi polscy* (Warszawa: Wydawnictwa Artystyczne i Filmowe, 1993); Małgorzata Niezabitowska and Tomasz Tomaszewski, *Remnants: the last Jews of Poland* (New York: Friendly Press, 1986); Małgorzata Niezabitowska and Tomasz Tomaszewski, *Die letzten Juden in Polen* (Schaffhausen: Edition Stemmle, 1987).

37 Łukasz Baksik, *Macewy codziennego użytku* (Wydawnictwo Czarne: Wołowiec, 2012).

It should be noted that there have been no detailed studies on a broader scale concerning the attitude of Poles to the destruction of Jewish cemeteries. The subject did however appear in a survey conducted by Krzysztof Malicki in 2011, in which 1,068 residents of the Podkarpacie province participated. When asked about the "destruction of Jewish memorial sites," 14.8% of respondents stated that such behaviour should be condemned but not punished, while 80% felt that it should also be punished. In turn, a rather ambiguous question about "the lack of care for ancient synagogues and Jewish cemeteries" gave the following results: 52.8% of respondents answered "it should be condemned, but not punished," 25.2% expressed the opinion that "it should be condemned and punished," 19.5% of the respondents had no clear opinion, and 2.5% did not see anything wrong with it.[38]

---

38 Krzysztof Malicki, *Poza wspólnotą pamięci: życie i Zagłada Żydów w pamięci mieszkańców regionu podkarpackiego* (Warszawa: Wydawnictwo IFiS PAN, 2017), 140.

Chapter 8

Jewish Initiatives to Protect Cemeteries

The subject of this book is the destruction of Jewish cemeteries, but another issue which needs to be addressed is the question of actions taken by Jewish organizations and individuals—Jews living in Poland, as well as emigrants and their descendants—to remove and reduce the effects of destruction and prevent further destruction. The following chapter is merely an attempt to touch on such activity; the issue definitely deserves a broader, separate study.

As early as the end of 1944, Jewish Committees got to work cleaning up cemeteries, recovering gravestones that had been taken away, repairing perimeters, and commemorating Shoah victims. The committees operated in extremely difficult conditions—Shoah survivors were often destitute, and the new state deprived Jewish organizations of the property of pre-war Jewish communities, whose sale could have been used to finance the securing of cemeteries. In the first post-war years, cleaning up work was carried out in among others, the cemeteries in Biała, Białystok, Bielsko, Chorzów, Dąbrowa Tarnowska, Garwolin, Gorlice, Góra Kalwaria, Hrubieszów, Kalisz, Katowice, Kielce, Kłodzko, Kraków (by 1946 the perimeters of the cemeteries at Miodowa Street and Szeroka Street had been repaired or partially rebuilt—with over 500,000 zloties spent on the latter),[1] Krosno, Kutno, Lublin, Łańcut, Łódź, Łowicz, Łuków, Mielec, Nowy Sącz, Otwock, Sandomierz, Siedlce, Tarnów, Warsaw, and Włocławek.[2] The work was largely financed with funds from the American Jewish Joint Distribution Committee.

Dozens of cemeteries were handed over by the state for the use of the Jewish Religious Congregations (in 1949 renamed the Religious Union of the Judaic

---

1 AŻIH, Wydział Prawny Centralnego Komitetu Żydów w Polsce, ref. no. 303/XVI/150, Kraków WKŻ. Akta organizacyjne. Korespondencja dotycząca cmentarzy, 3.

2 AŻIH, Wydział Prezydium i Sekretariat Centralnego Komitetu Żydów w Polsce, ref. no. 303/I/246, Prezydium. Komisja Mieszana dla Współpracy CKŻP i Komitetu Organizacyjnego Żydowskich Kongregacji Wyznaniowych, 53.

Faith), half of which were cemeteries located in territories annexed from Germany after 1945. Over the next decades, the Religious Association of the Judaic Faith in the Republic of Poland performed ongoing cleaning operations and employed caretakers for the cemeteries they controlled (in 1987 these numbered 47). However, in view of the enormous scale of destruction and progressive nature of the destruction, the budget available to the Religious Association of the Judaic Faith in the Republic of Poland[3] did not ensure the cemeteries could be properly looked after.[4] Likewise, the Socio-Cultural Society of Jews in Poland cleaned up selected cemeteries using funds from the American Jewish Joint Distribution Committee (for example in 1958 the Socio-Cultural Society of Jews in Poland spent 600,000 zloties on cemeteries).[5] Also important were the efforts of the Religious Association of the Judaic Faith in the Republic of Poland and the Socio-Cultural Society of Jews in Poland to halt the destruction of cemeteries. This is attested to by the hundreds of pages of correspondence both organizations conducted with state offices.

To a limited extent—due such things as bureaucratic procedures—cemeteries were tended on the orders of individual donors (mainly emigrants) and landsmanshafts. Such was the case in, among others, Biłgoraj, Bobrowniki, Czeladź, Kęty, Kielce, Łaskarzew, Radomyśl Wielki, Radoszyce, Rypin, Sławków, Suwałki, Tarnogród, Żarki, and Żyrardów. Also active were members of Hasidic communities (including Abush and Josef Hirsch, Yechiel Kurtz, Asher Scharf), whose efforts mainly involved protecting the burial places of tzadiks.

Jews were also among the activists of the Social Committee for the Care of Jewish Cemeteries and Monuments in Poland, established in 1981. In 1983, the Nissenbaum Family Foundation commenced activities in Poland, one of its main statutory missions being to save Jewish cemeteries from destruction and care for places connected to the martyrdom of Jews during World War II. The foundation was officially registered in 1985. The impetus for establishing the Foundation

---

3   Budget of Religious Union of the Jewish Faith consisted of subsidies provided by Joint (in the years 1949–1950, 1957–1967 and from 1981), along with state subsidies and its own funds.

4   Paweł Wildstein, "Z działalności Zarządu Głównego Związku Wyznania Mojżeszowego w Rzeczypospolitej Polskiej," in *Kalendarz Żydowski–Almanach 1990–1991*, ed. Ryszard Schnepf (Warszawa: Związek Religijny Wyznania Mojżeszowego w Rzeczypospolitej Polskiej, 1991), 172.

5   AAN, Urząd do Spraw Wyznań, ref. no. 131/503, Związek Religijny Wyznania Mojżeszowego, 60.

was the desire of its founder, Zygmunt Nissenbaum, to save the Jewish cemetery in Warsaw's Bródno district, where his ancestors rest, from complete destruction and annihilation. In the following years, the Foundation carried out numerous works in Poland related to cemeteries, ohels and synagogues (including fencing off and cleaning up cemeteries, building and reconstructing ohels, renovation of buildings related to religious worship). By 1989, work had been carried out in, among other places, Bobowa, Buk, Góra Kalwaria, Kielce, Kolbuszowa, Krosno, Łódź (renovation of a pre-funeral building), Okuniew, Przysucha, Rzeszów, Słubice, Sopot, Wodzisław and Wolbrom. As early as 1985, the Foundation began work on one of its most important and largest projects, namely the rescue of the Bródno cemetery, which in the 1950s the authorities had planned to liquidate. Within three years, the Foundation had built an almost 2 kilometre-long perimeter around it, erected a monumental gate, removed rubbish, cut down wild vegetation, cleaned several thousand gravestones and paved an inner avenue leading to a lapidarium. The Foundation took direct care of this cemetery until 2012, when it was handed over to the Jewish Community in Warsaw, but also continued to carry out cleaning works on it after the handover. In 1989, the Foundation secured about 2,000 matzevahs which the Germans had laid in the Rypinkowski Canal in Kalisz during World War II. Foundation employees dug them out and took them to the local Jewish cemetery. The Foundation was also involved in the preparation of other projects related to Jewish cemeteries, which in the end were not implemented for reasons beyond its control. In 1988, the Foundation published the album *Żywym i umarłym* (For those alive and dead). The photographs in it by Jerzy Budziszewski (Joshua Budziszewski Benor) showed the disastrous condition of material objects of Jewish heritage in Poland, including cemeteries.[6] That same year, the book *Fundacja Rodziny Nissenbaumów. Ratowanie śladów kultury żydowskiej w Polsce. Żywym i umarłym* (The Nissenbaum Family Foundation. Saving traces of Jewish culture in Poland. For those alive and dead) was published by Poland's National Publishing Agency as commissioned by the Foundation.[7]

From the end of the 1980s, cemeteries in Lublin were attended to by the Sara and Manfred Frenkel Foundation and the Society for the Preservation of Jewish Culture Memorials in Lublin, established by Symcha Wajs.

---

6   Jerzy Budziszewski, *Żywym i umarłym* (Warszawa: Wydawnictwo Współpraca, 1988).

7   *Fundacja Rodziny Nissenbaumów. Ratowanie śladów kultury żydowskiej w Polsce. Żywym i umarłym*, ed. Radosław Piszczek (Warszawa: Krajowa Agencja Wydawnicza, 1988).

The Jewish Historical Institute played an important role as a centre providing consultation on matters related to the protection of cemeteries, collecting related archival materials, documenting the changing condition of cemeteries and intervening in cases of their destruction. In 1992, the Institute co-organized a conference on *Problems of protection and conservation of Jewish cemeteries in Poland*. Jan Jagielski, head of the Jewish Historical Institute's Monuments Documentation Department and at the same time, chairman of the Social Committee for the Care of Cemeteries and Monuments of Jewish Culture in Poland and the Eternal Remembrance Foundation, became an advisor to many social activists tending cemeteries. In 1989, together with Eleonora Bergman, Jan Jagielski drew up a list of Jewish cemeteries and preserved synagogues and in 1994, together with Urszula Kalińska, another list of 1056 cemeteries. Jan Jagielski developed the first guidelines for the protection of Jewish cemeteries, which were presented in 1993 during a conference attended by employees of the State Service for Protection of Monuments and published in a post-conference publication.[8] He was also the author of articles and books on Jewish cemeteries.

A significant change took place after 1989. The reborn Jewish communities, which formed part of the Union of Jewish Communities in the Republic of Poland, obtained the right of succession to the property of pre-war communities. This has enabled the communities to take possession of cemeteries and take care of the same independently, but at the same time imposes the obligation to maintain such sites in a proper condition, this being enforced by local authorities and conservation services. According to the Institute of National Heritage's data, in 2019 the communities forming the Union of Jewish Commuties in the Republic of Poland owned at least 117 cemeteries,[9] including some of the largest in Europe, namely those in Łódź (40 hectares) and Warsaw (33.5 hectares). This number is gradually increasing as a result of the property restitution process that includes that of pre-war Jewish communities. In 2000, under an agreement between the Union of Jewish Communities in the Republic of Poland and the World Jewish Restitution Organization, the Foundation for the Preservation of

---

8   Jan Jagielski, "Lapidaria na cmentarzach żydowskich," in *Studia i materiały. Ochrona cmentarzy zabytkowych: materiały szkoleniowe pracowników Państwowej Służby Ochrony Zabytków oraz materiały z konferencji Organizacja lapidariów cmentarnych Żagań – Kożuchów 20–23 czerwca*, ed. Wanda Puget (Warszawa: Ośrodek Ochrony Zabytkowego Krajobrazu, 1994), 62–66.

9   Data from the Department of Records and Registry of Monuments of the Institute of National Heritage.

Jewish Heritage was established and duly registered in 2002. The Foundation's tasks include restitution of property of former Jewish communities, including cemeteries (acting as a representative of the Union of Jewish Communities in the Republic of Poland), management of recovered properties and protection of objects of religious or historical importance. By 2022, the Foundation had become the owner of 153 Jewish cemeteries. To cover the costs of its activities, the Foundation allocates funds obtained from the restitution of real estate, donors and other sources, including the German government-funded European Jewish Cemeteries Initiative (ESJF).[10] During its 24 years of operations, the Foundation for the Preservation of Jewish Heritage has implemented many projects involving the cleaning up and fencing of cemeteries in Frampol, Gniewoszów, Kolno, Lesko, Miechów, Myszyniec, Przemyśl, Radom, Radoszyce, Rajgród, Szczebrzeszyn, Wiskitki and other locations. One of the Foundation's projects is "Adopt a Jewish Cemetery," the aim of which is to search for supporters in the battle to preserve cemeteries.

Also in 2002, a Rabbinical Cemeteries Commission was established, operating initially alongside the Foundation for the Preservation of Jewish Heritage, and today within the framework of the Union of Jewish Communities in the Republic of Poland. Its tasks include supervision of Jewish cemeteries and Jewish graves located in other locations. The Commission is the most important consultative and advisory body monitoring works in Jewish cemeteries based on halachic principles. The *Rabbinical Cemeteries Commission's Guidelines concerning the protection of Jewish cemeteries in Poland* constitute a key document defining the rules for carrying out work in cemeteries.

The Gęsia Jewish Cemetery Foundation, established in 1992, has restored a 19th-century water pump, original iron gates and an old-fashioned street lamp as well as paved many paths at a cemetery in Warsaw.

In 1995, the Łódź City Council, the Union of Former Łódź Residents in Israel, and the World Jewish Restitution Organization established the Monumentum Iudaicum Lodzense Foundation, which to this day supervises cleaning works at the Łódź cemetery.

---

10   Monika Krawczyk, "Kto odpowiada za materialne dziedzictwo Żydów polskich?," in *Ochrona dziedzictwa żydowskiego w Polsce*, vol. 2, ed. Marcin Bartosiewicz, Monika Krawczyk, Lesław Piszewski, and Jarosław Sellin (Warszawa: Fundacja Ochrony Dziedzictwa Żydowskiego, 2017), 21–28.

Numerous cemeteries (including those in Adamów, Białystok, Brzeziny, Brzostek, Chmielnik, Chorzele, Dobra, Gniewoszów, Jeleniewo, Koło, Myszyniec, Nowy Dwór Mazowiecki, Pilzno, Różan, Sławatycze, and Wyszków) have been restored, fenced off and commemorated on the initiative of emigrants from Poland and their descendants—private individuals and landsmanshafts (including the Association of Brzeziny Residents in Israel and the Association of Częstochowa Jews in Israel). The Avoseinu New York Heritage Foundation for Preservation of Jewish Cemeteries has taken care of cemeteries in Dubienka, Lesko, Narol, Mogielnica and Szczebrzeszyn. In 2001, the Polish Jewish Cemetery Restoration Project was established and has performed work on cemeteries in Iłża, Iwaniska, Łosice, Ożarów, Strzegów, Szadek, Tarłów, and Wąchock and cooperated on similar projects in Chmielnik and Karczew. Additionally, this organization planned works in Działoszyce, Połaniec, Tykocin, Opole Lubelskie, Żelechów and Jaśliska; however, for various reasons these were ultimately not undertaken. Thanks to Michael Traison's funds, access to about 20 cemeteries was marked out and the cemetery in Wysokie Mazowieckie was put in order. Most of these activities were carried out in cooperation with the Foundation for the Preservation of Jewish Heritage and Jewish communities. The American organization Friends of Jewish Heritage in Poland, established in 2016, collects funds for the conservation of Jewish cemeteries and synagogues in Poland, with the Foundation for the Preservation of Jewish Heritage being its main beneficiary. Meir Bulka's J-nerations Foundation rebuilt an ohel in Ostrowiec Świętokrzyski and took efforts to stop desecrating cemeteries in various towns, including Kalisz, Kazimierz Dolny, Klimontów, and Wiżajny.

Friends of Jewish Cemeteries in Poland is a descendants' group established to restore Jewish cemeteries in Poland. The organization serves primarily as an advisory resource to such projects. FJCP is an affiliate of Friends of Jewish Heritage in Poland and works with organizations engaged in preserving Jewish heritage or restoring Jewish cemeteries, educates others on activities about restoration projects in Poland, and identifies resources to support descendants and local town inhabitants.

Since 2005, the cemetery in Pszczyna has been cared for by the social activist Sławomir Pastuszka—a member of the Jewish Community in Katowice. Sławomir Pastuszka was also involved in similar projects in Bieruń, Dębowa, Czechowice-Dziedzice, Katowice, and Mikołów.

The cemeteries in Tarczyn and on Warsaw's Izbicka Street have been put in order by a group of volunteers led by Piotr Stasiak, associated with the Beit

Figure 8.1. A search for the grave of Rabbi Yaakov Horowitz at the destroyed cemetery in Mielec, 2015. Photo: Krzysztof Bielawski.

Warsaw Progressive Jewish Community, and Lech Widawski, member of the Ec Chaim reform synagogue. The Poland-Israel Education Centre, run by Łucja Lisowska of the Jewish Community of Warsaw has been involved in the protection of the cemetery in Białystok.

In recent years, there have been numerous cases of involvement in these efforts by representatives of Hasidic circles (including Israel Meir Gabai, Duvid Singer, and rabbis Naftali Horowitz, Pinchas Pomp, Mendel Reichberg,[11] Yehuda Leib Halstock, and Josef Singer) taking care of cemeteries where famous tzadiks are laid to rest and reconstructing their ohels.

Other Jewish organizations also carry out occasional works in cemeteries. Members of the Polish Union of Jewish Students and the Jewish Youth Organization have tidied up cemeteries in among other places, Dukla, Dynów, Krzepice, Trzciel, and Warsaw, and have collected up scattered bones in Białobrzegi and Nowy Dwór Mazowiecki.

---

11 Rabbi Mendel Reichberg passed away in 2011. He was a founder of American Society for the Preservation of Jewish Cemeteries and Historic Objects in Poland.

Operations are continued by the Nissenbaum Family Foundation,[12] which has carried out projects in the cemeteries at Gąbin, Kraków (Remuh), Kraśnik, Łódź, Różan and Szydłowiec. Over the past 15 years, the Foundation has brought order to cemeteries in Andrychów, Czechowice-Dziedzice, Jeleniewo, Krynki, Seroczyn, Szydłowiec and Warsaw (Bródno). It has fenced off the cemeteries in Busko-Zdrój, Krościenko nad Dunajcem, Muszyna, Sławatycze, Sochaczew (a section of the perimeter), Szydłów, and Wiślica; it has built the last section of the perimeter wall in Warsaw's Bródno district cemetery (on the side facing Rzeszowska Street as part of a joint project with the Jewish Community in Warsaw), and fenced off a monument commemorating the Jewish community of Zamość. In the spring of 2020, the Foundation replaced the first section of the perimeter wall of the cemetery in Gąbin. In addition to works related to fencing off and cleaning up cemeteries, the Foundation has completed projects involving the construction or renovation of ohels (in Lelów, Leżajsk, Rzeszów, and Szydłowiec) and has provided financial support for the renovation of synagogues in Bobowa, Lelów and Kraków (Remuh). The Foundation also looks after places related to the martyrdom of Jews during World War II, including since 1988 the mass grave at the Monument to the Joint Martyrdom of Jews and Poles on Warsaw's Gibalskiego Street.

An important part of the Foundation's operations is intervening where the sanctity of Jewish cemeteries is being violated. The Foundation has led to the eviction from cemeteries of several illegal users, suspension of construction works carried out on such sites and prevented new housing estates being built on former cemeteries. It has also been involved in recovering matzevahs stolen from cemeteries, including those in Kalisz, Sławatycze and Strzyżów. Thanks to the work carried out in the cemeteries of Leżajsk and Lelów, the Foundation has contributed to increasing the number of Jewish pilgrims visiting Poland.

Since 2004, as part of the Gidonim project, students of the Reut School in Jerusalem, have come to Poland dozens of times to tidy up and document cemeteries, including those in Częstochowa, Kraków, Piotrków Trybunalski, Sieniawa, Szczebrzeszyn, Tomaszów Mazowiecki and Ulanów. On the initiative of the Ahawas Tora Association, the cemeteries in Barcin, Łabiszyn, Rynarzewo, Strzelno and Żnin have been commemorated. In the years 2010–2019, a group

---

12   After the death of Zygmunt Nissenbaum in 2001, his wife Sonja Nissenbaum (22.11.1929 – 06.10.2018, Konstanz) became president of the Foundation and today his son Gideon Nissenbaum.

associated with the Jewish Community in Warsaw ran the Protect Jewish Cemeteries Foundation in Lublin, which carried out, among other things, renovation of the retaining wall of the 16th-century cemetery on Kalinowszczyzna Street.

Since 2014, the "From the Depths" Foundation has been interested in the state of cemeteries, recovering matzevahs located in various places, transporting them to cemeteries, and publicizing in the media cases of destruction of Jewish burial sites. The project was ceased after a few years.

In 2015, The European Jewish Cemeteries Initiative (ESJF) was set up. The organization is run by Rabbi Isaac Shapira and Philip Carmel, and its core objective is protecting and preserving Jewish cemetery sites across Europe through the accurate delineation of cemetery boundaries and the construction of walls and locking gates. So far, ESJF has fenced cemeteries in Błonie, Bychawa, Gniewoszów, Frampol, Józefów Biłgorajski, Korycin, Miechów, Mińsk Mazowiecki, Narew, Rzepiennik Strzyżewski, Seroczyn, Sochocin, Starowola, Wiskitki, and Zaklików. Moreover, ESJF is involved in educational activity.

Projects for organizing and commemorating cemeteries (including those in Dobra, Gostynin, Grybów, Krościenko nad Dunajcem, Kurów, Łabowa, Wola Michowa, Wronki, and Zamość) are supported by the the Association of the Jewish Historical Institute of Poland, allocating funds for these projects from its grants program. The POLIN Museum of the History of Polish Jews has also come to the rescue. Through its educational and popularizing activities (including the Virtual Shtetl website) it has encouraged local social activists and authorities to look after cemeteries and has provided advice on the subject. Among other things, the Museum's employees have brought about the recovery of matzevahs from the bottom of the Vistula River, organized the tidying up of the cemetery in Warsaw by pupils of the "Chocimska" Social Primary School (both these activities being carried out together with the Nissenbaum Family Foundation), motivated Krajenka's town authorities to recover some matzevahs and set up a lapidarium, and lobbied for the commemoration of the cemetery in Białogard. Since 2017 to 2024, the POLIN Museum has been cooperating with the Ministry of Culture and National Heritage and the Institute of National Heritage on a project to mark out Jewish cemeteries.

Restoring order to a devastated cemetery is a complex activity that usually involves regaining ownership of the cemetery plot, building a perimeter wall within historical boundaries (which is often hampered by buildings that have been constructed on the cemetery or its secondary division), the removal of many years of litter and vegetation, renovation of gravestones and structures (which often additionally requires the consent of the Conservator of Monuments), and then requires periodic cleaning and tending. Even in the case of just one cemetery, this means considerable costs and the necessity of involving a team of people.

It should be emphasized that providing effective care of all cemeteries exceeds the capabilities of those Jews living in Poland. According to the 2021 National Census, just over 17,156 Polish citizens declare their Jewish national and ethnic identities. The largest number of members is recorded by the Jewish communities (about 1,704 in number) and the Socio-Cultural Society of Jews in Poland (numbering 935), with some of them counted twice, being members of both entities. People who belong to other Jewish organizations are often also members of the Socio-Cultural Society of Jews in Poland or a Jewish Community. This small group of Shoah survivors and their descendants face the challenge of taking care of burial places left over from a community with a thousand-year history and, in 1939, numbering almost three and a half million people.

Summary

The cases of destruction of Jewish cemeteries in approximately 470 localities presented in this study show the complexity of the process that began with the seizure of power in Germany by the Nazis.

In the Third Reich, acts of destruction took place even before 1939, although in the light of the materials examined, these were not on any mass scale. Later, cemeteries, as property seized by the Gestapo, were gradually sold to various buyers. The Nazis removed gravestones from them, but as a rule, they complied with the law prohibiting the digging up of graves for a period of 30 years since the last burial. A significant number of cemeteries in the Third Reich survived the war in relatively good condition. There is no doubt, however, that in the event of the Nazi totalitarian system being consolidated, the cemeteries would have faced further destruction.

Large-scale destruction of Jewish cemeteries began following the outbreak of World War II. Cemeteries were devastated as a result of actions by the German military and police units as well as the occupying administration. These actions were a form of antisemitic repression and the occupying forces' management of property. In the conquered territories, the Germans destroyed hundreds of cemeteries, also coercing the involvement of forced labourers and prisoners of war in such acts. At the same time, cemeteries were deprived of their natural guardians for decades to come through the genocide of about 90% of all Jews living in Poland.

Apart from a brief, unspecified reference concerning the removal of matze-vahs from the cemetery in Lesko "by Soviets,"[1] source materials contain no information about any possible cases of Jewish cemetery destruction on the orders of the Soviet authorities on Polish territory occupied by the USSR in the period from September 17th 1939 to June 22nd 1941.

Some of the local population took an active part in the destruction of Jewish cemeteries—either illegally or with the consent of the authorities. This process began during the war and continues to this day. Many people are charged with

---

1   Trzciński and Wodziński, *Cmentarz żydowski w Lesku*, 17.

stealing and smashing gravestones, dismantling perimeter walls and cemetery buildings, digging up graves and other acts of destruction and desecration. These have not only been "ethnic" Poles, but also members of various minorities—for example, in 1942 gravestones from the cemetery in Wielkie Oczy were stolen by displaced Ukrainians from Trościaniec,[2] and in 1994 the cemetery in Nowy Dwór Mazowiecki was dug up by a Roma family.[3]

The post-war Polish state played a significant role, weakening the position of the already few Jewish organizations, depriving them of their right of succession to the property of pre-war Jewish communities, nationalizing private real estate, adopting laws that did not take into account Jewish religious law and tradition, taking steps to destroy cemeteries, and failing to provide them with sufficient care. The antisemitic campaign initiated in 1968 by the authorities (and taken up by some members of the public) forced around 13,000 Jews to emigrate from Poland, causing thousands more graves to be left untended. Local officials often contravened the regulations concerning cemeteries; for example, failing to carry out exhumations in those cemeteries earmarked for construction.

It has only been with the democratization of life in Poland that significant changes have been brought about in this matter. However, despite numerous legal acts, the regulations are still disregarded, and cemetery plots are sold, their ownership transferred under perpetual usufruct, and buildings are erected or roads are constructed on them.

After 1989, with the reorganization of the economic system, the process of destruction included an increased role played by private entrepreneurs, for whom cemeteries became desirable investment plots.

The stories featured in this book show a cross-section of the people responsible for destroying cemeteries. These were not only uneducated people, but also representatives of the social elite, the inhabitants of towns as well as villages. Many acts of vandalism were committed by minors. Numerous cases mentioned indicate participation by peasant folk. The perpetrators also included educated people occupying prominent positions (including officials, some of high rank), and often respected by the local community. In one of the towns near Warsaw, a house was built in the cemetery by a teacher. In Brańsk and Sobienie-Jeziory, the destruction was somewhat legitimized by Catholic priests, who for decades walked on pavements made of matzevahs in front of their presbyteries

---

2   Majus, *Wielkie Oczy*, 336–337.

3   Małgorzata Łuka, "Pochówek na podwórku," *Express Wieczorny*, October 10, 1994.

and churches. A similar problem couldn't be solved by the directors and teachers of the 3rd High School in Inowrocław, where until 2011 the courtyard was made up of hundreds of fragments of smashed gravestones.

In the literature on this subject one can often find information about the total destruction of cemeteries by the Germans during the Second World War. This is due either to ignorance or a deliberately cultivated biased historical policy featuring two fundamental errors. The first is the suggestion of the "complete destruction of the cemetery." Such an action would entail the removal of all above-ground elements of the cemetery and the complete exhumation of the deceased, including their ashes. However, such cases did not take place. Even in two cemeteries in Kraków's Podgórze district, where the Germans established a concentration camp in Plaszow during the war, there are still relics of gravestones to be found to this day, and bones were excavated during the earthworks carried out in 2016. The second error is to attribute the destruction of cemeteries exclusively to Germans. In fact, the cemeteries that were to a greater or lesser extent destroyed by Germans during the war were also destroyed following the war, with the participation of some of the local population and the authorities. At the other extreme were cemeteries that managed to avoid destruction at the hands of the Germans or on their orders, and the perpetrators of their destruction were the local population (with this process often already beginning during the war) and the post-war authorities. One can also identify cemeteries destroyed by both the Germans and the local population or only by the local population, but in both cases without the participation of the post-war authorities. This applies mainly to cemeteries located in remote places, on the slopes of hills or in villages, and thus not subject to urbanization.

Destruction of cemeteries included the destruction of graves, gravestones, buildings, perimeters and other infrastructure, as well as a cemetery's vegetation. Human remains were dug up and often ended up being taken to gravel pits. Gravestones were commonly used to line roads and courtyards, as kerbstones and building material, as grinding wheels, or re-used as gravestones in the cemeteries of various denominations. Cemeteries were converted into parks, squares, horticultural plots and rubbish dumps, and many of them were built upon. In two cemeteries in the southern part of Kraków, the Germans established a forced labour camp, which later became the Plaszow concentration camp.

For the Jewish population, the destruction of their cemeteries was one more very severe form of repression and humiliation. Often Jews themselves were forced by the Germans to dig up graves and smash gravestones. They had to witness the disappearance of cemeteries where members of their families and widely respected rabbis and tzadiks lay buried.

The present state of research into Jewish cemeteries in Poland does not make it possible to determine how advanced this destruction process is. This would require researchers having detailed inventories of all the cemeteries—about one thousand two hundred—on the territory of present-day Poland, prepared before the outbreak of the Second World War, along with similar documentation from later years. Such inventories, however, would be far from perfect due to the specific nature of cemeteries. While it is possible to assess the number of destroyed gravestones, demolished buildings and cemetery perimeters, estimating the degree of damage to the graves themselves, understood as burial sites, would still be of key importance. There are still thousands of people buried in so many cemeteries, even if all above-ground traces have been removed.

To illustrate the scale of the damage caused the above-ground features, basic statistical data has been prepared for the Mazowieckie Province, within which there are 142 Jewish cemeteries, whose state of preservation is relatively reliably documented. The number includes medieval cemeteries in Gostynin and Warsaw, whose exact locations are unknown. Only four cemeteries have their original, pre-war perimeters, and only in the case of 13 cemeteries have their relics (gate pillars, sections of walls, low earth embankments) been preserved. 41 cemeteries have been re-fenced since 1945, with this only being accomplished after 1989 in at least 22 cases. Pre-funeral buildings survived in only two localities (in Pruszków, an unused facility, with a preserved table for the ritual washing of bodies, and in Żyrardów, now a residential building). At least 31 cemeteries have been fully or partially built upon. According to the nearest approximation, all the cemeteries in the Mazowia province together contain about 138,500 gravestones in various states of repair. Accounting for this large number is the cemetery at No. 49/51 Okopowa Street in Warsaw (one of the largest Jewish cemeteries in Europe), where approximately 90,000 gravestones have survived.[4] However, this cemetery also underwent extensive destruction. According to various sources, by 1939 anywhere between 120,000 and 150,000 Jews had been buried there.[5] Even adopting the lowest figure of 120,000 people buried there would mean that as many as 30 thousand gravestones are missing.

---

4   Data based on the census conducted by Przemysław Isroel Szpilman – director of the cemetery in the years 2002–2020.

5   Kroszczor and Zimler, *Cmentarz żydowski w Warszawie*, 5.

The number of matzevahs in the cemetery on Warsaw's Wincentego Street, due to their arrangement in piles, is not known—for these statistics, an approximate figure of 40 thousand gravestones was adopted (for comparison: in the years 1926–1930 alone, some 9,741 people were buried in this cemetery). 2,189 gravestones have survived in Szydłowiec (where half of the cemetery plot has been built upon), and some 1,210 in Otwock. In four cemeteries between 401 to 500 gravestones have survived; in three others between 201 to 300; in seven others between 101 to 200; and in 57 cemeteries between 1 to 100 gravestones (including 27 cemeteries where the number of matzevahs does not exceed 10).[6] Some 67 cemeteries (47.1% of all cemeteries in the Mazowia province) are completely devoid of matzevahs. The gravestones that are preserved usually constitute a small percentage of the original figure. The cemetery in Wiskitki is a good example of this. Based on an analysis of the births and deaths records and taking into account the demographic changes in the local Jewish community,[7] it can be assumed that during the approximately one hundred years of the cemetery's active operation, about 2,000 people were buried there. Currently, there are about 85 stelae within its boundaries, including a significant number that are damaged. This is therefore only about 4% of all the gravestones originally erected there.

There are no Jewish cemeteries in Poland that have not been to a greater or lesser extent destroyed. Thousands of graves have been destroyed, and the removal and demolition of gravestones has left many graves unmarked, preventing family members—if they survived the Shoah—from finding the burial place of their loved ones. The destruction of cemeteries must also be viewed in terms of Europe's material heritage. We have irretrievably lost objects that testified to the culture and history of the Jewish community on Polish soil.

The destruction of cemeteries continues to this day, although not on the same scale as in the years of the People's Republic of Poland—mostly because it involves less participation by the state. In addition, without proper care, cemeteries deteriorate as a result of the passage of time, weather conditions, and natural causes.

The reasons behind all this destruction remains a question requiring research and much more discussion. The following attempts at answering that question

---

6   The number of matzevahs was quoted on the basis of data from the websites www.cmentarze-zydowskie.pl, www.cemetery.jewish.org.pl, www.sztetl.org.pl.

7   The Jewish population in Wiskitki: 1827—192 individuals, 1857—552 individuals, 1880—1602 individuals, 1897—1138 individuals, 1921—951 individuals.

should be treated as merely introductory, far from exhausting the subject. In the case of the Germans, the reason was a program of antisemitism, the intention to completely exterminate the Jewish population, obliterate all traces of them, and steal their property. The post-war Polish state contributed to the destruction of cemeteries through an authoritarian attitude towards the Jewish community, attempts to restrict religious life in the country, nationalization of the property of Jewish communities, the process of urbanization, clumsy attempts to solve the problem of abandoned cemeteries of various denominations, and a failure to take proper care of historical monuments. Also significant was the covert or open antisemitism of many officials and decision-makers, their insensitivity, and their ignorance of Jewish culture and halachic principles.

As Tomasz Wiśniewski maintains, in the case of the general population (although this also applies to state officials), the main reason was a desire to use this abandoned, "unclaimed" raw material, and not antisemitism.[8] A similar conclusion can be drawn upon reading Marcin Zaremba's article on so-called looting, i.e. the "appropriation of property left unattended, abandoned or vacated by the owner, usually as a result of warfare or a natural disaster." The author has analyzed the intensity of the phenomenon, including during the Galician massacre of 1846, the first weeks of World War II, the period following the Third Reich's aggression towards the Soviet Union, the period following the extermination of the Jewish population, and in the post-war period. This concerned not only cemeteries, but also defensive castles and private estates. Looting was committed by people of various origins, not necessarily from the lower social orders, revealing a selective prohibition and condemnation of theft by applying it only to "what's ours," which made it possible to seize property belonging to "strangers," i.e. non-Poles,[9] defined in ethnic, religious and social categories. An example may be the thefts that occurred at the Muslim cemetery in Studzianka, where after the First World War, when the Tatar community was reduced to one family, the inhabitants began to take away the headstones. Wacław Świątkowski wrote about this in 1929: "The cemetery is being desecrated by new purchasers of these backwaters, who smash the sandstone headstones to make whetstones

---

8   Consultation with Dr. Tomasz Wiśniewski on June 10, 2018.

9   Marcin Zaremba, "Gorączka szabru," *Zagłada Żydów. Studia i Materiały*, no. 5 (2009): 193–220

for sharpening scythes. In vain the parish priest rebukes them from the pulpit for this sacrilege [...]. The vandalism keeps being repeated."[10]

After 1945, the phenomenon of looting also affected Catholic cemeteries in Poland, although these were acts by a relatively small group, condemned by the general public. Thefts in cemeteries, which came under the category of "alien," i.e. mainly Jewish and Protestant, were on a much larger scale and long-lasting in nature. This was especially true for the so-called Recovered Territories, where Jewish cemeteries were utterly foreign to the settlers who came from Eastern Poland, the graves being Jewish or German and involving people with whom they had never had contact.

Looting in cemeteries can be associated with the demoralization of some of society as a result of the war. Joseph Tenenbaum, in his book *In Search of a Lost People. The Old and New Poland*, quoted Józef Olszewski, the director of the Political Department at the Ministry of Foreign Affairs in the years 1945–1948 who, commenting on the plundering of the former KL Auschwitz-Birkenau camp, complained of "the savagery left behind by the Nazis." This was to manifest itself in the activities of whole gangs digging up cemeteries and robbing corpses of gold teeth and even clothing.[11]

Some people are of the opinion that the looting was additionally exacerbated by difficult climatic conditions (which resulted in the felling of trees in cemeteries and the theft of wooden matzevahs) and the lack of building materials.[12] It is worth recalling the story of Jochwed Kantorowicz, who in the years 1943–1944 hid with her sister in a dugout near the Jewish cemetery in Tarczyn. In the middle of winter, cold, exhausted, and desperate, the women decided to "dig up a fresh corpse, remove its clothes and wear them," but eventually gave up the idea.[13] One may wonder whether those perpetrators of such thefts at other cemeteries were in a similarly dramatic situation.

Nor did the historic character of some cemeteries constitute a protection against their destruction. The peasant tearing a 17th-century matzevah from the

---

10 Wacław Świątkowski, *Podlasie. Piąta wycieczka po kraju* (Warszawa: Wacław Świątkowski, 1929), 70.

11 Joseph Tenenbaum and Sheila Tenenbaum, *In Search of a Lost People. The Old and New Poland* (New York: Literary Licensing, 1948), 140–148; Monika Adamczyk-Garbowska, "Trzy wizyty w Auschwitz," *Zagłada Żydów. Studia i Materiały*, no. 14 (2018): 450.

12 Consultation with Dr. Monika Polit on April 29, 2019.

13 AŻIH, Relacje. Zeznania ocalałych, ref. no. 301/2493, Jochwed Kantorowicz's testimony, 16.

ground did not consider the fact that he was destroying a monument from the Baroque period and a precious epigraph. It is unlikely he even thought in such categories. For him, the value of the gravestone was limited to its usefulness.

The motives for destroying cemeteries due to their being "ownerless" and "alien" and a lack of respect for material heritage should not be treated as justification for such acts. As Aleksander Hertz wrote, classifying Jews (and consequently also their cemeteries) as foreign is the basis of antisemitism.[14] The perception of Jewish cemeteries as an alien cultural element was (or in fact, still is today) accompanied by antisemitism and the conviction that they are of less value, with the frequent dehumanization of Jews, which is permanently representative of some Poles. In surveys conducted in Poland in the years 1975-1977 and 1993-2007, antipathy towards Jews was declared by between 38% and 51% of the respondents, whereas in the years 1981–1991 the figures for this group ranged between 16% and 24%.[15] Antisemitism was particularly intense in the post-war period, in 1956, in the years 1967–1968, and in the second decade of the twenty-first century.

Jewish cemeteries were destroyed not only as a result of the actions of the Third Reich. The post-war Polish state and part of the local population share the blame for their destruction to an enormous degree. An awareness of this complicity—in addition to perceiving cemeteries as burial places and a part of European cultural heritage—should be one of the reasons for taking proper care of them.

The publication of this book is merely one stage in researching the history of Jewish cemetery destruction. Anybody wishing to share their accounts and memories of this process, or having knowledge about gravestones outside cemeteries, are kindly requested to contact the author (e-mail address: info@cmentarze-zydowskie.pl).

You may also support the Foundation for the Preservation of Jewish Heritage in Poland, where the author works, at www.fodz.pl.

---

14 Aleksander Hertz, *Socjologia nieprzedawniona* (Warszawa: Państwowy Instytut Wydawniczy, 1992), 396.

15 Cała, *Żyd – wróg odwieczny?*, 616–617.

Sources

Archival Sources

1. **Archives of the Emanuel Ringelblum Jewish Historical Institute (Archiwum Żydowskiego Instytutu Historycznego im. E. Ringelbluma, AŻIH)**
   a. Archiwa Wojewódzkich Komisji Historycznych, ref. no. 303/XX/558.
   b. Archiwum Ringelbluma, ref. no. ARG I 743. Ring. I/438, ARG I 1085. Ring. I/943.
   c. Centralny Komitet Żydów w Polsce, ref. no. 303/I/246, 303/X/16, 303/XVI/130, 303/XVI/150, 303/XVI/176, 303/XVI/178.
   d. Dokumenty niemieckie 1939–1944, ref. no. 233/59.
   e. Komitet Żydowski i Wojewódzki Komitet Żydowski w Lublinie, ref. no. 355/37.
   f. Relacje. Zeznania ocalałych, ref. no. 301/17, 301/188, 301/248, 301/567, 301/1349, 301/1792, 301/1216, 301/2455, 301/2493, 301/2600, 301/2652, 301/3546, 301/3546, 301/5503, 301/5862, 301/ 6043, 301/6669.
   g. Towarzystwo Społeczno-Kulturalne Żydów w Polsce, ref. no. 325/45, 325/55, 325/217.
   h. Zbiór pamiętników Żydów ocalałych z Zagłady, ref. no. 302/277.
   i. Związek Religijny Wyznania Mojżeszowego w Polsce, ref. no. 360.
   j. Żydowski Instytut Historyczny, ref. no. 310/82.

2. **Archives of the Institute of National Remembrance (Archiwum Instytutu Pamięci Narodowej, AIPN)**
   a. Akta spraw sądowych, ref. no. IPN BU 626/16.
   b. Główna Komisja Badania Zbrodni Hitlerowskich w Polsce, ref. no. GK 182/83, IPN BU 3076/168,
   c. Ministerstwo Spraw Wewnętrznych w Warszawie, ref. no. IPN BU 00170/52/3, 0296/134, 00231/205/6, 1585/3607, 00231/205/6, 00170/429, 00945/2713/J, 0296/134, 1585/7150, 1585/7150, 1585/7150, 1585/832, 1585/7150, 1585/21506.
   d. Oddziałowa Komisja Ścigania Zbrodni Hitlerowskich przeciwko Narodowi Polskiemu, ref. no. Ds. 38/67.
   e. Wojewódzki Urząd Spraw Wewnętrznych w Częstochowie, ref. no. Ka 010/75.
   f. Wojewódzki Urząd Spraw Wewnętrznych w Łodzi, ref. no. IPN Ld PF10/522.

3. **Archives of the Majdanek State Museum (Archiwum Państwowego Muzeum na Majdanku)**
   a. Spuścizna Roberta Kuwałka, ref. no. XXIV–30/1/9.

4. **Emanuel Ringelblum Jewish Historical Institute (Żydowski Instytut Historyczny im. E. Ringelbluma, ŻIH)**
   a. Dział Dokumentacji Dziedzictwa: Dąbie, Sandomierz, Sochaczew (no reference numbers)
   b. Institute of National Heritage (Narodowy Instytut Dziedzictwa, NID)
   c. Karty cmentarzy no 3634, 10133, 14164.

5. **Karta Centre Archives (Archiwum Ośrodka Karta)**
   a. Kolekcja Bogdana Łopieńskiego, ref. no. OK 1600 0098 0001, OK 1600 0176 0003, OK 1600 0193 0001.

6. **New Records Archive (Archiwum Akt Nowych, AAN)**
   a. Ambasada RP w Berlinie, ref. no. 474/875.
   b. Ministerstwo Administracji Publicznej, ref. no. 1098, 199, 794.
   c. Ministerstwo Gospodarki Komunalnej, ref. no. 9/10, 9/18, 9/20, 9/23, 9/29, 9/32, 9/38, 9/39, 9/46, 9/53, 9/64.
   d. Ministerstwo Gospodarki Terenowej i Ochrony Środowiska, ref. no. 1/30, 1/31 1/24, 1/33.
   e. Ministerstwo Opieki Społecznej w Warszawie, ref. no. 15/696.
   f. Ministerstwo Ziem Odzyskanych, ref. no. 196/496.
   g. Polska Zjednoczona Partia Robotnicza. Komitet Centralny w Warszawie, ref. no. 237/XVIII/22.
   h. Urząd do Spraw Wyznań, ref. no 5b/31, 9/357, 13/377, 13/381, 14/462, 14/469, 19/482, 22/417, 22/434, 22/447, 24/549, 24/552, 24/686, 25/579, 25/581, 45/476, 75/32, 131/503, 131/505, 131/510, 131/511, 131/516, 131/517, 131/518, 131/520, 132/218, 132/283, 132/305, 132/306, 132/314, 132/318, 132/323.

7. **Shalom Foundation (Fundacja Shalom)**
   a. Collection of works from the "History and Culture of Polish Jews" competition, ref. no. 262/V/2004.

8. **State Archives in Katowice (Archiwum Państwowe w Katowicach, AP Katowice)**
   a. Urząd Wojewódzki w Katowicach, ref. no. 1/714

9. **State Archives in Kielce (Archiwum Państwowe w Kielcach, AP Kielce)**
   a. Urząd Wojewódzki w Kielcach, ref. no. 1080/1067, 1080/1071, 1080/1079.
   b. Urząd Wojewódzki Śląski w Katowicach, ref. no. 185/366.
   c. Urząd Wojewódzki Kielecki II, Ref. no. 305/1519.

10. **State Archives in Kielce, Sandomierz Branch (Archiwum Państwowe w Kielcach, Oddział w Sandomierzu, AP Sandomierz)**
    a. Akta gminy Szydłów, ref. no. 28/78.

11. **State Archives in Lublin (Archiwum Państwowe w Lublinie, AP Lublin)**
    a. Prezydium Powiatowej Rady Narodowej i Urząd Powiatowy w Puławach, ref. no. 746/39.
    b. Rada Żydowska w Lublinie, ref. no. 891/177.
    c. Urząd Okręgu Lubelskiego, ref. no. 498/30.

12. **State Archives in Łódź (Archiwum Państwowe w Łodzi, AP Łódź)**
    a. Przełożony Starszeństwa Żydów w Getcie Łódzkim, ref. no. 1081.

13. **State Archives in Olsztyn (Archiwum Państwowe w Olsztynie, AP Olsztyn)**
    a. Prezydium Powiatowej Rady Narodowej i Urząd Powiatowy w Giżycku, ref. no. 2542/9/523.

14. **State Archives in Przemyśl (Archiwum Państwowe w Przemyślu, AP Przemyśl)**
    a. Akta miasta Przeworska, ref. no. 137/1399.

15. **State Archives in Warsaw, Otwock Branch (Archiwum Państwowe w Warszawie, Oddział w Otwocku, AP Otwock)**
    a. Urząd Miasta i Gminy Karczew, ref. no. 78/193/50.

16. **State Archives in Siedlce (Archiwum Państwowe w Siedlcach, AP Siedlce)**
    a. Starostwo Powiatowe w Siedlcach, ref. no 62/29/19.
    b. Urząd Wojewódzki w Siedlcach, ref. no. 1336.

17. **Yad Vashem Archive**
    a. a. YV Relations Department, ref. no. O.3/1316.

Primary Sources

"06.1942, Warszawa-getto. Raport 'Oneg Szabat'. Gehenna Żydów polskich pod okupacją niemiecką" in *Archiwum Ringelbluma. Ludzie i prace "Oneg Szabat"*, vol. 11, ed. Szymon Morawski and Beata Jankowiak-Konik. Warszawa: Żydowski Instytut Historyczny im. E. Ringelbluma, 2013.

Cohn, Willy. *Żadnego prawa – nigdzie. Dziennik z Breslau 1933–1941*. Wrocław: Via Nova, 2010.

Czerniaków, Adam. *Adama Czerniakowa dziennik getta warszawskiego*, ed. Marian Fuks. Warszawa: Państwowe Wydawnictwo Naukowe, 1983.

Dzieje Żydów w Polsce. Wybór tekstów źródłowych XI–XVIII wiek, ed. Paweł Fijałkowski. Warszawa: Żydowski Instytut Historyczny, 1993.

"Folklor," in *Archiwum Ringelbluma. Konspiracyjne Archiwum Getta Warszawy. Utwory literackie z getta warszawskiego*, vol. 26, ed. Agnieszka Żółkiewska, Marek Tuszewicki. Warszawa: Żydowski Instytut Historyczny im. E. Ringelbluma, 2017.

Grasberg-Górna, Anna. "Dziennik. 25.08.–4.09.1942." in *Archiwum Ringelbluma. Konspiracyjne Archiwum Getta Warszawy. Dzienniki z getta warszawskiego*, vol. 23, ed. Katarzyna Person, Michał Trębacz, and Zofia Trębacz. Warszawa: Żydowski Instytut Historyczny im. E. Ringelbluma, 2015.

Huberband, Szymon. "Dziennik 9–19.05.1942," in *Archiwum Ringelbluma. Konspiracyjne Archiwum Getta Warszawy. Pisma rabina Szymona Huberbanda*, vol. 32, ed. Eleonora Bergman and Anna Ciałowicz. Warszawa: Żydowski Instytut Historyczny im. E. Ringelbluma, 2017.

Huberband, Szymon. "Memoriał w sprawie ratowania zabytków kultury żydowskiej," in *Archiwum Ringelbluma. Konspiracyjne Archiwum Getta Warszawy. Pisma rabina Szymona Huberbanda*, vol. 32, ed. Eleonora Bergman and Anna Ciałowicz. Warszawa: Żydowski Instytut Historyczny im. E. Ringelbluma, 2017.

Huberband, Szymon. "Zagłada bożnic, bejt ha-midraszy i cmentarzy," in *Archiwum Ringelbluma. Konspiracyjne Archiwum Getta Warszawy. Pisma rabina Szymona Huberbanda*, vol. 32, ed. Eleonora Bergman and Anna Ciałowicz. Warszawa: Żydowski Instytut Historyczny im. E. Ringelbluma, 2017.

Huberband, Szymon. *"Życie religijne podczas wojny,"* in *Archiwum Ringelbluma. Konspiracyjne Archiwum Getta Warszawy. Pisma rabina Szymona Huberbanda*, vol. 32, ed. Eleonora Bergman and Anna Ciałowicz. Warszawa: Żydowski Instytut Historyczny im. E. Ringelbluma, 2017.

Makower, Henryk. *Pamiętnik z getta warszawskiego. Październik 1940 – styczeń 1943*. Wrocław: Ossolineum, 1987.

Materiały źródłowe do historii Żydów Mławy i powiatu mławskiego w XVIII–XX wieku, ed. Leszek Arent, Piotr Grochowski, and Przemysław Miecznik. Mława: Towarzystwo Przyjaciół Ziemi Mławskiej, 2016.

NN, "Wspomnienia z pierwszych miesięcy okupacji w Warszawie. 09.1939–01.1940 r." in *Archiwum Ringelbluma. Konspiracyjne Archiwum Getta Warszawy. Getto warszawskie*, part 1, vol. 33, ed. Tadeusz Epsztein and Katarzyna Person. Warszawa: Żydowski Instytut Historyczny im. E. Ringelbluma, 2016.

Pamiętniki żołnierzy baonu "Zośka": Powstanie Warszawskie, ed. Tadeusz Sumiński. Warszawa: *Nasza Księgarnia*, 1959.

Plonski. David, Yurek. [no title], in *We remember. Testimonies of twenty-four members of Kibbutz Megiddo who survived the Holocaust*, ed. Denise Nevo and Mira Berger. New York: Shengold Publishers, 1994.

Proces ludobójcy Amona Goetha przed Najwyższym Trybunałem Narodowym, ed. Nachman Blumental. Warszawa – Kraków – Łódź: Centralna Żydowska Komisja Historyczna w Polsce, 1947.

Ringelblum, Emanuel. *Kronika getta warszawskiego wrzesień 1939–styczeń 1943.* Warszawa: Czytelnik, 1988.

Szlachter Wojtkowska, Ilana. "Zwykłe życie." *Biuletyn Żydowskiego Instytutu Historycznego w Polsce*, vol. 1–2/185–186 (1998): 116.

Urban, Kazimierz. *Cmentarze żydowskie, synagogi i domy modlitwy w Polsce w latach 1944–1966. Wybór materiałów.* Kraków: Zakład Wydawniczy Nomos, 2006.

"Wydział Statystyczny," in *Archiwum Ringelbluma. Rada Żydowska w Warszawie*, vol. 12, ed. Szymon Morawski, Beata Jankowiak-Konik. Warszawa: Żydowski Instytut Historyczny im. E. Ringelbluma, 2014.

Zelkowicz, Józef. *Notatki z getta łódzkiego 1941–1944.* Łódź: Wydawnictwo Uniwersytetu Łódzkiego, 2016.

Żydzi polscy 1648–1772: źródła, ed. Adam Kaźmierczyk. Kraków: Uniwersytet Jagielloński. Katedra Judaistyki, 2001.

Secondary Literature

Abraham-Diefenbach, Magdalena, Jenny Gebel, and Michał Szulc. "Lębork," in *Śladami żydowskimi po Kaszubach. Przewodnik. Jüdische Spuren in der. Kaschubei. Ein Reisehandbuch*, ed. Mirosława Borzyszkowska-Szewczyk and Christian Pletzing. Gdańsk – Lübeck – München: Academia Baltica, Instytut Kaszubski w Gdańsku, 2010.

Adamczyk-Garbowska, Monika. "'Pan/Pani żyje?'. Zamość po Zagładzie w wybranych wspomnieniach, relacjach i reportażach z języku jidysz," in *Żydzi w Zamościu i na Zamojszczyźnie. Historia – kultura – literatura*, ed. Weronika Litwin, Monika Szabłowska-Zaremba, and Sławomir Jacek Żurek. Lublin: Towarzystwo Naukowe Katolickiego Uniwersytetu Lubelskiego, 2012.

Adamczyk-Garbowska, Monika. "Trzy wizyty w Auschwitz." *Zagłada Żydów. Studia i Materiały*, no. 14 (2018): 450.

Appel, Binyamin. "In the Years of the German Extermination of the Jews," in *Yiskerbukh fun der Tshekhanover yidisher kehile*, ed. A. Wolf Yassini. New York: JewishGen, 2013.

Baksik, Łukasz. *Macewy codziennego użytku.* Wydawnictwo Czarne: Wołowiec: 2012.

Bałaban, Majer. *Historja i literatura żydowska ze szczególnem uwzględnieniem historji Żydów w Polsce*, vol. 3. Lviv: Zakład Narodowy im. Ossolińskich, 1925.

Bałaban, Majer. *Przewodnik po żydowskich zabytkach Krakowa.* Kraków: Stowarzyszenie Solidarność – B'nei Brith, 1935.

Bałaban, Majer. *Zabytki historyczne Żydów w Polsce.* Warszawa: Instytut Nauk Judaistycznych, 1929.

Bartosz, Adam. *Cmentarz żydowski w Tarnowie. Przewodnik.* Tarnów: Komitet Opieki nad Zabytkami Kultury Żydowskiej w Tarnowie, 2019.

Bauman, Janina. *Zima o poranku.* Kraków: Znak, 1989.

Bednarek. Małgorzata. *Sytuacja prawna cmentarzy żydowskich w Polsce 1944–2019.* Kraków – Budapest – Syracuse: Austeria, 2020.

Bednarczyk, Ryszard. *Gliwicka 66. Inwentaryzacja kirkutu w Tarnowskich Górach*. Tarnowskie Góry: Tarnogórska Fundacja Kultury i Sztuki, 2018.

Berendt, Grzegorz. "Żydzi," in *Encyklopedia Gdańska*, ed. Błażej Śliwiński. Gdańsk: Fundacja *Gdańska*, 2012.

Bergman, Eleonora and Jan Jagielski. "Ślady obecności. Synagogi i cmentarze," in *Następstwa Zagłady Żydów. Polska 1944–2010*, ed. Feliks Tych and Monika Adamczyk-Garbowska. Lublin–Warszawa: Wydawnictwo UMCS, Żydowski Instytut Historyczny im. E. Ringelbluma, 2011.

Bergman, Eleonora. *Cmentarz żydowski w Grodzisku Mazowieckim. Studium historyczno-konserwatorskie*. Warszawa: Stołeczna Pracownia Dokumentacji Dóbr Kultury, 1990.

Bieberstein, Aleksander. *Zagłada Żydów w Krakowie*. Kraków–Wrocław: Wydawnictwo Literackie, 1985.

Bielawski, Krzysztof. *Zagłada cmentarzy żydowskich*. Warszawa: Więź, 2020.

Bieniaszewska, Anna. *Shalom znad Drwęcy. Żydzi Golubia i Dobrzynia*. Toruń: Wydawnictwo Adam Marszałek, 2016.

Bis, Wojciech, and Wiesław Więckowski. "Cmentarz żydowski w Węgrowie w świetle sondażowych badań archeologicznych." *Rocznik Liwski* 9 (2016–2017): 110–111.

Blätter, Franz. *Warszawa 1942. Zapiski szofera szwajcarskiej misji lekarskiej*. Warszawa: Wydawnictwo Naukowe PWN, 1982.

Blushtein, Avraham. "Di Brisker Gas," in *Sefer Mezrich*, ed. Yitzchak Ronkin and Binem Heller. Tel Aviv: Ha-Merkaz ha-Mezritshai be-Israel ve-Irgune bene irenu be-tefutsot, 1978.

Borkowski, Maciej, Andrzej Kirmiel, and Tamara Włodarczyk. *Śladami Żydów. Dolny Śląsk, Opolszczyzna, Ziemia Lubuska*. Warszawa: Muzeum Historii Żydów Polskich POLIN, 2008.

Brilling, Bernhard. *Die jüdischen Gemeinden Mittelschlesiens. Entstehung und Geschichte*. Stuttgart: W. Kohlhammer, 1972.

Buczkowski, Janusz. *Tak było. . . .* Kielce: Biuro Wystaw Artystycznych w Kielcach, 2015.

Budziszewski, Jerzy. *Żywym i umarłym*. Warszawa: Wydawnictwo Współpraca, 1988.

Cała, Alina. *Asymilacja Żydów w Królestwie Polskim 1864–1897*. Warszawa: Państwowy Instytut Wydawniczy, 1989.

Cała, Alina. *Wizerunek Żyda w polskiej kulturze ludowej*. Warszawa: Oficyna Naukowa, 2005.

Cała, Alina. *Żyd – wróg odwieczny? Antysemityzm w Polsce i jego źródła*. Warszawa: Żydowski Instytut Historyczny im. E. Ringelbluma, 2012.

Canin, Mordechaj. *Przez ruiny i zgliszcza. Podróż po stu zgładzonych gminach żydowskich w Polsce*. Nisza: Warszawa, 2018.

Cieśla, Romuald. *Blask dawnych Krzepic*. Krzepice: UMiG w Krzepicach, 2007.

Cybertowicz, Jan, and Jarosław Kotuniak. *Z dziejów Osięcin i okolic*. Osięciny–Włocławek: Lega, 2006.

Czechowicz, Jerzy. *Zarys historii Żydów w Jarosławiu i okolicy*. Rzeszów: Wydawnictwo Edytorial, 2015.

Czubala, Dionizjusz, and Piotr Grochowski. *O tym nie wolno mówić... Zagłada Żydów w opowieściach wspomnieniowych ze zbiorów Dionizjusza Czubali*. Toruń: Wydawnictwo Naukowe Uniwersytetu Mikołaja Kopernika, 2019.

Czwojdrak, Dariusz. "Kłódki grobowe z cmentarza żydowskiego w Osiecznej." *Zeszyty Osieckie*, no. 17 (2009): 29.

Delowicz, Jan. *Gmina wyznania mojżeszowego w Żorach 1511–1940*. Żory: Towarzystwo Miłośników Miasta Żory, 2018.

Domańska, Hanna. *Kamienne drzewo płaczu*. Gdańsk: Krajowa Agencja Wydawnicza, 1991.

Domański, Paweł. *Izraelici w Żabnie*. Żabno: Mała Poligrafia Redemptorystów w Tuchowie, 2003.

Dombrowski, Danuta, and Abraham Wein. "Zgerzsher Yidn unter der daytschisher groyl-okupatzye," in *Sefer Zgerzsh: tsum ondenk fun a Yidisher kehile in Poyln*, ed. Dawid Stokfisz. Tel Aviv: Irgun yotsei Zgerzsh be-Israel, 1975.

Einhorn, Ignacy, Tomasz Jamróg, and Tamara Włodarczyk. *Dzieje społeczności żydowskiej w Kłodzku w XIX–XX w.*. Warszawa: Fundacja Ochrony Dziedzictwa Żydowskiego, 2006.

Elsner, Irena. *Żydzi w Lęborku i w powiecie lęborskim do 1945*. Amberg: Elsir, 2017.

Felder, Aaron. *Yesodei Smochos*. New York: Rabbi Aaron Felder, 1978.

Fershtenberg, Leib. "Oyf di hurbus," in *Pinkas Sokhatshev*, ed. Avraham Shmuel Shtein and Gabriel Weissman. Jerusalem: Irgun Yotsei Sokhatshov be-Israel: 1962.

Fijałkowski, Paweł. "*Obrządek pogrzebowy Żydów polskich w świetle badań archeologicznych. O potrzebie badań archeologicznych nad historią i kulturą Żydów w Polsce*." *Biuletyn Żydowskiego Instytutu Historycznego w Polsce*, no. 3/151 (1989): 25.

Friedman, Esther. *Daleka droga do domu*. Kraków: Ambrozja, 1997.

Gałosz, Wojciech, Marcin Karetta, Jacek Proszyk, and Artur Szyndler. *Cmentarz żydowski w Oświęcimiu. Historia, symbole, przyroda. The Jewish Cemetery in Oświęcim. History, Symbols, Nature*. Oświęcim: Centrum Żydowskie w Oświęcimiu, 2018.

Ganzfried, Salomon. *Code of Jewish law. Kitzur Schulchan Aruch. A compilation of Jewish laws and customs*. New York: Hebrew Publishing, 1927.

Gańczyk, Barbara, Bartłomiej Grzanka, Adam Maliński. *Kłodawskie cmentarze*. Kłodawa: Ireneusz Niewiarowski, 2015.

Gładyś, Beata. "Rozwój chasydzkiego ośrodka pielgrzymkowego w Leżajsku." *Peregrinus Cracoviensis* 17, (2006): with.

Głowacka-Penczyńska, Anetta, Tomasz Kawski, and Witold Mędykowski. *The first to be destroyed. The Jewish community of Kleczew and the beginning of the final solution*. Boston: Academic Studies Press, 2015.

Grabski, August, and Albert Stankowski. "*Życie religijne społeczności żydowskiej*," in *Następstwa Zagłady Żydów. Polska 1944–2010*, edited by Feliks Tych and Monika Adamczyk-Garbowska. Lublin–Warszawa: Wydawnictwo UMCS, Żydowski Instytut Historyczny im. E. Ringelbluma, 2011.

Grabski, August. "Współczesne życie religijne Żydów w Polsce," in *Studia z dziejów i kultury Żydów w Polsce po 1945 roku*, ed. J. Tomaszewski. Warszawa: Trio, 1997.

Grossman, Moshe. "A Burial Place and a Memorial," in *Yizkor-Buch Kurov. Sefer Yizkor. Matzevot zikaron Laayaratenu Kurov*, ed. Moshe Grossman. Tel Aviv: Irgun yotsei Kurov be-Israel, 1955.

Gruszkowski, Krzysztof. *Nad starym Bugiem w Sławatyczach*. Biała Podlaska: ARTE, 2012.

Halkowski, Henryk. *Żydowski Kraków. Legendy i ludzie*. Kraków – Budapest: Austeria, 2009.

Hertz, Aleksander. *Socjologia nieprzedawniona*. Warszawa: Państwowy Instytut Wydawniczy, 1992.

Hoffman, Zygmunt. "Noc Kryształowa na obszarze Wrocławskiego Nadodcinka SS." *Biuletyn Żydowskiego Instytutu Historycznego w Polsce*, no. 2/98 (1976): 75–96.

Hońdo, Leszek. *Cmentarz żydowski w Tarnowie*. Kraków: Wydawnictwo Uniwersytetu Jagiellońskiego, 2001.

Hońdo, Leszek. *Dom przedpogrzebowy przy żydowskim nowym cmentarzu w Krakowie*. Kraków: Universitas, 2011.

Hońdo, Leszek. *Nowy cmentarz żydowski w Krakowie*. Kraków: Księgarnia Akademicka, 2005.

Jachimek, A. "Geshendet oych nochn toyt," in *Sefer Zlochev*, ed. Yaakov Freund. Tel Aviv: Ha-Vaad ha-Tsiburi Shelyad Irgun Yotsei Zlotsev ba-Arets uva-Tefutsot, 1971.

Jagielski, Jan. "Lapidaria na cmentarzach żydowskich," in *Studia i materiały. Ochrona cmentarzy zabytkowych: materiały szkoleniowe pracowników Państwowej Służby Ochrony Zabytków oraz materiały z konferencji Organizacja lapidariów cmentarnych Żagań – Kożuchów 20–23 czerwca*, ed. Wanda Puget. Warszawa: Ośrodek Ochrony Zabytkowego Krajobrazu, 1994.

Janicki, Paweł. "Eksterminacja Żydów w powiecie tureckim w latach 1941–42." *Kwartalnik Historii Żydów*, no. 1/241 (2011): 86.

Jonca, Karol. *"Noc kryształowa" i casus Herschela Grynszpana*. Wrocław: Wydawnictwo Uniwersytetu Wrocławskiego, 1998.

K., J. "Cmentarze żydowskie – ciągła troska Związku," in *Kalendarz Żydowski 1984– 1985*, ed. Ewa Świderska. Warszawa: Związek Religijny Wyznania Mojżeszowego w Polsce, 1985.

Karczewski, Marian. *Czy można zapomnieć?*. Warszawa: PAX, 1969.

Kermish, Joseph. *To live with honor and die with honor!...*. Jerusalem: Yad Vashem, 1986.

Kichelewski, Audrey. "'Pomóc naszym braciom z Polski...'. Działalność Jointu na rzecz społeczności żydowskiej w PRL w latach 1957–1967," in *Społeczność żydowska w PRL przed kampanią antysemicką lat 1967–1968 i po niej*, ed. Grzegorz Berendt. Warszawa: Instytut Pamięci Narodowej, 2009.

Kirmiel, Andrzej. "Żydowskie ślady na Ziemi Lubuskiej," in *Makom tov – der gute Ort – dobre miejsce. Cmentarz żydowski Frankfurt nad Odrą / Słubice*, ed. Eckard Reiss and Magdalena Abraham-Diefenbach. Berlin: Vergangenheits Verlag, 2012.

Klimowicz, Teresa, Paweł Sygowski, Monika Tarajko, and Andrzej Trzciński. *Cmentarze żydowskie. Podręcznik dobrych praktyk w ochronie dziedzictwa lokalnego*. Lublin: Stowarzyszenie Studnia Pamięci, 2018.

Kolbuszewski, Jacek. *Cmentarze*. Wrocław: Wydawnictwo Dolnośląskie, 1996.

Kopciowski, Adam, Marta Kubiszyn, Andrzej Trzciński, and Marzena Zawanowska. *Śladami Żydów. Lubelszczyzna*. Lublin: Stowarzyszenie Panorama Kultur, 2011.

Koper, Mariusz. "Zapomniane sztetl – Lubycza Królewska. Śladami nieistniejącego," in *Żydzi w Zamościu i na Zamojszczyźnie. Historia – kultura – literatura*, ed. Weronika Litwin, Monika Szabłowska-Zaremba, and Sławomir Jacek Żurek. Lublin: Towarzystwo Naukowe Katolickiego Uniwersytetu Lubelskiego, 2012.

Kopówka, Edward. *Żydzi w Siedlcach 1850–1945*. Siedlce: Stowarzyszenie Tutaj Teraz, 2009.

Kotarba, Ryszard. *Niemiecki obóz w Płaszowie 1942–1945*. Warszawa–Kraków: Instytut Pamięci Narodowej, 2009.

Kowalski, Rafał. *Płoccy wypędzeni. Marzec '68*. Płock: Muzeum Mazowieckie, 2018.

Kowalski, Rafał. *Raz jeszcze. Żydzi – Płock – Polska*. Płock: Muzeum Mazowieckie w Płocku, 2016.

Krajewska, Monika. "'Świadkiem niech będzie ten kamień'. Genesis 31:52." in *Kalendarz Żydowski 1986–1987*, ed. Ewa Świderska. Warszawa: Związek Religijny Wyznania Mojżeszowego w Polsce, 1987.

Krajewska, Monika. *A Tribe of Stones. Jewish Cemeteries in Poland*. Warszawa: Polish Scientific Publishers Ltd, 1993.

Krajewska, Monika. *Czas kamieni*. Warszawa: Interpress, 1982.

Krajewska, Monika. *Le temps des pierres*. Warszawa: Interpress, 1983.

Krajewska, Monika. *Time of Stones*. Warszawa: Interpress, 1983.

Krajewska, Monika. *Zeit der Steine*. Warszawa: Interpress, 1982.

Krajewski, Stanisław. "Powojnie, *od 1944 do dziś*," in *POLIN. 1000 lat historii Żydów polskich*, ed. Barbara Kirshenblatt-Gimblet, Antoni Polonsky. Warszawa: Muzeum Historii Żydów Polskich POLIN, 2014.

Krasucki, Eryk. *Historia kręci drejdlem. Z dziejów szczecińskich Żydów*. Łódź: Księży Młyn, 2018.

Krawczyk, Monika. "Kto odpowiada za materialne dziedzictwo Żydów polskich?," in *Ochrona dziedzictwa żydowskiego w Polsce*, vol. 2, ed. Marcin Bartosiewicz, Monika Krawczyk, Lesław Piszewski, and Jarosław Sellin. Warszawa: Fundacja Ochrony Dziedzictwa Żydowskiego, 2017.

Kroczyński, Hieronim. *Kronika Kołobrzegu*. Kołobrzeg: Wydawnictwo Le Petit Café, 2000.

Kropp, Brigitte. *"Auf den Spuren der judischen Gemeinde von Deutsch Krone,"* in *Heimatstadt-Heimatkreis Deutsch Krone*, ed. Hans-Geord Schmeling. Bad Essen: Verein Deutsch Krone Heimathaus e.V.: 1996.

Kroszczor, Henryk, and Henryk Zimler. *Cmentarz żydowski w Warszawie*. Warszawa: Państwowe Wydawnictwo Naukowe, 1983.

Krzyżanowski, Łukasz. *Dom, którego nie było. Powroty ocalałych do powojennego miasta*. Wołowiec: Wydawnictwo Czarne, 2016.

Kubit, Bożena. *Max Fleischer i jego dzieło. Historia żydowskiego cmentarza i domu przedpogrzebowego w Gliwicach*. Gliwice: Muzeum w Gliwicach, 2018.

Kuwałek, Robert, and Marta Kubiszyn. "Miasteczko polsko-żydowskie na Lubelszczyźnie," in *Dziedzictwo kulturowe Żydów na Lubelszczyźnie. Materiały dla nauczycieli*, ed. Marta Kubiszyn, Grzegorz Żuk, and Monika Adamczyk-Garbowska. Lublin: Zakład Kultury i Historii Żydów UMCS, Ośrodek "Brama Grodzka – Teatr NN", 2003.

Kuwałek, Robert, and Weronika Litwin. *Izbica. Opowieść o miejscu*. Warszawa: Fundacja Ochrony Dziedzictwa Żydowskiego, [no date].

Kwiatkowski, Jerzy. *485 dni na Majdanku*. Lublin: Wydawnictwo Lubelskie, 2018.

Kwiek, Julian. *Nie chcemy Żydów u siebie. Przejawy wrogości wobec Żydów w latach 1944– 1947*. Warszawa: Nieoczywiste, 2021.

Lemański, Wojciech. *Z krwi, kości i wiary. Wojciech Lemański w rozmowie z Anną Wacław- ik-Orpik*. Warszawa: Agora, 2013.

Łabęcka, Halina, and Zbigniew Łabęcki. *Cmentarz żydowski w Opolu, ul. Poniatowskiego. Studium konserwatorskie rozszerzone*, manuscript. Opole: Halina Łabęcka, Zbigniew Łabęcki, 1987.

Łagiewski, Maciej. *Macewy mówią*. Wrocław: Zakład Narodowy im. Ossolińskich, 1991.

Łagiewski, Maciej. *Stary cmentarz żydowski we Wrocławiu*. Wrocław: Muzeum Architektury, 2006.

Mahler, Ozjasz. *Przewodnik po żydowskich zabytkach Krakowa*. Kraków: Ozjasz Mahler, 1935.

Majer, Diemut. *"Narodowo obcy" w Trzeciej Rzeszy. Przyczynek do narodowo-socjalistycznego ustawodawstwa i praktyki prawniczej w administracji i wymiarze sprawiedliwości ze szczególnym uwzględnieniem ziem wcielonych do Rzeszy i Generalnego Gubernatorstwa*. Warszawa: Wydawnictwo Prawnicze, 1989.

Majus, Krzysztof Dawid. *Wielkie Oczy. Studia z dziejów wieloetnicznego galicyjskiego miasteczka*. Przemyśl: Południowo-Wschodni Instytut Naukowy, 2013.

Malicki, Krzysztof. *Poza wspólnotą pamięci: życie i Zagłada Żydów w pamięci mieszkańców regionu podkarpackiego*. Warszawa: Wydawnictwo IFiS PAN, 2017.

Maśliński, Maciej Zenon. "Ostrowskie lapidaria – cmentarze żydowskie," in *Ostrowskie Studia. Studia Iudaica Ostroviensia*, vol. II, ed. Jarosław Biernaczyk. Ostrów Wielkopolski: Gmina Miasto Ostrów Wielkopolski, 2009.

Meed, Vladka. *On both sides of the wall: memoirs from the Warsaw ghetto*. New York: Schocken Books Inc, 1999.

Modrzewska, Krystyna. "Czaszka z monetami z XVIII w. z Lublina-Kalinowszczyzny." *Wiadomości Archeologiczne* 22, no. 2 (1955): 214–215.

Moskal, Grzegorz, Michał Rapta and Wojciech Tupta. *Mroczne sekrety willi "Tereska": 1939–1945*. Wadowice: Grafikon, 2009.

Müller-Madej, Stella. *Dziewczynka z Listy Schindlera*, ed. Aleksander Bartłomiej Skotnicki. Kraków: Wydawnictwo AA [no date].

Myrcik, Jan. *Pro Memoria. Cmentarz żydowski w Cieszowej*. Tarnowskie Góry: Dom Kultury im. W. Roździeńskiego, 2011.

"Nasi sąsiedzi –Żydzi". Z dziejów relacji polsko-żydowskich na Kielecczyźnie w XX wieku, ed. Agnieszka Dziarmaga, Dorota Koczwańska-Kalita, and Edyta Majcher-Ociesa. Kielce: Instytut Pamięci Narodowej, 2017.

Niedzielska, Magdalena. *Cmentarz żydowski*. Toruń: Wydawnictwo Adam Marszałek, 2010.

Niezabitowska, Małgorzata, and Tomasz Tomaszewski, *Ostatni. Współcześni Żydzi polscy*. Warszawa: Wydawnictwa Artystyczne i Filmowe, 1993.

Niezabitowska, Małgorzata, and Tomasz Tomaszewski. *Die letzten Juden in Polen*. Schaffhausen: Edition Stemmle, 1987.

Niezabitowska, Małgorzata, and Tomasz Tomaszewski. *Remnants: the last Jews of Poland*. New York: Friendly Press, 1986.

Nowak, Gabriela. "O żydowskich stelach nagrobnych w Płocku." *Nasze Korzenie*, no. 6 (2009): 97.

Pakman, Leon. "A binel zichronot," in *Sefer Biala Podlaska*, ed. Moses Joseph Feigenbaum. Tel Aviv : Kupat Gmilut Hesed a»sh kehilat Biala Podlaska, 1961.

Pastuszka, Sławomir. *Cmentarz żydowski w Czechowicach-Dziedzicach*. Kraków: Wydawnictwo Jak, 2019.

Paszkowski, Wiesław. *Cmentarz żydowski w Częstochowie*. Częstochowa: Muzeum Częstochowskie, 2012.

Penkalla, Adam. *Żydowskie ślady w województwie kieleckim i radomskim*. Radom: Tramp, 1992.

Pęziński, Piotr. *Na rozdrożu. Młodzież żydowska w PRL 1956–1968*. Warszawa: Żydowski Instytut Historyczny im Emanuela Ringelbluma, 2014.

Piątkowski, Sebastian. *Radom w latach wojny i okupacji niemieckiej. 1939–1945*. Lublin–Warszawa: Instytut Pamięci Narodowej, 2018.

Piorr, Ralf, and Peter Witte. *Ohne Rückkehr: Die Deportation der Juden aus dem Regierungsbezirk Arnsberg nach Zamosc im April 1942*. Essen: Klartext Verlag, 2012.

Piotrowski, Marek. "Próba rekonstrukcji obrządku pogrzebowego ludności żydowskiej na podstawie badań archeologicznych cmentarza w Wyszogrodzie." *Rocznik Mazowiecki* 9 (1987): 216–221.

Piszczek, Radosław, ed. *Fundacja Rodziny Nissenbaumów. Ratowanie śladów kultury żydowskiej w Polsce. Żywym i umarłym*, Warszawa: Krajowa Agencja Wydawnicza, 1988.

Podolska, Joanna. *Spacerownik. Łódź żydowska*. Łódź: Agora, 2009.

Połomski, Franciszek. "Zawłaszczenie i sprzedaż cmentarzy żydowskich w latach II wojny światowej na Śląsku. Ze studiów nad prawem własności w III Rzeszy." *Studia nad faszyzmem i zbrodniami hitlerowskimi* 11, no. 815 (1987): 304–328.

Proszyk, Jacek. *Cmentarz żydowski w Bielsku-Białej*. Bielsko-Biała: Urząd Miejski w Bielsku-Białej, 2002.

Radwański, Kazimierz. "Odkrycie renesansowych i barokowych nagrobków żydowskich na cmentarzu Remuh w Krakowie." *Biuletyn Krakowski* 2 (1960): 64.

Ratajczyk, Maciej. "Cmentarz żydowski w Koźminie Wielkopolskim." *Kwartalnik Historii Żydów*, no. 3/259 (2016): 743.

Reiss, Eckard. "Makom tov – der gute Ort – dobre miejsce. Cmentarz żydowski Frankfurt nad Odrą / Słubice. Makom tov – der gute Ort – a good place. The Frankfurt an der Oder / Słubice Jewish Cemetery," in *Makom tov – der gute Ort – dobre miejsce. Cmentarz żydowski Frankfurt nad Odrą / Słubice*, ed. Eckard Reiss and Magdalena Abraham-Diefenbach. Berlin: Vergangenheits Verlag, 2012.

Romanowicz, Tomasz. *Dzieje społeczności żydowskiej w Głownie*. Głowno: Poligrafia, 2014.

Rosenberg, Göran. *Krótki przystanek w drodze z Auschwitz*. Wołowiec: Wydawnictwo Czarne, 2014.

Rozmus, Dariusz. *Cmentarze żydowskie ziemi olkuskiej*. Kraków: Oficyna Cracovia, 1999.

Rozmus, Dariusz. *Prawne i badawcze wyzwania archeologii żydowskiej*. Sosnowiec: Wyższa Szkoła Humanitas, 2022.

Rozmus, Dariusz. "Zagadnienie ochrony prawnej zabytków ze starego cmentarza żydowskiego w Pilicy." *Roczniki Administracji i Prawa* 2015, no. XV (2), 93.

Rudawski, Michał. *Mój obcy kraj?*. Warszawa: Agencja Wydawnicza Tu, 1996.

Sabor, Agnieszka. *Sztetl. Śladami żydowskich miasteczek. Działoszyce, Pińczów, Chmielnik, Szydłów, Chęciny. Przewodnik*. Kraków: Austeria, 2005.

Sanocka-Tureczek, Katarzyna. "Cmentarze na obszarze obecnego województwa lubuskiego w latach 1945–1975." *Ziemia Międzyrzecka* IV, (2008): 118–119.

Sapir, Yoav A. "Bolszewo," in *Śladami żydowskimi po Kaszubach. Przewodnik. Jüdische Spuren in der. Kaschubei. Ein Reisehandbuch*, ed. Mirosława Borzyszkowska-Szewczyk and Christian Pletzing. Gdańsk – Lübeck – München: Academia Baltica, Instytut Kaszubski w Gdańsku, 2010.

Sas-Jaworski, Andrzej. *Dzieje Żydów kazimierskich*. Warszawa: Subdan Agencja, 1997.

Schiper, Ignacy. *Cmentarze żydowskie w Warszawie*. Warszawa: Maor, 1938.

Simonstain Cullman, Peter. *Historia gminy żydowskiej z Piły od roku 1641 do Holokaustu*. Piła: Stowarzyszenie Inicjatyw Społecznych Effata, 2017.

Skoczek, Renata. "*Cmentarz żydowski w Chorzowie. Okoliczności związane z jego likwidacją*," in *Żydzi na Górnym Śląsku w XIX i XX wieku*, ed. Barbara Kalinowska-Wójcik, Dawid Keller. Rybnik–Katowice: Muzeum w Rybniku, Instytut Historii Uniwersytetu Śląskiego w Katowicach, 2012.

Skwara, Marian. *Pruszkowscy Żydzi. Sześć dekad zamkniętych Zagładą*. Pruszków: Powiatowa i Miejska Biblioteka Publiczna im. H. Sienkiewicza w Pruszkowie, 2007.

Sławiński, Piotr. "Dzieje i przestrzenna organizacja cmentarzy," in *Cmentarze żydowskie w Sandomierzu*, ed. Piotr Sławiński. Sandomierz: Armoryka, 2011.

Sobota, Jerzy, and Andrzej Trzciński, *Cmentarze żydowskie w Międzyrzecu Podlaskim*. Lublin: Wydawnictwo UMCS, 2009.

Spychalski, Stefan. "Dyskryminacja ludności żydowskiej na terenie b. rejencji opolskiej," *Biuletyn Żydowskiego Instytutu Historycznego w Polsce*, no 3/91. 1974.

Stankowski, Albert, and Piotr Weiser. "Demograficzne skutki Holokaustu," in *Następstwa Zagłady Żydów. Polska 1944–2010*, ed. Feliks Tych and Monika Adamczyk-Garbowska. Lublin – Warszawa: Wydawnictwo UMCS, Żydowski Instytut Historyczny im. E. Ringelbluma, 2011.

Stendig, Jakub. "Dewastacja cmentarzy, bóżnic i zabytków żydowskich Krakowa pod-czas okupacji hitlerowskiej," in *W 3-cią rocznicę Zagłady ghetta w Krakowie*, ed. Michał Borwicz, Nella Rost, and Józef Wulf. Kraków: Centralny Komitet Żydów Polskich, 1946.

Stola, Dariusz. *Kraj bez wyjścia. Migracje z Polski 1949–1989*. Warszawa: Instytut Pamięci Narodowej, 2010.

Stroop, Jürgen. *Żydowska dzielnica mieszkaniowa w Warszawie już nie istnieje!*. Warszawa: Instytut Pamięci Narodowej, 2009.

Sygowski, Paweł. "Cmentarze żydowskie Zamojszczyzny – stan badań, stan zachowania, uwagi konserwatorskie," in *Żydzi w Zamościu i na Zamojszczyźnie. Historia – kultura – literatura*, ed. Weronika Litwin, Monika Szabłowska-Zaremba, and Sławomir Jacek Żurek. Lublin: Towarzystwo Naukowe Katolickiego Uniwersytetu Lubelskiego, 2012.

Szlezynger, Piotr, and Iwona Zawidzka. *Żydowski Wiśnicz*. Kraków: Piotr Szlezynger and Iwona Zawidzka, 2016.

Szynowłoga-Trokenheim, Guta. *Życie w grobowcu*. Warszawa: Ypsylon, 2002.

Śliwiński, Krzysztof. "Nasz cmentarz żydowski," *Więź*, no. 4/294. 1983.

Świątkowski, Wacław. *Podlasie. Piąta wycieczka po kraju*. Warszawa: Wacław Świątkowski, 1929.

Tenenbaum, Joseph, and Sheila Tenenbaum. *In Search of a Lost People. The Old and New Poland*. New York: Literary Licensing, 1948.

The Jerusalem Talmud, Moed Katan 2:4.

Tokarska-Bakir, Joanna. *Okrzyki pogromowe, Szkice z antropologii historycznej Polski lat 1939–1946*. Wołowiec: Wydawnictwo Czarne, 2012.

Tryczyk, Mirosław. *Drzazga. Kłamstwa silniejsze niż śmierć*. Kraków: Znak, 2020.

Trzaskowska, Grażyna. "Cmentarz żydowski przy ul. Gwarnej we Wrocławiu w świetle zachowanych materiałów archiwalnych." Unpublished manuscript, Wrocław, [date unknown].

Trzciński, Andrzej, and Marcin Wodziński. "XVI-wieczne macewy ze starego cmentarza żydowskiego w Przemyślu," in *Żydzi i judaizm we współczesnych badaniach polskich, t. II, Materiały z konferencji*, ed. Pilarczyk, Krzysztof, and Stefan Gąsiorowski. Kraków: Księgarnia Akademicka, 2000.

Trzciński, Andrzej, and Marcin Wodziński. *Cmentarz żydowski w Lesku. Część 1. Wiek XVI i XVII*. Kraków: Księgarnia Akademicka, 2002.

Trzciński, Andrzej. *Świadkiem jest ta stela. Stary cmentarz żydowski w Lublinie*. Lublin: Wydawnictwo Uniwersytetu Marii Curie-Skłodowskiej, 2017.

Trzciński, Andrzej. *Cmentarz żydowski w Hrubieszowie. Nagrobki niewykorzystane do pomnika-lapidarium i zakopane obok lapidarium*, manuscript. Lublin: Andrzej Trzciński, 1997.

Tylman, Hercke, Hirshel Gothelf, and Shlomo Jakubowicz. "Tsvangs-arbet," in *Pinkas Sokhatshev*, ed. Avraham Shmuel Shtein, Gabriel Weissman. Jerusalem: Irgun Yotsei Sokhatshov be-Israel: 1962.

Vinecour, Earl, and Chuck Fishman, *Polish Jews: the final chapter*. New York: New York University Press, 1977.

Walerjański, Dariusz. "Zatarty ślad – historia cmentarzy żydowskich w Gliwicach," in *Żydzi gliwiccy*, ed. Bożena Kubit, Aleksandra Turek. Gliwice: Muzeum w Gliwicach, 2006.

Wardzyńska, Maria. *Był rok 1939. Operacja niemieckiej policji bezpieczeństwa w Polsce. Intelligenzaktion*. Warszawa: Instytut Pamięci Narodowej, 2009.

Wasiutyński, Bohdan. *Ludność żydowska w Polsce w wiekach XIX i XX. Studjum*. Warszawa: Wydawnictwo Kasy im. Mianowskiego, Instytut Popierania Nauki, 1930.

Weizman, Yechiel. *Unsettled Heritage: Living next to Poland's Material Jewish Traces after the Holocaust*. Ithaca: Cornell University Press, 2022.

Węgrzynek, Hanna. "Praktyki medyczne we wczesnonowożytnej Polsce i ich wpływ na funkcjonowanie oskarżeń o mord rytualny." *Czasy Nowożytne*, no 25 (2012): 109–110.

Wiatr, Ewa. "Historia cmentarza," in *Monumenta et Memoria. Cmentarz żydowski w Łodzi*, ed. Leszek Hońdo. Łódź: Wydawnictwo Hamal Andrzej Machejek, 2016.

Wildstein, Paweł. "Z działalności Zarządu Głównego Związku Wyznania Mojżeszowego w Rzeczypospolitej Polskiej," in *Kalendarz Żydowski–Almanach 1990–1991*, ed. Ryszard Schnepf. Warszawa: Związek Religijny Wyznania Mojżeszowego w Rzeczypospolitej Polskiej, 1991.

Wirsching, Andreas. "Jüdische Friedhöfe in Deutschland 1933–1957," *Vierteljahrshefte für Zeitgeschichte* 50, no. 1. 2002.

Wiśniewski, Tomasz. *Nieistniejące mniejsze cmentarze żydowskie. Rekonstrukcja Atlantydy*. Białystok: Kreator: 2009.

Włodarczyk, Edward. *Z dziejów Żydów skierniewickich*. Skierniewice: Wojewódzka Biblioteka Publiczna w Skierniewicach, 1993.

Włodarczyk, Tamara, and Jerzy Kichler. *Przewodnik po żydowskim Wrocławiu*. Wrocław: Ad Rem, 2016.

Wodziński, Marcin. *Groby cadyków w Polsce*. Wrocław: Towarzystwo Przyjaciół Polonistyki Wrocławskiej, 1998.

Wodziński, Marcin. *Hebrajskie inskrypcje na Śląsku XIII–XVIII wieku*. Wrocław: Towarzystwo Przyjaciół Polonistyki Wrocławskiej, 1996.

Woronczak, Jan Paweł. *"Cmentarz żydowski w Kromołowie jako tekst kultury"*. University of Wrocław, 1999.

Wyszyński, Stefan. "Biskup Lubelski do Przewielebnego Duchowieństwa w sprawie cmentarzy, mogił i miejsc straceń." *Wiadomości Diecezjalne Lubelskie*, no. 8 (1946): 293–297.

Zaremba, Marcin. "Gorączka szabru." *Zagłada Żydów. Studia i Materiały*, no. 5 (2009): 193–220.

Zawidzka, Iwona. *Przewodnik po cmentarzu żydowskim w Bochni*. Bochnia: Muzeum im. prof. S. Fischera w Bochni, 2018.

Zenderowski, Wojciech. "Barczewo. Macewy i metalowe krzyże." *Wiadomości Barczewskie*, no 5 (2010): 8.

Zieliński, Konrad. *Stosunki polsko-żydowskie na ziemiach Królestwa Polskiego w czasie pierwszej wojny światowej.* Lublin: Wydawnictwo UMCS, 2005.

Ziontek, Artur. *Żydzi Kosowa Lackiego.* Kosów Lacki: Miejsko-Gminny Ośrodek Kultury w Kosowie Lackim, 2016.

Ziółkowska, Anna. *Obozy pracy przymusowej dla Żydów w Wielkopolsce w latach okupacji hitlerowskiej. 1941–1943.* Poznań: Wydawnictwo Poznańskie, 2005.

Ziółkowski, Janusz. "Międzynarodowe Targi Poznańskie w przeszłości i obecnie." *Przegląd Zachodni*, no. 5–6 (1955): 206–207.

Żywień, Michał. "Cmentarz żołnierski w Krzykach." In *Kalendarz wrocławski.* Wrocław: Towarzystwo Miłośników Wrocławia, 1967.

Theses

Gwiazdowicz, Agnieszka. "Cmentarze żydowskie w Lelowie jako miejsca (nie)pamięci." BA diss., University of Warsaw, 2016.

Hajduk, Małgorzata. "Cmentarze żydowskie w badaniach archeologicznych. Podsumowanie dotychczasowego stanu badań." MA diss., University of Warsaw, 1993.

Herzberg, Nina. "Społeczność żydowska w Wejherowie i okolicach w ujęciu koncepcji miejsc pamięci." BA diss., University of Gdańsk, 2014.

Jankowska-Nagórka, Anna. "Deteutonizacja" Dolnego Śląska w latach 1945–1949 jako przykład polityki władz Polski Ludowej wymierzonej przeciwko niemczyźnie." PhD diss., Pedagogical University in Kraków, 2017.

Panz, Karolina. "Zagłada żydowskich mieszkańców Nowego Targu w perspektywie mikrohistorycznej – głosy, obrazy, przybliżenia i oddalenia." PhD diss., University of Warsaw, 2018.

Legal Acts

"Okólnik nr 11 Ministra Gospodarki Komunalnej z dnia 3 sierpnia 1964 roku w sprawie stanu prawnego nieczynnych cmentarzy, stanowiących własność Państwa, pozostających w zarządzie i użytkowaniu organów resortu gospodarki komunalnej oraz finansowania, porządkowania i konserwacji tych cmentarzy," Dziennik Urzędowy Ministerstwa Gospodarki Komunalnej, no 11/1964.

"Ustawa z dnia 23 lipca 2003 roku o ochronie zabytków i opiece nad zabytkami," Dziennik Ustaw no. 162/2003.

"Ustawa z dnia 31 stycznia 1959 roku o cmentarzach i chowaniu zmarłych," Dziennik Ustaw no. 11/1959.

"Ustawa z dnia 6 lipca 1972 roku o zmianie ustawy o cmentarzach i chowaniu zmarłych," Dziennik Ustaw no. 27/1972.

Press

Bikont, Anna. "Mieli wódkę, broń i nienawiść." *Gazeta Wyborcza*, June 15, 2001.

Biuletyn Żydowskiej Agencji Prasowej, August 28, 1946.

Biuletyn Żydowskiej Agencji Prasowej, January 27, 1948.

Biuletyn Żydowskiej Agencji Prasowej, June 3, 1945.

Biuletyn Żydowskiej Agencji Prasowej, November 12, 1945.

Bojanowski, Michał. "Czy mury runą?." *Chidusz*, no. 2. 2019.

Boratyn, Iwona. "Nie te czasy na takie bajania." *Gazeta Wyborcza*, June 13–14, 1998.

Dołęga Szczepański, Jan. "*Żyrardowiacy."* *Fołks Sztyme,* January 19, 1990.

Dymarczyk, Dariusz. "Profanacja czy tchórzostwo." *Wiadomości Wałeckie,* May 27, 2014.

Fijałkowski, Paweł. "Kamienne owoce czasu." *Fołks Sztyme,* January 6, 1989.

Filar, Alfons. "Przesyłka z Sarnak." *Perspektywy*, June 23, 1973.

Januszewski, Radosław. "Szkoła Tysiąclecia." *Rzeczpospolita* , October 27, 2001.

Kantor, Leszek Leo. "Płonące zboże i czerwone porzeczki." *Gazeta Wyborcza*, November 21, 2012.

Kąkolewski, Krzysztof. "Umarły cmentarz." *Tygodnik Solidarność*, December 16, 1994.

Kichler, Jerzy. "Agonia cmentarza, czyli rzecz o wrocławskim kirkucie." *Midrasz*, no. 4/198, 2017.

Krzemińska, Agnieszka. "Tam, gdzie dusze wiecznie czekają." *Polityka*, October 24, 2017.

Łuka, Małgorzata. "Pochówek na podwórku." *Express Wieczorny*, October 10, 1994.

M., A. "Nocna obława na hieny cmentarne. Likwidacja 12-osobowej bandy na cmentarzu żydowskim w Warszawie." *Express Wieczorny*, December 14, 1946.

Palester-Chlebowczyk, Małgorzata. "Ochrona cmentarzy żydowskich." *Tygodnik Solidarność*, July 24, 1981.

Rostkowski, Dariusz. "Warsztat nagrobkami wykładany." *Express Wieczorny*, May 28, 1999.

Ryss, Robert. "Dziedzictwo niczyje." *Gazeta Chojeńska*, July 3, 2007

Sobolewski, Janusz. "Zabytki powiatu grajewskiego." *Rajgrodzkie Echa*, no. 7/306. 2016.

"Spotkanie w Przemyślu," *Tygodnik Solidarność*, June 2, 1981.

Susid, Włodzimierz. "Cmentarz żydowski na Bródnie." *Słowo Żydowskie*, June 2, 1995.

Terczyńska, Beata. "Nagrobki w rzece." *Nowiny*, August 29, 2005.

Wąsacz, Małgorzata. "Po żydowskim cmentarzu na Wzgórzu Dąbrowskiego nie ma już śladu." *Gazeta Pomorska*, June 7, 2006.

Zasada, Stanisław. "*Macewy z jeziora."* *Rzeczpospolita*, September 6, 2002.

Zbrożek, Konrad. "Cmentarza już nie ma." *Gazeta Warmia i Mazur*, January 11, 1996.

Online Sources

Adler, Horst. "Noc Kryształowa" i pogrom Żydów w Świdnicy." Accessed June 30, 2020. http://www.mojemiasto.swidnica.pl/?p=1047.

"Apel o upamiętnienie." Accessed June 30, 2020. https://jewish.org.pl/opinie/apel-o-upamitnienie-ydow-6850/

Bielawski, Krzysztof and Małgorzata Frąckowiak. "Mikołów." Accessed June 30, 2020. http://www.cmentarze-zydowskie.pl/mikolow.htm

Bielawski, Krzysztof. "Biała Podlaska." Accessed June 1, 2020. http://cmentarze-zydowskie.pl/bialapodlaska.htm.

Bielawski, Krzysztof. "Iława." Accessed June 1, 2020. http://cmentarze-zydowskie.pl/ilawa.htm.

Bielawski, Krzysztof. "Skorogoszcz." Accessed June 30, 2020. http://www.cmentarze-zydowskie.pl/skorogoszcz.htm.

Bielawski, Krzysztof. "Września." Accessed June 1, 2020. http://cmentarze-zydowskie.pl/wrzesnia.htm.

Dąbrowski, Eugeniusz. "Krynki. Macewy żydowskie wywoziły tiry." Accessed June 30, 2020. https://www.youtube.com/watch?v=2Szcnb9Da0A&t=238s.

Derecki, Włodzimierz. Accessed June 30, 2020. https://www.1944.pl/archiwum-historii-mowionej/wlodzimierz-derecki,837.html.

"Epilog działań Nieformalnej Grupy Kamieniarzy Magurycz. Rok 2006." Accessed June 30, 2020. http://www.magurycz.org/spr2006.pdf;

Ginsberg, Abraham. "Understanding of the value of Jewish cemeteries." Accessed June 30, 2020. https://sztetl.org.pl/en/tradycja-i-kultura-zydowska/religia/jak-rozumiec-wartosc-zydowskich-cmentarzy.

Gołąbek, Michał. "Brzeziny żyją na macewach." Accessed June 30, 2020. http://www.e-kalejdoskop.pl/wiadomosci-a230/brzeziny-zyja-na-macewach-r669/pdf.

Grążawski, Piotr. Accessed June 30, 2020. https://www.facebook.com/piotr.grazawski.7. https://web.archive.org/web/20160309084125/http://www.roztocze.net/newsroom.php/21919_Niemcy_ul%C5%BCyli_%C5%BBydom_.html.

Gromek-Gadkowska, Aleksandra. "Likwidacja cmentarza żydowskiego w Opatowie.", Accessed June 30, 2020. http://gadkowski.pl/publikacja/likwidacja-cmentarza-zydowskiego-w-opatowie.

Ignatiew, Radosław Jacek. "Postępowanie o umorzeniu śledztwa." Accessed June 30, 2020. http://ipn.gov.pl/ftp/pdf/jedwabne_postanowienie.pdf.

Januszkiewicz, Julita. "Boisko na cmentarzu – Sokoły", Accessed June 30, 2020. https://poranny.pl/boisko-na-cmentarzu-sokoly/ar/5135140.

Jaworski, Adam. "Niemcy ulżyli Żydom." Accessed June 30, 2020.

John Paul II. "Homilia kaliska Ojca Świętego." Accessed: May 25, 2022. https://info.kalisz.pl/pope/index.htm.

Karpeta, Adrian. "Rybnickie Pokłosie." Accessed June 30, 2020.

Kozubal, Marek. "Macewy znalezione w żłobie dla konia." Accessed June 30, 2020. http://archiwum.rp.pl/artykul/1273416-Macewy-znalezione-w-zlobie-dla-konia.html?_=Rzeczpospolita-1273416?_=8

Leszczyńska, Joanna. "Brzeziny: zaniedbane dziedzictwo." Accessed June 30, 2020. http://www.dzienniklodzki.pl/artykul/96658,brzeziny-zaniedbane-dziedzictwo,id,t.html.

Miller, Monika. "Co z matką noworodka znalezionego na cmentarzu?" Accessed June 30, 2020. http://www.radio.kielce.pl/post-73222.

Musiolik, Franciszek. "Opowieść o likwidacji cmentarza żydowskiego w Rybniku." Accessed June 30, 2020. https://www.youtube.com/watch?v=UP866a8uXpI

"Naczelny rabin w Kamiennej Górze." Accessed June 30, 2020. http://www.kamiennagora.pl/pl/aktualnosci/naczelny-rabin-w-kamiennej-gorze.html

Piotrowski, Maciej. "Szkoła życia na cmentarzu." Accessed June 30, 2020. https://www.tygodnikprzeglad.pl/szkola-zycia-na-cmentarzu/.

Stankiewicz, Dariusz. "Cmentarze żydowskie, miejsca egzekucji, zbiorowe mogiły na terenie województwa podlaskiego." Accessed June 1, 2020. http://bialystok.jewish.org.pl/page5.html.

Storick, Herman. "Interview with two Jeleniewo residents." Accessed June 30, 2020. http://cmentarze-zydowskie.pl/jeleniewo_wywiad.htm.

Ulas Urbański, Juliusz. "*Święta Kuczek już nie będzie. Żydzi w Leżajsku.*" Accessed June 30, 2020. http://ulas2.republika.pl/ulas.htm

Wajkselfisz, Efraim. "In Liberated Kutno." Accessed June 30, 2020. https://www.jewishgen.org/yizkor/kutno/kut401.html

Wiśniewski, Tomasz. "Park Centralny." Accessed June 30, 2020. https://www.youtube.com/watch?v=NCC6n1N-8DU

Żygawski, Jakub. "Lokalizacja dawnych zamojskich cmentarzy w oparciu o archiwalne opracowania kartograficzne z XVIII–XX wieku." Accessed June 30, 2020. http://zamosc.ap.gov.pl/images/AZ2015/007-034.pdf.

Oral history

POLIN Museum of the History of Polish Jews, Oral History Collection, ref. no. 311, 549, 589, 1032.

USC Shoah Foundation, Visual History Archive, ref. no. 16713, 20367, 22839, 23991, 24854, 27274, 28548, 29827, 54163, 55570, 6642, 6655, 7556.

Index of Towns

Index of Names

www.ingramcontent.com/pod-product-compliance
Ingram Content Group UK Ltd.
Pitfield, Milton Keynes, MK11 3LW, UK
UKHW021548050225
4464UKWH00032B/600